NEW WORLD LITERATURE

New World Literature

TRADITION AND REVOLT IN LATIN AMERICA

By Arturo Torres-Rioseco

UNIVERSITY OF CALIFORNIA PRESS
BERKELEY AND LOS ANGELES
1949

UNIVERSITY OF CALIFORNIA PRESS
BERKELEY AND LOS ANGELES
CALIFORNIA

◇

CAMBRIDGE UNIVERSITY PRESS
LONDON, ENGLAND

PRINTED IN THE UNITED STATES OF AMERICA
BY THE UNIVERSITY OF CALIFORNIA PRESS

Acknowledgment

THE AUTHOR WISHES TO MAKE GRATEFUL ACKNOWLEDGMENT TO MISS ZENIA SACKS AND TO MRS. RUTH J. WARNER FOR THEIR VALUABLE HELP IN PREPARING THE MANUSCRIPT OF THIS BOOK

Contents

Chapter I ◇ Introduction

NOW THAT the termination of the war has put an end to a series of official platitudes concerning Hispanic America and has reduced that continent to its true significance, the publication of this book seems to me especially opportune. The Spanish American nations, even united, do not form a great power, and bear very little weight, therefore, in shaping the destiny of the world. It would be useless self-deception to believe the flattery and praise heaped upon us from abroad; rather it is essential that we be fully aware of our worth and of our importance and that we ourselves discover the truth of our existence.

In spite of the rage of Pan-Americanism that has exalted our imagination for several years, we must confess that our mutual ignorance of each other still prevails: that in Latin America we do not really know one another; that our approximation to the United States is more apparent than real. We have merely deluded ourselves with speeches, good-will missions, spectacular projects, "the good neighbor policy," and with other high-sounding trivialities, but the individual continues uninformed and confused, and the spirit remains in its obscurity of old. Without knowing the American "man" and his soul, it is futile to seek revelations in proposed programs and in objective formulae; words are meaningless, and the fraternal gesture inconsequential. All that we have achieved is a kind of mental sloth, an admission of incapacity, limiting ourselves to statistical compilations and commentaries.

My intention in this book is to delve into the spiritual life of my continent; its literature serves me as a base upon which to explore and understand the "man." And the prime definition of the "Spanish American man" is found in the light of his aesthetic attitude toward life.

At this moment of human history, the world, abandoning concepts of material and scientific greatness, appears to seek a new moral orientation to save itself from the chaos which looms threateningly in the foreground; and there appears to me a providential design in the fact that our continent was peopled by men from Spain, Portugal, and England, men who exalted above all values that of human dignity.

We must remember this historic truth every moment. As Americans, we aspire to the expression of our free will, our dignity; to the fulfillment of our endowments as rational beings. We desire liberty even for the errors in our thinking, since only physical violence perpetrated by the individual is dangerous to society. We do not want a totalitarian state, a political Frankenstein's monster, to stifle our minds and to crush our hearts. In the words of Walt Whitman, the duty of every citizen is to resist stubbornly, for lost liberty, once yielded, is very difficult to regain.

The task that I have set myself is not an easy one, for, in order to know intimately the twenty Spanish American literatures, one would need the Benedictine patience, the eclectic tolerance, and the unselfish wisdom of a Marcelino Menéndez Pelayo. I confess that I do not possess these qualities. But I do possess, on the other hand, a constantly impelling disquietude and a great enthusiasm. This uneasiness is concerned with everything related to the future of our America and to the Latinity of our continent. I note with deep regret that on all sides the noble colonial architecture is retreating before the advance of those iron-and-cement cages which, for lack of definitive stylistic qualities, are summarily termed "skyscrapers." It must be very modern to carry the classic patio to the top of a building; it must be very agreeable to ride twenty stories in an elevator, instead of strolling through the spacious corridors of our old houses; to press a button for air conditioning instead of opening the yawning windows to the sun and the wind; to cultivate roses and jasmine on pianos and radios! It must be agreeable—for the ultramodern souls!

I remark with misgivings the disappearance of the twisted, climbing street; the pleasant, narrow lane, with its clean, adobe-walled houses, the flower-laden balconies; the cobblestoned pavement. Today's street must be straight; it must have enormous structures, street lights, neon signs, wires, rails, electric bells, American shops.

The tree, following the example of the horse, will become a prehistoric phenomenon. The young woman of today no longer appears on the balcony, but in the tea room or in the bar; in the lobby of the Palace Hotel, on the golf course, or in the jockey club, or playing bridge, or tennis, or badminton. If she has not gone out, then surely she must be in the living room, smoking Lucky Strikes. All to the greater glory of our god—Progress!

I see with regret that our theater—that noble institution created in the sixteenth century on the Iberian peninsula, and developed by great writers such as Lope de Rueda, Gil Vicente, Lope de Vega—is fading from the scene. And the efforts of a García Lorca or of a thousand drama enthusiasts will not suffice to revive it, because our youth prefers Hollywood scenarios.

There is a great cultural crisis in Spanish America. After abandoning the models which Spanish culture had afforded us during the colonial period, we turned to the treasure chests of beauty and learning that France generously proffered to us. We approached that culture bare, avid with hunger and thirst, and we returned elegantly dressed and with firm step, our wants satisfied, even satiated. Through France we were introduced to ancient Greek civilization and we memorized the *Prière sur l'Acropole* (Prayer on the Acropolis) of Renan; through French culture we glimpsed the wisdom of the Orient. We discovered the advances of Western science from French scholars; our philosophers were disciples of Voltaire, Rousseau, Lamennais, Compte, and Bergson; our critics, of Sainte-Beuve, of Brunetière, of Taine; our novelists, of Balzac, Flaubert, and of Zola; our painters, of Cézanne; our sculptors, of Rodin; our poets, of Verlaine.

And our approach to the important problems of the world was French, which indicates that our psychology was being transformed along with our new independent existence, thanks to the cultural influence of that great nation. Without France it is impossible to explain the development of our Hispanic American culture. But the day came when the decadence of the West was loudly proclaimed and the French spirit began to waver and subside like a weak flame before contrary winds.

Hispanic America, having lost its guiding star, then turned to Portugal and Spain, which, unfortunately, had nothing to offer. It was then that those light, pleasant forms of culture appeared: sports, illustrated magazines, Negro music, superficial condensations of scientific essays, detective stories and murder mysteries, infantile comic strips in the newspapers, radio programs, movies, records, lectures, and television. The flamboyant optimism of the popular culture of North America began to conquer the world. In vain rose the protesting voice of the learned José Enrique Rodó; and equally fruitless were his attempts to open new paths to the young thought of the continent, to point out the dangers of the immediate success of utilitarian culture.

Our intellectual middle class, composed of educators, politicians, writers, and professional men, refused to heed the call. There arose semispecialists, semitechnicians, semistatesmen—the practical men who preached against the liberal arts, against Latin and philosophy; the materialists who scorned imagination and aesthetic values. We are weakening our character in this way, sacrificing our individuality, abandoning even our democratic gains, because, as Rodó had warned us, we are forgetting to be thinking, ardent citizens; *men,* rather than merchants of learning and of patriotism. And we create universities that have everything but universality; institutions that do not form the student's character, but arouse in him only the desire for a diploma and a title; schools in which memorizing ability takes the foreground and scientific investigation is unknown.

Our politicians were experts in party machinations; they were electoral technicians, masters of combinations and alliances, able leaders of other men of their kind. But very few ever had a clear, exact conception of what their nations mean in the world, or a philosophy of government that would allow them to administer the state intelligently and with dignity. From this stems Spanish American demagogy, the electoral victories gained so easily by deceit and cynicism, the seeming hopelessness of the multiple problems that the politician cannot solve.

It is this lack of orientation, these nebulous ideals, that occasion my uneasiness. Yet, though I know that our Hispanic American continent is pursuing a wrong path, I have great faith in its chance for salvation. I know that we are all aspiring toward a better world, that the democratic sentiment is alive in our people, that we have a strong feeling for justice, and that we are always ready to defend with our lives the cause of liberty. And this produces in me great enthusiasm.

We are the heirs to a very rich artistic heritage; five empires have bequeathed to us inexhaustible cultural treasures; Spaniards, Portuguese, Mayas, Aztecs, and Incas have stamped their personality on the history of the world through their heroism and aesthetic sense. We must be worthy of this heritage and not allow ourselves to be overcome by illusions and fallacies.

How many times have we heard from the lips of men who are ignorant of the tradition of their culture: "If the English had discovered and colonized our continent, we would now be as great as the Yankees, but since we have all the defects of the Spaniards and Portuguese, we are condemned to be a second-rate people"!

This is a crass error. We are inferior in an age in which a mechanical conception of the world dominates, in which industry and commerce are the yardstick by which the greatness of nations is measured, in which the accumulation of material possessions is the ultimate purpose of all human activities. But the world of tomorrow may be different; the world of the future should be different; and then the great country will be the one whose life is most just and most full, the one that does not exploit its people, the one that educates all its children, the one that will digress from its everyday course to theorize with its philosophers, dream with its poets, feel with its musicians. Beauty is not incongruous amidst humility. Justice is not impossible anywhere, as long as men are being bettered individually.

We must admit the failure of our political, economic, and social systems; and when we attempt the transformation of our society we must keep in mind certain racial qualities that may be put to use. Hispanic American peoples possess the faculty of imagination and dream. Not in vain have we lived more than three centuries in the shade of Don Quijote; not in vain have we accompanied Camões through fantasy and across unending seas; nor was it in vain that we followed Santa Teresa into metaphysical realms. "Who will be weakling enough to deny the strength of Spanish vigor?" wrote Rubén Darío.

We have approached almost all the problems of our short life with an idealistic attitude. We have believed in the sanctity of treaties, in the settlement of conflicts by means of arbitration, in the rights of man, in democracy and liberty. At times—too often, unfortunately—we have been mistaken, but, like Don Quijote, we continue to believe that lambs are enemy forces and that windmills are giants. And as long as we maintain this faith we will succeed in converting unhappy reality into a marvelous ideal.

I could cite in this connection the theory of the majority of Hispanic American sociologists, philosophers, and statesmen. Nevertheless, I shall let these words of Oliveira Lima, commenting upon the idealistic attitude of Brazil, suffice:

> America did not learn liberty by itself. The seed of representative institutions was transported from abroad and germinated here. Europe transmitted its culture to the New World. The fundamentals of Brazilian civilization are Portuguese. From Portugal came its laws and also its ethical norms, generating peace through the equilibrium of the social

forces. Peace is unfortunately still an ideal, but one which shall be attained; for notwithstanding its periodic eclipses, right resists all, as morality resists, as faith resists, as do all those creations of the mysterious instincts of the collective soul acting under the pressure of social laws. Having constructed its own noble edifice on such a firm base, Portugal gave to the Brazilian people perpetuity, and achieved immortality through this work.[1]

When we hear a man speak of "the mysterious instincts of the collective soul," we feel as though we were in the presence of a New World visionary, much closer to the sentimental humanitarianism of a Rousseau than to the utilitarianism of a Bentham. And this is a very typical Hispanic American attitude.

I once attended a convention of Spanish American educators in Washington. A Mexican delegate arose and delivered an eloquent address on some topic. "Very inspired," said an American lady who was seated next to me, "but I just cannot get anything out of it." Actually it was an accomplished oratorical outburst, but it was also a chaotic ideological maze. Here we find grounds for serious meditation. The Spanish American soars to a high emotional plane when he speaks; he is possessed with inspiration; he is in a fervor of artistic creation. His brain contains a given quantity of ideas, and he merely allows them to move about and combine at will, without any organized method. In his exposition he is somewhat of a romanticist; he generally wields a powerful emotional influence over his audience, to whom he succeeds in conveying the ardor of his convictions. If, however, his speech is later submitted to the test of cold analysis, it is apt to reveal only a series of commonplaces and platitudes.

The North American, on the other hand, delivers his talk with cool deliberation; he organizes his ideas methodically and tries to make his public understand the meaning of his thought. Ideas and concepts, as he presents them, have genuine objective values, without the excessive intervention of the individual element in their communication.

---

[1] For note to chapter i see page 217.

We see here that the Spanish American continues faithful to the qualities of his race. He expresses himself artistically, in his own way, and introduces, quite evidently, the subjective factor. The ideas are uttered in rhythmic form, tinted with emotion and imbued with the personality of the orator. The romantic creative process is always complicated, which explains why the American lady could not "get anything out of it." This Spanish American attitude is common even in the most trivial conversation. A young man begins to speak and before long is so intricately involved in elegant phraseology and circumlocutions that he loses the threads of what he is saying, and comes to conclusions entirely contrary to those which his premises had suggested. He is simply engaging in a conventional dialectic form, a beautiful, rhythmic mental exercise.

To proceed, then, we note that a facet of this idealistic attitude toward life is the Hispanic American's preference for certain aesthetic activities. If I were asked which trait is most typical of the Brazilian character, I should say it is lyricism. Oratory has flourished in Brazil with even greater exuberance than in Chile or Argentina. Brazilian statesmen and historians adorn their speeches, and even their technical treatises, with ornate language not far removed from poetic expression. Lyrical is the nature of Nepomuceno and Villalobos; lyrical is, often, the form of Portinari. And how could we deny the lyricism of Manuel Bandeira, Murilo Mendes, and Cecília Meireles? It is a very Portuguese lyricism, that of the old Galician-Portuguese anthologies, very un-Spanish, and therefore difficult to find in other Latin American countries.

The region formerly called New Granada, that is, the zone which was liberated by Bolívar, has been distinguished ever since the early days of our independent existence by its zeal for measure and purity of diction. From there came forth the undaunted Juan Montalvo, who tried to continue the *Quijote* in Ecuador; the great Andrés Bello, who remains till today the most complete intellectual that our continent has produced; the first Spanish

American philologist, Rufino José Cuervo; the severely exacting critic, Miguel Antonio Caro; the elegant novelist, Manuel Díaz Rodríguez; the poet of the most perfect form in our language, Guillermo Valencia; and prose writers and poets without number who cultivated beauty of style and lexicographic purity. It is already axiomatic that the best Spanish in America is spoken in Colombia and it probably would not be far-fetched to attribute this fact to the noble tutelage of these writers.

The influence of the Mayas, those exquisite builders of temples, and of the Aztecs, who excelled in the construction of imposing pyramids, is keenly felt even today among the Mexican people. Mexico had already in the sixteenth century famous architects, sculptors, and painters who had been born in the New World or had come from Spain. This double heritage has affected, therefore, the plastic and pictorial genius of contemporary Mexicans, who have brought American painting to its fullest realization. It is common to speak of Diego Rivera, José Clemente Orozco, and Alfaro Siqueiros as if they were the only great Mexican artists. But when I begin to think of some of my friends, such as Roberto Montenegro, Ramos Martínez, Tamayo, Orozco Romero, Carlos Mérida, Lazo, Frida Rivera, María Izquierdo, and a hundred others, and when I recall those thousands of children whom I have seen in Mexican schools—seven-year-olds who wielded their brushes with the enthusiasm of the old masters of the Renaissance—I am tempted to err on the side of exaggeration and state that everyone in Mexico is a painter!

In Chile, a cosmic passion pervades us. The social drama of our people and of the whole world moves us deeply. Uneasy and tormented, we wander afar in search of spiritual serenity, and finally, having become imbued with mysticism, turn our gaze once again upon our own country. We are cosmopolitan and dramatic. It seems that the omnipresence of the sea has impelled us to journey through all the continents. During the past century, eternal globetrotters were such notable figures as Blest Gana, Vicuña Mac-

Kenna, and Pérez Rosales. And in our times we find D'Halmar traveling through India; Juan Marín in the interior of China; Pablo Neruda in Java, Argentina, Spain and, finally, in Mexico; and Gabriela Mistral enjoying in her nostalgia twenty years of absence from her native land.... Some day we shall all return to our country, each with his apostolic creed, with a Messianic gesture, and before the cold realism of the positivists we will enter again our inner abodes and will remain, wrapped in fantasy, facing the sea and the mountains.

Everything is transformed in America under the influence of the climate and atmosphere. European institutions are brought to our continent; they retain their name, but soon lose their essence. We have witnessed the shameful spectacle of the utter failure of the English type of parliamentary government in our countries; the sheer waste of state funds in useless, fantastic enterprises; the decadence of our universities; the death of our theater, government, economy, education, Church. Everything on the surface is the same as it is in Europe, but in essence it is all different. Only art seems to resist the attacks of the environment without suffering a decline of quality in the evolutionary process. Since colonial times our literature has been undergoing modifications, especially in its more popular aspects, but even this without losing its intrinsic value. Although its external forms may be those of Europe, Spanish American literature has gradually acquired a personality of its own, until it has become the revelation of a new type of man and of a different world. This New World passed through several stages of evolution before finding its voice of today, and my object is to define these changes, from their first manifestations to the present; to sketch, though it be only with general strokes, the complete picture of our literary formation, or rather of the literary expression of the New World.

Before we plunge into the subject matter, I believe it necessary to study briefly the cultural state of our continent at the time of the appearance of its first literary efforts. A literature cannot be conceived in a vacuum, since it is the result of a society, of a special way of viewing life at a particular time and by a particular group of men. Mexico City in the sixteenth century is our scene—but Santo Domingo or Lima would do just as well, since the history of the colonization of America was merely repeated in different geographical areas. I choose Mexico City because Spanish culture of the sixteenth century had its richest flowering there. The Spaniards are the heroes of this cultural drama, although without the Aztecs the dramatic conflict would not have existed. It is for this reason that I deem it necessary to say a few brief words on the indigenous culture before continuing with the higher forms of Spanish civilization, and then to describe finally the clash between the two cultures. The result, most obviously, was the complete destruction of the native culture, in Mexico as well as in all the empires, towns, and tribes invaded by the Spaniards. Therefore, the term *colonial culture in America* should be considered as a general introduction applicable to all the Spanish American countries.

I leave for historical treatises the enumeration of the names of all the writers engendered in an epoch of easy improvisation, an era in which the Church, the sword, and the pen were the only roads to distinction. I pause only before the most outstanding literary figure of the whole colonial period, Sor Juana Inés de la Cruz, the living symbol of a restless people, oppressed by the political and religious imperialism of her time. Like that people, Sor Juana was a rebel, very much an individual, and even when she bowed to the will of her superiors in the order, she left her protest engraved in indelible characters. One modern critic, after studying the works of Sor Juana, spoke of her "frustrated vocation." As a nun, perhaps. She endured a great deal and commented more than once on the stupidity of her religious sisters, but in the end she offered her life to save those ingenuous, simple cell-companions. As a poetess, no. I would place her among the five or six best poets in the Spanish language, and, of course, I consider her *the* great poet of the colonial era. The entire colonial culture flowers in the ardor of her verse.

A hundred years of sterility, monotony, and routine go by. America during the eighteenth century was a field of lilies and shadows. And so was Spain; hardly could be heard the mellifluous but trite song of Meléndez Valdés. But at its end the skies were set aflame with revolution; deafening thunder presaged the death of kings. America, having struggled in seemingly endless turmoil, finally was awakened by the bared sword of Bolívar. Ten nations rallied about the hero. Bolívar built this new world, gave it its institutions and its frontiers, and in a delirium of grandeur burst forth from the summit of Mount Chimborazo in a song of victory.

We new nations then turned against Spain and rejected its tutelage. Upon achieving our independence, we lost at a stroke all the culture acquired during three centuries: there followed a notable cultural decline in the formerly great cities of the Viceroyalty, and for a while we reverted almost to barbarism. Cultural institutions suffered greatly; old customs were uprooted, and even the language began to degenerate. But soon there was a reaction, starting from the very interior of our democratic organism, and we came forth triumphant, with renewed energy, with the virile voice of a free people. America sought and found her own voice, a voice which rose, not as a mere "geographical expression," but as a vigorous new theory of cultural values.

The environment then began to wield great influence upon artistic creation. As the man himself changed, so did his expression, and our continent was enriched with an infinite variety of tones and shades. In the burning tropics appeared poets of exalted imagination and rich, warm color; in the high plateaus or in the temperate zones, Mexico and Chile, the expression became refined and aesthetic conception more subtle; in the great prairies of Brazil, Uruguay, and Argentina, the man of the fields, the man of the savage interior, the man of the *sertões* and the plains alone under the skies, felt the primary impulse of the artist in direct contact with the earth. From that stem the harsh, genuine literature that is represented in Brazil by *Os Sertões* of Euclides da Cunha, and in Argentina by the *Facundo* of Sarmiento and, even more, by the *Martín Fierro* of Hernández. This is the dry, virile voice of the plains that I shall attempt to explain in the essay, *Martín Fierro*. This is literature of a typically American group of men; literature conscious of its creative purpose and of its stylistic medium, literature formed originally by folkloric elements and later elevated to the category of great artistic creation.

I have often commented upon the fortunate bifurcation of our literary path. On one side we have the most cultured forms of European literature, especially those of France, and on the other side the more popular forms, based upon direct observation of phenomena. The latter type of literature is perhaps of less permanence, although it is more genuinely ours because of the local color and the idiomatic, regional nature of expression. We could not remain eternally in the Indianist stage, nor wrapped in the Negro or gaucho phases; and we were rather tired of our little Mussets and of our would-be Byrons. It was then that French influence, instead of being applied directly on particular writers, began to form a general atmosphere in America. It was impossible to escape from the determining tendencies, whether Parnassian or symbolist. One had to write elegantly, with French exquisiteness. The great Spanish literary figures of the times, Juan Valera, Pereda, Pardo Bazán, Pérez Galdós, did not interest us greatly. Insolently we declared that the Spaniards lacked style, that they did not know how to write, that they were prosaic. And at home our first serious stylistic movement was in preparation, the first school that was to restore us, after the death of colonial literature, to the current of universal letters. We gave that tendency the generic appellation of modernism; and in that school arose America's greatest poet, Rubén Darío, and its greatest critic, José Enrique Rodó.

Rubén Darío marks the appearance of poetic genius. He was somewhat of a romanticist because the times in which he lived were never clearly defined and most of the lyric poets wavered between the cold perfection of Leconte de Lisle and the sentimental intensity of Verlaine.

Darío had the gift of internal rhythms, of harmony of phrase, and of symbolic originality. His vocabulary is amazingly rich, his fund of human experiences unique. He sang objectively of the past, present, and future of his America, and even became a civic poet. At times he was unjust in his Hispano-American zeal, as when he summarized so negatively the moral culture of the United States:

> even though you seem to have everything,
> one factor is lacking—God.

And then again he expressed the anguish of a whole continent with the question:

> Will so many millions of us have to speak English?

Finally, having realized that it was possible for the two continents to live in amicable intercourse, he exclaimed with the Brazilian statesman, Fontoura Xavier:

> May this grand Union have no end.

It is obvious, then, that Darío was not of those poets who dwelt in ivory towers. Very much on the contrary, he vibrated with his people and with his race, and more than once there appears in his work the echo of the mixture of blood which coursed through his veins, for, like Gonçalves Dias, he had Indian, Negro, and Spanish forefathers. Briefly, then, we may state that Rubén Darío is the greatest poet of America and that his name may well rank among those of the six best poets of the Spanish language.

José Enrique Rodó, in my opinion, is a highly gifted prose writer. In literary and philosophical subjects he was the most cultured man of his time. He dedicated his whole life to study and meditation; his moral stature was always indisputable; he cultivated his style as did the old Spanish writers, but he renovated the architecture of prose, investing it with a soaring French grace.

His idealism led to the formation of a new school of thought.

With the teachings of his work, *Ariel,* he became the leader of a generation. Perpetuated by his disciples, the Arielists, his philosophy held sway from 1900 until 1918. In that year a strong North American current began to be felt in Latin America, thus reducing the admiration for French thought. Rodó was the chief victim of this approximation to the *mores* of the United States, since he had always opposed the utilitarianism of the Anglo-Saxon people. And the truth is that, viewed in the light of a persistent pragmatism, his theories have proved inadequate for the material development of Spanish America. Nevertheless, I believe that they will once again have their hour of glory, when scientific mechanism has led us to absolute skepticism.

The year 1918 was a crucial one for us. The death of Rodó seemed to put a sudden end to fine prose of the French type. Two years previously, in 1916, Rubén Darío had died, and with him, the *preciosista* poetry. Everywhere now, literary Americanism, New Worldism, regionalism, and nativism were the keynotes of artistic production. Although European modes continued to influence our taste, there already had arisen a desire to create genuinely national art. The same phenomenon appeared shortly before in the United States, where, about 1914, a very American type of poetry came to the fore. Robert Frost, Carl Sandburg, Edgar Lee Masters, and Vachel Lindsay heralded the great lyrical revolution that was to culminate in Ezra Pound and T. S. Eliot. Frank Norris led the way to Sinclair Lewis, Willa Cather, Hemingway, John dos Passos, Faulkner, and Steinbeck.

We witnessed a continent-wide movement of renovation, which in Spanish America meant the death of modernism, and paradoxically, in Brazil, the birth of another type of modernism, although the latter is really an entirely different phenomenon. The lyric vanguard made its appearance with a series of such schools as creationism, stridentism, and surrealism, the majority of which, fortunately, are no longer in existence. New names of daring authors were sounded; thunderous manifestoes were proclaimed;

magazines, more warlike than poetic, were begotten. Rhyme and the usual rhythms were summarily discarded; the sonnet was exiled; punctuation was scorned, as were grammar and common sense. Free verse, exaggerated metaphors, and verbal motorism held sway. But even this period was not entirely barren of fruitful development; new findings enriched the poetic instrument; and though hundreds of poets were drowned in their own madness, several remained as representatives of an era of spiritual and moral anarchy. The modernists of the school of Rubén Darío, horrified by the new groups, mournfully announced the arrival of the anti-poet. All this indicated the presence of a saving vitality, and in fact the chaos did disappear when the poets tried to interpret the clash of the various economic, political, and social forces. The leftist poets, once Communist theorists, surged forward seriously and were actively involved in the Spanish civil war. There were César Vallejo, Pablo Neruda, Nicolás Guillén, actors in the great drama of a young continent, fighting at the side of their Spanish brothers, García Lorca, Rafael Alberti, Miguel Hernández. Much may be expected from these poets so intensely thrust into the social struggle, so forcefully opposed to the past.

About 1918 there appeared also several novelists who shocked readers accustomed to the French type of novel. These writers were the interpreters of a revolutionary sentiment, the defenders of the Indian, the Negro, of the broken, lost, debauched derelict in the city slums, of the jungle laborer on the rubber plantations—in short, of all the oppressed. Our novel, which since its inception at the beginning of the nineteenth century had been a sad imitation of the European, began an independent existence, Americanized in content as well as in form. At times, as in some Ecuadorian and Mexican works, it bordered on excessive exaggeration and bad taste, but on the other hand it has produced masterpieces such as *Los de abajo* (The Underdogs) by Mariano Azuela; *Cantaclaro* by Rómulo Gallegos; *Don Segundo Sombra* by Ricardo Güiraldes; *El Mundo es ancho y ajeno* (Broad and Alien Is the World) by

Ciro Alegría. Contrary to the opinion of Ortega y Gasset, I believe that the novel is only beginning to reveal its multiple possibilities and that in its character as a hybrid genre it is destined for a rich future in America. I say this especially because the novel has ceased to be a purely literary form and has penetrated into all the intellectual activities of man, becoming biography, history, philosophy, and science. Instead of finding itself impoverished, the novel has acquired myriad aspects in its constant search for revelation. Whether or not it is the same genre which used to adhere to the prescribed formulae of composition is a question which does not disturb the young writers of Spanish America; unconcerned, unheeding, they care only to create works which will interest and stir the reader.

Whenever I write "Spanish America," I am assailed by doubt. Shall I consider Brazil also? Even more, will the Brazilians resent being included in the geographical concept of "Spanish America"? It would not be just. "Spanish (or Hispanic) America" is—at least to me—a spontaneous, almost organic concept. And it is only right, if one thinks of *Hispania* and not of *Spain,* that it should be a term devoid of any belligerent connotation, an ingenuous mode of expression to include the entire continent. On the other hand, "Latin America" is a concept loaded with ideology, and therefore with dynamite; it is a term treasured by the French, because it contains cultural implications; but it is extremely difficult for me to accept when I think of such countries as Paraguay or Bolivia. To go on: "Indo-America" is an inaccurate, confusing term, especially when one recalls Cuba, Haiti, and even Brazil itself. As for "Ibero-America," when we employ this term the analytical process has already taken place, and we find it highly artificial. I shall continue, therefore, to use the concept of Hispanic or Spanish America.

The evolutionary process of Brazilian literature is considered generally similar to that of the rest of the continent. Despite the great differences in the systems of colonization of Portugal and

Spain, the culture is identical from the very beginning. The sixteenth and seventeenth centuries produced a kind of Renaissance literature which seems more fitting to the urban flourishing of the Spanish empire than to the mining or rural social organization of the Portuguese. Narrative letters, chronicles, epics, histories, tales of travel, academies—that whole thundering mechanism, laden with exaggeration, beauty, falsity, and revelations—is common to both cultures.

Even in our lives as independent nations the parallels continue. Every cultural evolution, every new ideology, tendency, or school reached America with the same facility with which our gold arrived in Europe. Romanticism, realism, naturalism, Parnassianism, symbolism, modernism—all had their representatives in the Spanish-speaking peoples. For a Castro Alves, we had an Almafuerte; for a Casimiro de Abreu, a Zenea; for a Euclides da Cunha, a Sarmiento; for an Olavo Bilac, a Rubén Darío; for a Cecília Meireles, a Gabriela Mistral; for a Mário de Andrade, an Alfonso Reyes.

I was once asked at a literary convention: "In your opinion, which is the best Chilean work?" Without hesitation I answered: "*Don Quijote*." And I should be very proud if I could add to my list of Chilean, or rather Hispanic American, works, *Dom Casmurro, Os Sertões, Canaan, Angústia,* and *Fogo morto*. And I would enrich Brazilian literature with *Facundo, Martín Fierro, Tradiciones peruanas, Ariel, Prosas profanas, Geometría moral, El Casamiento de Laucha,* and *Los de abajo.*

I should like to appeal to Spanish American youth to abandon the usual domestic and foreign policies of their respective countries. We, who have inherited a great European cultural treasure, have a great American mission to fulfill. Shall we waste this treasure on the daily squabbles of political parties? Shall we continue formulating empty phrases about a Pan-Americanism built on loose sands? Shall we cultivate false local patriotism until it is converted into a continental drama?

Even the social struggle seems of little transcendency when I think of America. Let us not forget that the *left* of yesterday is the *center* of today and can be the *right* of tomorrow! America, one and indivisible, as the orators are wont to say, remains on its bedrock foundation. It is united by the work of its artists, thinkers, and men of letters, by a Bolívar, a Martí, a Rubén Darío, an Alfonso Reyes, a Portinari, an Orozco, a Villalobos. This is our America, the America for which we live, keep vigil, and suffer. Toward its more nearly perfect construction we dedicate our powers, some with the brush, the chisel, or the pen, others with the microscope, but most with the hammer and the plow.

Writing these essays, I am attempting to fulfill an important task: the interpretation of the spiritual values of America.

Chapter II ◇ Colonial Culture in America

LITERATURE, the expression of life, should be studied as one of the many aspects of a society. I therefore begin this series of essays with a rapid commentary on the colonial civilization of Mexico, the most important cultural center of Hispanic America during the sixteenth century. For a definitive study of this subject we should have to analyze all the efforts of the Spaniards in such colonies as Santo Domingo, Lima, New Granada, and Córdoba, in which there was a magnificent cultural flowering. However, I shall not delve quite so far, for various reasons. In the first place, these essays are more an over-all survey than a specialized, minute investigation. Secondly, it is impossible at present to obtain adequate information on the colonial culture of the previously mentioned centers. And lastly, through our study of Mexico, we are obtaining an indirect glimpse of the culture of the other advanced regions of that era. Conditions, dates, and names may vary somewhat, but the Hispanic colonies were virtually alike in formation and development. For example, we find that sixteenth-century Lima, as well as Mexico City, boasted schools for native, mestizo, and Spanish children, a university, printing, religious processions, dramatic presentations in convents and in the open air, and a sumptuous court, overflowing with official poets imported from Spain and with pompous scholars. Lima and Cuzco figured among the most advanced intellectual centers, since not only did they receive distinguished European men of learning, but they also made possible the appearance of native writers of true greatness, such as Garcilaso de la Vega and the brilliant orator, Doctor Espinosa y Medrano, called *el Lunarejo*. The court of the Viceroys of Lima was famed throughout the world for its amazing number of writers and for the literary efforts of the viceroys themselves. What is said of Mexico, then, may be applied equally to Peru. The similarity lies not only in the cultural sphere, but in the entire orbit of human activities and events as well.

It would be absurd to expect colonial Mexico to produce a native culture, one typically, originally its own. For only countries that have achieved complete independence of thought and political action can find their own voice. The colonial culture of Mexico, therefore, was that of Spain, but transplanted into a strange environment and brought into contact with different racial groups. All the institutions of the mother country—the *audiencia,*[1] archbishoprics, convents, monasteries, municipal councils, universities, judicial tribunals, the Inquisition—flourished in Mexico as well and demonstrated clearly the great power of Charles V (Charles I of Spain). As a cultural entity, Mexico was always to Spain and to the rest of the world a nation composed of soldiers, friars, lawyers, adventurers, nobles, businessmen, gunsmiths, silversmiths, tailors, scholars and poets—all white men and all of the Spanish tongue. The vitality and the original, picturesque culture of the great mass of Indians were known only to specialists and travelers. When Cortés arrived in Mexico to conquer empires, exploit mines, create new kingdoms, and destroy native temples, he symbolized the indomitable will of Spain over a people rent with anarchy. The struggle between the two races was mortal. Cortés triumphed, and the Aztec had to speak Spanish, render homage to Charles V, and kneel in somber cathedrals. There came an abrupt end to the temple of the sun, to the pyramid of the moon, and to the cruel human sacrifices. In 1521 the Indian began his hard apprenticeship, a novitiate which has not yet been terminated. The Indian of Mexico, Yucatán, Guatemala, the Chibcha and the Quechua, the Araucanian and the Guaraní, began the tragic march toward the heights of an alien culture.

The language of the whites, the mestizos, and of the majority

[1] For notes to chapter ii see page 217.

of the Indians during colonial times was Spanish. The Mexicans used this linguistic medium in order to become acquainted with the material and intellectual world and to explain in literature their concepts of beauty. Almost all literary historians are agreed that Mexican literature is only a branch of the Spanish and that nothing but the difference of environment has caused in it certain discrepancies in form and background from the works of the mother country. The question arises then: is this difference in literary production sufficiently noticeable to reveal whether a given author is Spanish or Mexican? The Spanish American critic will seek proofs of Americanism wherever possible. For example, several Mexican writers have tried to prove that there are Mexican characteristics in the work of the dramatist Juan Ruiz de Alarcón, one of the four great pillars of the Spanish theater of the Golden Age. They find in the plays of Alarcón a certain moderation, an extremely personal conception of morality, and even stylistic peculiarities foreign to the Spanish temperament. Biographers and critics consider Sor Juana Inés de la Cruz a genuinely Mexican poetess, and assert that her work, deviating from the paths of Spanish lyricism of the Golden Age, acquires a regional tone. However, I maintain that if this local note does exist, it is not clearly determinable, and hence I shall study the colonial writers as true representatives of Spanish culture.

My purpose is to investigate some of the aspects of that culture in Mexico, especially in the sixteenth century. I wish to establish from the beginning that I hold the highest opinion of the native culture that existed in Mexico at the time of the Spaniards' arrival. In order to construct their temples and pyramids, the Aztecs must have been able to boast a long cultural tradition; in order to compose their calendars they must have been considerably advanced in abstract thought and scientific learning. Through their sculpture, painting, and hieroglyphic writing we may surmise the intensity of their internal life. Their principal activities were war and religion, and consequently their entire educational system centered about these two vital ends.

When a male child was born, the medicine woman, according to Sahagún, would address him in the following words: "Here you have sprung forth and shall flourish; here you have been separated from your mother as a chip is cut from a rock; this is your cradle, the place where you rest your head. This house is only your shelter, your dwelling; your true land is elsewhere, on the fields where wars are waged and battles are fought; war is your right and your occupation: you shall toast the sun with the blood of your enemy." If the newborn infant was a female, the invocation was different: "You shall remain in your home as does the heart within the body; you shall neither leave it nor become accustomed to going elsewhere; you shall keep alive the coals of the hearth; you shall be like the rocks upon which is placed the receptacle. Here our God surrounds you; here you shall work, and your task shall be to bring water and to grind the maize on the *metate:*[3] here you are to toil by the coals of the firepan."

The goal of Aztec education was to develop a body of steel and a soul filled with fanatical zeal. Throughout the entire year the children were bathed in cold water; they were dressed with only the indispensable garments, and made to sleep on hard beds. At the age of four the male children carried water and light burdens, and at seven they learned the profession of their fathers. The little girls learned domestic tasks, and upon reaching womanhood were dedicated to the cult of the gods and to the service of their husbands. Children were taught to tell the truth at all times, and lying was severely punished; furthermore, there was instilled into them a love for the helpless and the poor, and they were constantly engaged in useful labors. Above all, idleness was despised.

García Icazbalceta gives us interesting details of the native schools and educational methods:

> The Aztecs did not have public schools similar to ours today. Instead, the schools for boys, adjoining the temples, were places of retirement, maintained by the priests for their own benefit. The young girls cleaned the temple and did the manual labor; there they were taught moral prin-

ciples, but were denied all intellectual knowledge. There existed an institution called *Quico-Yan,* where the youths learned to sing and dance. The children were divided into two groups: those who attended the *Calmecac* and those who went to the *Telpuchcalli.* The first school, for the children of the nobility, prepared its pupils for the service of the priests; it emphasized especially the memorization of ritual chants dealing with historical episodes and the study of hieroglyphics. Boys and girls of the middle class attended the *Telpuchcalli,* where they received an education similar to that afforded by the *Calmecac.* However, they were subject to a more rigid discipline, almost military in character. On the other hand, the great mass of the people received no education at all.[3]

It is known from the unanimous testimony of the writers of the time and from the study of native pictures that the Aztecs had books on varied subjects: history, travels, genealogy, criminal and civil law codes, calendars, mythology, astrology, topographical maps, plans of cities, financial statements and accounts of tributes, land and property rights, statutes and legal actions, songs, hymns to the gods, and the like. They were well versed, also, in arithmetic, astronomy, geometry, national geography, poetry, and gymnastics. They were fond of sports, and especially of the dance, ball games, and the *volador.*[4] In the words of Orozco y Berra:

> They held in great esteem dancing and singing, and therefore the kings and lords maintained official dancers. In private celebrations the dancers were few, but on the occasion of public festivals their number increased to thousands. The musicians, seated on fine palm mats, occupied the center, while the dancers formed about them concentric circles, ever widening as they receded from the music.[5]

In every city of reasonable importance there were places reserved for ball games. The players, unclothed except for deerskin leggings and gloves to protect their hands, indulged in a game of tossing the ball through a stone ring on a wall or in the corner of a building.

The Mexicans were especially fond of architecture, sculpture, painting, feather work, textiles, and pottery, and even created a kind of theater, the stage being placed in the center of a market or in the patio of a temple.

The primitive civilizations of Mexico are noted for their artistic works, but their art was not based on canons of beauty or on subjective emotion. Rather, it was the product of a religious conception of the universe. From the time of the Mayas until that of the Aztecs, the nature of the aboriginal painting was always determined by the severe, rigid dogma of their supernatural beliefs. There emerged a symbolic art in the early civilization, wherein the mystic element of the ceremonies and rituals bore close resemblance to magic. Architecture was the most important artistic form and included in its complex character both painting and sculpture. Of course, I refer here only to monumental, religious, and military structures—temples, pyramids, and forts—since the more simple type of construction, based on inferior materials, disappeared at the time of the Spanish conquest. The pyramids and temples served a dual purpose: they were places of worship and sacrifice and, at the same time, fortresses. The most common architectural type of Mexico is the pyramidal form, and we find temples and palaces constructed on superimposed planes.

Decorations abound in Mexican architecture, and the most typical symbol is that of Quetzalcoatl, the plumed serpent. The interior walls of many temples are adorned with the faces of gods and devils, and on all the religious buildings there are many symbolic reliefs. The common purpose of priest and warrior in the erection of these structures is proved by the fact that the temples generally were built around squares, offering thus the aspect of modern fortifications. One of the most famous temples in Mexico is that of Quetzalcoatl, in Teotihuacán. Its popular appellation, "la ciudadela" (the citadel), is indicative of the fortress-like character of its construction.

The first impression that one receives of Mexican sculpture is mystery-boding, even terror-inspiring. The power of magic revealed in the gods, devils, and symbolic masks unsettles our conception of realistic art. We must remember that the Mexican artist was steeped in an atmosphere of religion and that his creations interpreted natural and divine forces far beyond the understanding of the masses. The monstrous nature of this sculpture was the means employed by the upper classes to keep the people in constant fear and awe of the natural powers that the sculptor symbolized in grotesque figures. Sculpture was only a part of the decorative plan of religious structures. The Mayas reached an extraordinary level of development in this art; their bas-reliefs, with figures in profile, are exquisite, and their mastery of line is apparent in the drawing of feathers, birds, animals, and human faces.

The Toltec culture reveals a development of technique never surpassed by the other races, as the pyramid of Quetzalcoatl in Teotihuacán amply proves. There the influence of Mayan art is manifest in a new aspect of the plumed serpent. The Toltecs introduced into Yucatán not only columns in the form of the serpent, but also the use of caryatids.

The Mexican sculptor had no realistic conception of his art, and consequently did not attempt to imitate nature. He was the interpreter of a barbarian cosmogony, and hence reduced all his experiences to a few symbols, such as the serpent, the eagle, and the tiger.

Ritual dominated also in Mexican painting, which was therefore ornamental and symbolic. Landscapes were unknown, and the representation of objective reality was deformed, in accordance with the desires of the priestly caste. Painting, as we have already indicated, was merely part of architecture, and even today, fretwork, animals, and human figures may be observed in the mural reliefs. Perspective is nonexistent in the pictorial groups, and the figures are distributed one above the other, with the purpose of conveying the impression of distance. However, the line of the horizon is always conspicuously lacking. In spite of the fact that the Mexican painters were limited to religious expression, they have left us, in manuscripts, frescoes, and ceramics, definite proof of their technical perfection.

One wonders, when confronted with evidence of the refinement of these races, how they could possibly have fallen so easily into the hands of the Spanish conqueror. Clearly, we must attribute that collapse to their religious beliefs. Montezuma was fully convinced that some day the god Quetzalcoatl would come to put an end to his reign; and so, when Cortés appeared, the emperor believed that his destiny was realized, as Hernan Cortés himself relates in his *Cartas* (Letters), and Bernal Díaz in his celebrated *Historia* (History). Furthermore, since the Mexican peoples were divided and torn by constant warfare, Cortés profited by the situation, contracting advantageous alliances with the enemies of Montezuma. The year 1521 marks the end of the native Mexican civilization. The Spaniard had come to the New World to conquer, to destroy, and to re-create. Too intolerant to permit the coexistence of any other religion with the Catholic, the conqueror razed the temples, burned the sacred books, and annihilated the higher ranks of Mexican nobility.

Churches and palaces were built upon the ruins of the ancient native temples. Within a few years the Aztec capital was converted into a European city, the center of a new civilization. Cathedrals, buildings of plateresque architecture, private houses of stone and iron, resembling fortresses rather than homes, arose everywhere. The Spanish governmental mechanism began to function, staffed by an enormous, unwieldy bureaucracy. The marvelous tales recounted about New Spain attracted a multitude of soldiers, priests, and adventurers. But there were great tasks to be done, for millions of Indians had to be assimilated into the Spanish civilization, and the conquerors were not common highwaymen or thieves—as English historians have asserted,—but men entrusted with a religious and cultural mission.

I have said that the first missionaries destroyed valuable cultural and religious documents. Although I am in agreement with García Icazbalceta with respect to the exaggerations of many historians on that question, especially concerning the destructive work of Juan de Zumárraga, the first Archbishop of Mexico, who has been accused of burning the Aztec writings, we must conclude that these historians are in essence correct. In the words of Padre José de Acosta:

> In the province of Yucatán, where the bishopric of Honduras is located, there were certain books in which the native scholars had noted down their calendar system and their ancient customs. All were things which indicated great inquisitiveness and diligence. But it seemed to one of our priests that they were tokens of sorcery and magic, and he decided that they should be burned, a deed that was later lamented, not only by the Indians, but also by the Spaniards, who wanted to learn the secrets of the land. The same thing has taken place in other spheres, since some members of our order, believing that everything is superstition, have destroyed many documents of ancient, secret things, that would be very useful to me.... The cause of this is a stupidly applied zeal, because not knowing, and not even wanting to know the civilization of the Indians, they assert, without reflection or examination, that everything native is mere witchcraft, and that, since the Indians are just drunkards, they cannot know or understand anything.[6]

This religious zeal, which to other historians, to opponents of Spain, and to Protestants, was only ignorance and fanaticism, had so calamitous an effect that even Cortés bemoaned it. But, according to Padre Jesús Sánchez, those dark days were followed by a period of enlightenment in which the great loss that the world had suffered was assessed at its true value. Thus, other missionaries tried to repair the damage done by their spiritual brothers. They learned the native tongues and taught Spanish to the Indians; they studied the history, the customs, and even the religion of the land; they wrote grammars and dictionaries, and published books, at times in three languages. Five priests landed in Mexico with Cortés; soon thereafter, the mendicant orders sent representatives to the New World. First were the twelve famous Franciscan friars, whose arrival is so beautifully described by Bernal Díaz; the Dominicans were not long in following; later came the Augustinian monks, and lastly the Jesuits. Some of these priests, such as Gante, Witte, and Daciano, were of royal blood. Beyond a doubt, these missionaries were truly heroic; they did not venture in search of earthly possessions, but aspired to the kingdom of Heaven. In general, they were cultured men, anonymous heroes of unsung deeds, humble teachers, great scholars and martyrs. History has been ungrateful to them. The most outstanding of them, Padre las Casas, has been slandered throughout the centuries by his own fellow countrymen, who blame him for having originated the "black legend" of the Spanish conquest.

During the sixteenth century, many of the missionaries opposed bitterly those governors who deviated from the path of righteousness and ethical conduct. It would be difficult to assert that their religious propaganda was more effective than their cultural influence. We do know one thing: that their interest for the well-being of the Indians was sincere; ample proof of this is afforded by the long battle which they waged against the *encomenderos*,[7] the traditional oppressors of the natives. In effect, only part of the work of the priests was strictly religious, since they devoted themselves to offering the Indians every kind of learning: reading, writing, arithmetic, history, geography, painting, music, and industrial arts.

Among the first missionaries were two whose names belong today to history, Fray Pedro de Gante and Fray Toribio de Benavente, whom the Indians called *Motolinía* because of his poverty and humility. Herbert I. Priestley, commenting upon the importance of these clergymen, says:

> The conquerors, led by Cortés himself, reverently kissed the robes of these saintly men when they reached the capital, displaying a humility which had its intended effect on the Indians. The influence of the friars was sedulously courted because of their power as representatives of the church, but more practically because their hold over the Indians would tend to make the latter better vassals and laborers. Then too it was advisable to stand well with the friars, for their reports to the king's ministers might bring great good or evil. Cortés submitted, on a staged occasion, to being flogged by a friar for non-attendance at mass, so that his example might quiet the complaints of natives who had received similar treatment.[8]

And Bernal Díaz relates in his *Historia* that Cortés, upon learning of the arrival of the first missionaries, sent special welcoming delegations to receive them and ordered that they be rendered homage all along the road to Mexico City. In fact, so great was his zeal that he ordered tents to be built to shelter the holy travelers, so that they would not have to sleep in the open air.

The Franciscans built schools next to their churches. At first they forced the Indian nobility to send their children to these schools, but soon compulsion was no longer required. Within a short time some of these children learned so much that they in turn became teachers of the men of their own race and held classes in the patios of churches and monasteries. Fray Pedro de Gante was the founder and principal of Mexico City's first school, called San Francisco de México. This school boasted an attendance of a thousand students, many of whom were children of the old Aztec nobility. The pupils received elementary education and religious instruction. Later they were given music lessons, and were taught drawing, Latin, and industrial arts. Soon there were painters, sculptors, engravers, carpenters, masons, tailors, and shoemakers among the Indians. Fray Pedro de Gante is the originator of the objective method of teaching, employing figures and objects which graphically represent new ideas; this form of pedagogy is the natural outgrowth of the hieroglyphic characters of the Aztecs. Gante wrote a series of books with beautiful symbols and attractive colors which represented friars, soldiers, buildings, and sacred scenes. His method was later adopted by all the missionaries. A French monk, Fray Jacobo de Tastera, who did not even know Spanish, caused the principal mysteries of the Catholic faith to be portrayed on a large canvas; then, showing it in his classroom, he would ask the best student to explain to his companions the meaning of the paintings. The missionaries would hang illustrative pictures on the walls and, as they lectured, would indicate the scenes with a pointer. Accustomed to hieroglyphics, the Indians adopted this method for writing out their own catechisms and prayer books, inserting European letters occasionally and thus creating a kind of hybrid writing.

Fray Pedro de Gante succeeded in founding a church, a hospital, and an excellent school which was at the same time a center of fine arts and of industrial training. He was the great propagator of the culture of his century, not only in Mexico, but also in the other colonies. His objective method was applied in Quito and Lima with equally notable results.

Bishop Zumárraga, who has been blamed by all historians for the destruction of the Aztec books, repaired, through his great interest in the advancement of the Indians, the harm he had done previously. In 1536 he founded, exclusively for the natives, the Academy of Santa Cruz de Tlaltelolco, where instruction in religion, ethics, reading, writing, Latin grammar, rhetoric, philosophy, music, and Mexican medicine was offered. This institute boasted famous teachers: Fray Arnaldo de Basacio, a French scholar; Fray Juan Focher, a professor of the University of Paris; Fray Andrés de Olmos, a celebrated linguist; Fray Juan de Gaona, a graduate of the University of Paris; Fray Francisco de Bustamante, the most distinguished orator of his time; and Fray Bernardino de Sahagún, defender of the Indians and a noteworthy historian.

Some of the best students of this school later became teachers of the children of the Creoles and Spaniards, a fact which speaks most highly of the intelligence of the vanquished race and of the humanitarianism and democratic sentiment of the conquerors. Others dedicated themselves to the dissemination of Catholicism among their people, and a few even became "mayors" and governors of native provinces.

But the work of the missionaries was not restricted to the Indians. The mestizos, offspring of Spaniards and Indian women, were generally forsaken, and either died or became social outcasts. To remedy this tragic situation, the viceroy, Antonio de Mendoza, founded the Academy of San Juan de Letrán, for the purpose of training the mestizos for the teaching profession. This institute may be considered the first normal school in the Americas. One of the most interesting aspects of San Juan de Letrán was the introduction of vocational instruction. Here the students were divided into two groups with different careers in prospect: those who gave evidence of superior intelligence and industry could follow a course in literature and the liberal arts; those who showed less aptitude acquired mechanical skills and practical trades.

The children of the Spaniards and of the Creoles could not attend any of the above-mentioned schools. There existed for them private schools with special teachers at fixed salaries. One of these private teachers was the famous humanist Francisco Cervantes de Salazar, author of the well-known *Diálogos* (Dialogues). The Augustinian monks and the Jesuits also engaged actively in education: the former, limiting themselves to the instruction of Creoles and Spaniards, founded several important academies; the latter, concentrating on higher education ever since their arrival in Mexico in 1572, also established secondary schools and seminaries, among them the prominent San Ildefonso (1583).

Enthusiasm for the quest of culture ran so high that, according to García Icazbalceta, Mexico was virtually becoming depopulated because so many young men went to Spain to complete their education! Of course, the statement of the distinguished scholar is exaggerated, since only the rich families could afford to send their sons to Spain. On the other hand, the racial division of education produced a veritable chaos. The problem became so pressing that the religious orders and the civil authorities addressed a joint petition to the King of Spain, requesting that he create a "university replete with instruction in all the sciences, one in which Indians and Spaniards might be educated in the Catholic faith and in other faculties." Without awaiting the approval of the entreaty, the viceroy, Antonio de Mendoza, appointed professors to teach the most popular sciences of the time, and promised the creation of the university. In fact, he offered some of his private property to the new institution. And thus, in 1551, only thirty-two years after the arrival of Cortés in Mexico, the University of Mexico was founded by a royal decree of Charles V, the edict bearing the signature of Prince Philip. The ordinance granted to the University the sum of 1,000 gold pesos a year and bestowed upon it the organization and privileges of the University of Salamanca. In 1555 the Pope confirmed its foundation, conceding to the University the title of "Pontifical."

Thus, on January 25, 1553, the Royal and Pontifical University of Mexico was inaugurated. Luis de Velasco, Viceroy of New Spain, the members of the *audiencia,* government officials, and representatives of the religious orders were in attendance. A solemn mass was celebrated and the various regents of the new institution were named. Classes began on June 3, 1553, with a prayer delivered in Latin by the scholar mentioned above, Cervantes de Salazar. Among the first professors were several of European fame, as the learned author of the *Diálogos* recounts, and the principal courses of study included civil and canon law, theology, liberal arts, rhetoric, grammar, medicine, and the Otomí language.

The establishment of the University marks the apogee of Mexican culture and provides indisputable proof of that Spanish idealism which those who see in the conquest only brutality and plundering would deny. In the same year, 1551, the foundation of the University of San Marcos was decreed. For more than a hundred years these two universities were the only institutions of higher learning on our continent.

In the capital of Mexico, as in Lima, all literary genres were cultivated, with the single exception of the novel, which, because of its social nature and possible utilization as a means of propaganda, was expressly prohibited. Let us note the learned words of the wife of Charles V, who stated in a royal edict:

> I have been informed that many works of fiction, in the vernacular tongue, and of other than religious subject matter, such as *Amadís de Gaula*[9] and others, have been brought to the Indies; as this is very bad

for the Indians, and a thing which they should not know of or read, I order, consequently, that henceforth no one shall be allowed to take works of fiction or of secular subject matter to those territories. Only to be permitted are those which treat of Christian religion and morality, with which works the Indians and other inhabitants may practice the art of reading, and with which they may busy themselves.

But such decrees then, as others like them today, were at times impossible to enforce. The fact is that some novels were smuggled into the country between sacred works and reached the avid eyes of the Creoles. And not only did chivalric novels of the cycle of *Amadís* and *Palmerín* make their way into the New World, but also such very dangerous material as copies of the picaresque tale *Lazarillo de Tormes,* and of the *Quijote.* In short, other reasons than the interdiction must be adduced to explain the complete absence of the Spanish American novel during that period. Printing facilities were in the hands of the priests, who naturally reserved them for the publication of doctrinal works and for the dissemination of Catholic dogma. The epic poem and the chronicle, actual or fantastic, replaced the novel to a certain extent. It is interesting to note that when the novel finally appeared, three centuries later, its first fruit was *El Periquillo Sarniento,* a work of the picaresque type!

If poetry did exist among the natives, none of it has definitely been uncovered. There are critics who accept the authenticity of the poems of *Netzahualcoyotl* in Mexico, as there are others who believe in the Quechua origin of *Ollanta.* It is an established fact that some of the missionaries wrote plays and poetry in native tongues, and more than one scholar has indulged the fancy of attributing these works to Aztec or Quechua poets. The problem still exists, and those scholars who take great pleasure in tormenting themselves needlessly are still struggling with such transcendental questions. What we may actually assert is that certain oral legends of the Indians came to form part of compositions written by Spanish poets of the sixteenth century. Naturally, these legends stimulated the writers to continue exercising their own imaginations and to produce what could be called the nativist cycle of Latin American literature.

Poetry was abundantly cultivated in Mexico and Lima in the sixteenth century. The Church employed it as an aesthetic complement to its religious ceremonies, and for use in its processions and on triumphal arches. Christmas carols and verses to the Virgin and to the saints burst forth like wildflowers. The University inaugurated poetic tourneys and contests in which there was everything—except poetry. Poets arrived from Spain and established themselves at the courts of Lima and Mexico. Valbuena says that poets in Mexico were as abundant as manure. For example, three hundred of them appeared at a literary competition. I feel very little interest toward these lyricists; rather, I prefer the descriptive poetry of a Bernardo de Valbuena and the Renaissance epic, *La Araucana,* of Alonso de Ercilla.

Without doubt, the theater had positive merit during that period. It was of great social importance in Mexico and Lima, and it served as the instrument of Catholic dogma elsewhere. Among the Indians, it had developed from the dance, after the latter means had become incapable of expressing the psychological conflicts or the historical events of the race. There is only a short step between the dances that the Mexican Indians offered to their gods (dances in which men and women took part, disguised with masks, and in which simpletons did the contrary of what was told them) and the real comedy in the period of its formation. Mexican chroniclers describe to us Indian performances in which characters appeared, feigning infirmities, sneezing, jumping about, and mocking each other. Those Spaniards who had just witnessed in Spain the naïve productions of Juan del Encina must have delighted in this native theater.

The missionaries used dramatic art to teach the Indians the mysteries of the Catholic faith; they themselves wrote plays in the native tongues and translated classical works of Lope de Vega and Calderón into the Mexican languages. Performances were given at the Epiphany, Corpus Christi, and Christmas ceremonies in the courtyards of the monasteries and churches. When the churches became too small to accommodate all the spectators, the friars built special chapels with many naves, each open on one side, so that the ceremonies could be seen from all parts of the structure. Finally, the performances took place in the open air. One of the favorite plays of the Tlascala Indians was the *Misterio de Adán y Eva* (Mystery of Adam and Eve), of interest even to us because of its ingenuous concept of the original sin. The play begins in a garden constructed with real and artificial trees. Adam and Eve appear, before the original sin. Eve is playing with an ocelot or leopard; in the trees, birds are gaily singing. However, in the next scene, after the sin, Eve approaches the wild cat, but the animal bares its teeth menacingly toward her. By means of that naïve symbol the Mexican Indian gleaned a moral principle which was really far beyond his ken.

Also, as in medieval Europe, historical themes were widely developed in the theater. The famous battles between the Moors and the Christians, and those of the conquest of the Americas, afforded abundant material for these works. Fortresses often served as settings, and at times thousands of actors took part. Among these plays, the *Conquista de Jerusalén* (Conquest of Jerusalem) and *Conquista de México* (Conquest of Mexico) are most worthy of attention. To illustrate the opinion that the Indians held of Cortés, we may note here that the Conqueror himself appears in one of these works—as chief of the Moslems!

Parallel to this theater in the native tongue there existed another in Castilian, one especially dedicated to the celebration of important religious occasions, that of Corpus Christi above all. After the processions, performances were offered, at once secular and religious. Nevertheless, the profane elements increased so alarmingly that certain presentations were soon forbidden. Bishop Zumárraga had to issue an order decreeing the exact form that processions were to take, and the good cleric took pains to observe how shameful and disrespectful a thing it was for men to go about masked and dressed as women, and to dance and jump about with indecent and licentious movements in the very presence of the Most Holy Lord.

So numerous were the restrictions and limitations imposed upon the religious theater that the people began to feel a need of secularizing the dramatic art. In fact, within a short time profane performances appeared and the theater acquired a professional character. The catechizer was forced to yield before the troupes from Spain, which wended their way from Mexico to Peru. The Mexican theater flourished so greatly that by the dawn of the seventeenth century it had given Spain one of its great dramatists, Juan Ruiz de Alarcón, who bears, or should bear, to Spain the same importance that Shakespeare does to England and Molière to France.

The tendency toward secularization is made evident in the works of a very curious writer of the sixteenth century, Fernán González de Eslava. In his *Coloquios espirituales y sacramentales* (Spiritual and Sacramental Plays) Eslava combines religious themes with others of a most temporal nature: for example, the arrival in Mexico of distinguished travelers, the appearance of highwaymen along the roads, the construction of forts, and the terrible effects of the plague. In short, Juan Ruiz de Alarcón, González de Eslava, and Sor Juana Inés de la Cruz place the Mexican colonial theater above that of many European countries of the period.

To complete the picture of the cultural life of Mexico in the sixteenth century, we would have to discuss in detail the work of the historians and chroniclers, of the epic and narrative poets, the refinements of court life, the academies of music, the great painters who worked on religious murals, the sculptors and architects, the silversmiths, the philosophers, and the scientists. Let it be enough here to recall that García Icazbalceta's *Bibliografía mexicana del siglo XVI* (Bibliography of Mexican Works of the Sixteenth Century) lists more than one hundred books of varied subject matter written and published in Mexico during that period. A full commentary would require a long dissertation on each one, and these essays are, I repeat, more in the nature of a survey than of minute, erudite researches.

Upon these solid cultural foundations, the roots of which penetrate deeply into the soil of America, those heroic, brutal, primitive yet cultured Spaniards were going to build a glorious edifice, an entire continent of adventures and future greatness. Had it not been for the exemplary stimulus given by the sixteenth-century Spaniards to the formation of cultural and spiritual values, Latin America would have been a savage, sterile, colonial territory. Spain gave us its blood, and that still courses through our veins. Spain gave us its spirit, and with it we have built a new world, in which we live with dignity and pride . . . and if at times there appears in us a spark of the madness of the *conquistador,* we are proud of that madness too.

Chapter III ◇ Sor Juana Inés de la Cruz

THE MEXICAN nun, Sor Juana Inés de la Cruz, is the most important literary figure of colonial Hispanic America. She lived during the second half of the seventeenth century, when the poetry of the Spanish Golden Age was obviously in decadence, redeemed only by the genius of Calderón. The great poets, such as Fray Luis de León, Quevedo, Góngora, and Lope de Vega, who had lent such brilliance to the literary production of that century of masters, had already passed into oblivion, and only minor names—Villegas, Bernardino de Rebolledo, Sor Violante do Ceo—figure among the contemporaries of Sor Juana. Of the poets of that period, some suffer from an exaggerated Gongorism,[1] and others, from an even more fatal malady, prosaism and vulgarity of theme and expression. Luis de Góngora should not bear the entire blame for that vertiginous descent toward bad taste and a poetic labyrinth, despite the accusations of almost every critic who has studied the era. The obscurity of Gongorism, which many have attacked, is only a desire to stylize poetry, to remove it from everyday, popular expression, to create the atmosphere of mystery and the loftiness indispensable to all aesthetic conception. If Góngora's poetry, with its continual use of Greek words and Latin phrases—which denote a solid classical foundation—and with its exuberance of metaphors and hyperboles, needs explanations and commentaries, the fault is not that of the poet, but of the reader, who does not know the mainstays of poetic technique.

In my opinion, the decline which began in the seventeenth century and lasted until 1900 is due to the dearth of real genius and the superabundance of ingenuity. In fact, the elements of

[1] For notes to chapter iii see pages 217–222.

sonorousness, brilliance, and elegance of diction which were introduced into the poetic idiom should have effected a fruitful rebirth of Castilian poetry. But Gongorism could not work miracles on Spanish literary sterility. It is futile to offer distinguished models when there are no poets to receive them. Therefore, in order to judge this movement we must study it as exemplified by Góngora himself, and by his most gifted disciple, Quevedo. I would say that Gongorism, next to the Italian school of the sixteenth century, is the most important and vigorous movement in the artistic history of Spain; for its influence was not limited to poetry, but invaded all the arts, and in some degree even the general expression of the Spanish-speaking man! The most evident proof of this lies in the fact that when there did arise, within and without Spain, serious poets who followed this euphuistic trend—as did Sor Juana Inés de la Cruz, in her *Primero Sueño* (First Dream), Mallarmé and Laforgue in France, Julio Herrera y Reissig in Uruguay, and almost the entire European and Hispano-American "vanguard,"—it served as a purifying, disciplinary force. Whether or not Sor Juana Inés de la Cruz was under the influence of Góngora, the circumstance does not affect our evaluation of her as the last great lyric poet of Spain and the first great poet of America. The significance of this fact transcends the cultural history of the Spanish-speaking peoples, as well as that of the world of literature. In observing that Sor Juana, though born in Mexico, is a poetess clearly Spanish in type, we are defining the whole process of Spanish colonization. For Spain continues to live in America, without any fundamental changes, as much in the sphere of institutions and customs as in the attitude of its people before the most vital problems of life—in the deep Iberian psychological root. This manner of understanding and expressing life, which carried Spain to the apogee of its greatness, passed as if by miracle to a world yet in the formative stage and gave it a spiritual significance that still is the prime reason for its existence. Sor Juana is a symbol and a realization, one more proof of the internal vigor of a race, and a justification of the Spanish effort in America.

The entire work of Sor Juana—plays, sonnets, ballads, little Christmas songs, critical writings—conforms with the best poetic inspiration of the Golden Age. It would be useless to try to discern in her work traces of Mexicanism, for they are nonexistent, whether in her sensibility or in her subject matter. Her occasional references to local events and her use of native words are not sufficient reason for characterizing her as a Mexican poetess; they serve merely to lend the grace of popular inspiration to her poetry.

In her role as a Spanish poetess Sor Juana fulfills a historic mission, that of linking two continents by means of her poetry and her insatiable intellectual curiosity. Not only did she perpetuate Spanish lyric verse in Mexico; she also maintained a close epistolary friendship with the great figures of the court. And even in her cell the nun held a kind of literary cenacle, which was attended by all the cultured men of the time, including the viceroy,—all eager to foster in the New World a renascence of the cultural atmosphere of the Iberian peninsula. In her work, and in the example she set for others, the genius of Sor Juana shone forth against the dull background of an era of general artistic decline.

If time had destroyed all the documents pertinent to the literary culture of colonial Mexico; if the world knew nothing of the great university founded in 1553, nor of the schools for Indians, Creoles, and Spaniards; nor of González de Eslava (author of the *Autos sacramentales*); nor of Juan Ruiz de Alarcón, the profound and discreet dramatist, whose play *La Verdad sospechosa* (The Liar) is of enduring significance; nor of Sigüenza y Góngora (although a century late, still almost a Renaissance figure)—were all this unknown, and were we to discover suddenly in an old convent a manuscript of the *Inundación castálida* of Sor Juana, we would believe we had encountered a poet of a highly advanced civilization. And in effect we would be right, for the nun lived spiritually in an ideal world of her own and conscientiously ignored the pettiness of the courtiers and writers who surrounded her.

It is very fortunate for us, I believe, that our literary formation did not undergo in colonial times what we have later called "literary Americanism," with its varied manifestations of Indianism, nativism, Negro poetry, gaucho literature, popular regionalism, and the like. All these tendencies have their reason for being and should exist; but it is much to be preferred that they be cultivated when a literature has already achieved its full development and acquired a distinctive personality. Only when the writer is master of his cultural heritage, and skilled in every phase of classical discipline, can he approach the rich fount of popular themes with the implements of the artisan. The evolution from the primitive to the cultured is difficult and slow; and obviously, once the models are at hand, it would be absurd for us to repeat an entirely useless historical process. Our literature, then, did not have to pass through that long evolution, but appeared from the very outset—be it in the *Araucana* of Ercilla or in the *Bernardo* of Valbuena—with an exalted sense of artistic expression.

The work of Sor Juana stands forth, then, as the flowering of a refined culture. She carries the *auto sacramental*[2] (that form so dear to the greatest Spanish poets) to its highest lyric expression in *El Cetro de José* (Joseph's Sceptre), *El divino Narciso* (The Divine Narcissus), and *El Mártir del Sacramento, San Hermenegildo* (Saint Hermengildus, Martyr of the Sacrament). She acquits herself with merit in her plays, *Los Empeños de una casa* (Domestic Difficulties), and *Amor es más laberinto* (Love is a Labyrinth), as well as in her *loas*[3] and *sainetes*.[4] Her prose is full of color and vitality in the famed *Respuesta a Sor Filotea* (Reply to Sister Filotea). Her strophes and sonnets in the Italian manner reveal a style worthy of the envy of even the great Spanish classicists of the sixteenth century. Her spontaneous ballads are of the more popular type, as are her ingeniously contrived quatrains. Especially charming is the one that begins:

Este amoroso tormento
que en mi corazón se ve,
sé que lo siento y no sé
la causa por que lo siento.[5]

Finally, Sor Juana reaches her definitive expression in her short religious compositions, sacred ballads, dirges, and especially in her Christmas songs, little masterpieces of charm and simplicity.

Her most transcendental, if not her best known, lyric work is the symbolic poem, *El Sueño* (Dream), in which she approaches only too frequently the *Soledades* (Solitudes) of Góngora. Literary critics generally assert that this poem is superior to the masterwork of the great Cordovan, but once again comparison is futile. *El Sueño* is an interesting document which reveals the subconscious and organic processes of sleep, as well as Sor Juana's flight of imagination, sustained by the metaphorical framework of Góngora.

Above all these manifestations of literary talent, Sor Juana possessed one outstanding gift, an insatiable Renaissance intellectual curiosity, an ever-pressing desire to acquire all kinds of knowledge, at the cost of sleeplessness, of sacrifice, and of controversy. For this reason, she became interested in literary theories, in matters of style and language; she cultivated varied metrical forms, employed several languages in her poems, coined words and popular expressions; she engaged in serious discourse on art, science, beauty, and education; she attempted to destroy prejudice and superstition, and pleaded for complete freedom of mind and soul. That all-pervading intellectual curiosity, which brought her to study mathematics, to read every book that fell into her hands, and to create an astronomical observatory equipped with the most modern instruments of her time, clearly defines her, and places her well in the history of her race.

In a fine essay written by Pedro Salinas on the Mexican nun, the Spanish poet denies that the personality of Sor Juana may be wholly summed up in her capacity as a poetess or as a nun; rather, Salinas asserts that the basic element of her character was the desire to learn, and that the drama of her life sprang from the constant clash between her inquisitive nature and the intellectually narrow environment in which she lived. "Neither poetic nor religious was the real soul of Sor Juana. If we take the word 'philosophy' in its original sense, as the love of knowledge, hers would be justly designated and accurately defined as the model philosophical soul."[6]

But the desire for learning did not jibe with her profession, nor with the limitations imposed upon her sex by the rigid moral canons of her epoch. This accounts, then, for her continual uneasiness, the restless tide of her emotions—in short, the drama of her existence.

> Harboring a philosophical soul in the body of a beautiful woman, and being confronted with the world of colonial Mexico of the mid-seventeenth century is not a very pleasant lot. How little there was, if one looked about her, to encourage the pure and profound desire, the "natural impulse" toward learning! How much there was, on the contrary, to combat it: the omnipresent, narrow dogmatism, enemy of free intellectual activity; the almost exclusive position of theology, religious doctrine, and rhetoric in the programs of studies; the restrictive duties imposed by the State, limiting the introduction of books, and maintaining the Argus of the Inquisition in constant vigilance over all free thought. Does this not explain to us why Sor Juana wrote poetry and became a nun?[7]

There is a certain amount of truth in all this. Nevertheless, I believe that Pedro Salinas exaggerates somewhat the intellectual sterility of the environment and that kind of orphanhood which he attributes to Sor Juana. Let us not forget that in Mexico City there were schools, a university, academies of music, theaters, and poets like Matías de Bocanegra, Carlos de Sigüenza y Góngora, Juan de Guevara, and Diego de Ribera, who, although mediocre, reveal that the Mexican literary atmosphere breathed in unison with the Spanish.

The greatest responsibility for the subjection and restriction of Sor Juana rests on the Church, the serious warnings of the Bishop of Puebla, and the tyranny of her confessor, Padre Núñez. We must remember that Viceroy Mancera invited her to the palace as a lady-in-waiting to his wife; that a later viceroy's wife, the Countess de Paredes, was her intimate friend and patron; that Sor Juana was for many years rather a prodigy, the object of attentions and praise, and received constantly the applause of the great writers of her time.

Salinas wonders: "If Sor Juana was an anomaly in seventeenth-century Mexico, what could have been her true era, the appropriate setting for her brilliance?" And his answer is: "A Renaissance court, or a present-day American university." Here, without realizing it, he is repeating the words of José María Vigil: "This has led me to believe that not only was Sor Juana superior to the epoch in which she lived, but that even today, despite the great progress that has been realized, she probably could not have found a social atmosphere befitting her aspirations except in a city of the United States of America, the nation that approximates most closely the solution to the problem of the emancipation of women."[8]

Sor Juana Inés de la Cruz led an exemplary life. She was born in a farmhouse in the town of Amecameca, near the volcano Popocatepetl, on November 12, 1651. Apparently destined to an obscure existence, without real personal development of any kind, in the anonymity of country life, Juana Inés changed the course of her future, living a constant adventure in an uninterrupted series of rich experiences. Her life passed as does a deep river, traversing infinite cities and countrysides, reflecting all the marvels of the earth. It bore the charm of the family atmosphere that surrounds precocious children, an environment filled with care and pampering, with few worries and warm affection. At the age of three—she tells us herself with agreeable pride—she learned to read. It happened this way: Her older sister used to go to study at the home of a teacher ("a friend," as they would say so elegantly in those times).

Juana would accompany her, and one day, "burning with the desire to know how to read," the child informed the teacher in her baby talk that her mother wanted her to be given lessons. The "friend," though taking Juana's words in jest, good-naturedly began to show her the alphabet, and with such success that the child learned how to read before her mother realized the deception—too late to avoid its effects. "In two years she learned how to read and write, to count, and to do the most intricate embroidery work, the latter with such skill and care that it might well have been her occupation, had such a course been necessary."[9]

From that moment on, her biography would be only a long commentary on her zeal for learning, the history of her reading, of her ardent desire to understand the world about her, and of her intellectual restlessness manifested so early. She was accompanied in her first adventure by the love of an older sister, lost to us in the silence of the past, and by the encouraging smile of a teacher, who shines forth in her life experience as the dawn of a new day. Juana was inordinately fond of books, and at seven years of age wrote a perfect *loa,* to win a volume as an award for her talent.

Taken to Mexico City when she was eight years old, she resided in the home of her grandfather. There she devoured an entire library in a short time, disobeying thus the pleas, and even the orders, of her parents. She asked her mother to send her to the University, and when she learned that women could not attend that institution, she wanted to enter—dressed as a man! Even at that early age, Juana Inés gave evidence not only of her great love of study, but also of an independent judgment, free from the prejudices and conventions of the time, especially in regard to the education of women.

Learning was for the child both an adventure and a discipline. She constantly reproached and punished herself for what she considered a lack of ability. When she did not learn as rapidly as she wished, she would deprive herself of her favorite delicacies; she would not eat cheese, because she had heard that cheese makes children foolish. When she began a new study, she would shorten her hair by several inches; and if, when it had regained its normal length, she had not completed her goal, she would cut it once again, because, in her words, "it was not fitting that a head so empty within should be so adorned without."

At first she read religious books, *autos sacramentales,* drama, and history, but gradually she began to delve into works of more profound content. She had a Latin instructor, and in less than twenty lessons she began to read that language, as is proved so amply by her numerous quotations from Latin religious and secular texts. She became extremely interested in nature and the heavens, and from that base she continued on to cosmography and astronomy. She progressed from the study of books to the use of maps, compasses, and quadrants, and finally began a little astronomical observatory.

Such precocious manifestations of talent and culture attracted the attention of the court, and the viceroy's wife, the Marquesa de Mancera, invited Juana Inés to be her lady-in-waiting. The prodigy lived for some time in the palace, where her beauty, wit, and learning brought universal acclaim. There she defended her honor against the envy of erudite courtiers, and her culture against their pedantry. It was there that forty scholars, commissioned by the viceroy to discover whether her wisdom was innate or superficial, exhausted her with irrelevant questions. But she emerged triumphant from the ordeal.

Occupied with her poetry and science, she did not enjoy long the ostentatious life of the court. We know nothing of that period during which the beauty of Juana Inés graced the salons of the viceregal palace. However, we may safely guess that many suitors vied for her affection and that perhaps one may have succeeded in leaving an indelible imprint upon the heart of the poetess. The scholars who have studied the life of this distinguished woman have tried to see in the subject matter of her sonnets a series of confessions and emotional revelations. Thus they have assumed the existence of a handsome gentleman with whom Sor Juana had fallen madly in love, a gentleman of social endowments so high that he was far above the poetess and thus beyond her reach. However, it would be dangerous to attribute a mundane meaning to her sonnets and to draw from them evidence for asserting that Juana was pursued by bold courtiers or that her affection for one was unrequited. Juana Inés was superior in intelligence and culture to all the men of her time, and it is not likely that she would entrust the disposition of her heart to the caprice of any man; or even less, that she would be a slave of jealousy. As all women do, she must have felt occasionally a sudden flame of love, but her good sense probably extinguished it at once. As all women do, she philosophized about love, jealousy, absence, affection, hate, and about the stupidity and ingratitude of men; so vehement and well founded are her protestations that she resembles, rather than a poetess, a victim lamenting some amorous treachery, or a woman hopelessly in love who weaves a garland of devotion for her lover.

Juana Inés knew that all women like to be adored by many men. But since a just equilibrium reigned within her, she hoped that, as a discreet woman, she would be requited only by the one to whom she had given her heart. She was continually disturbed about a problem of clashing emotions: which would represent greater displeasure to a woman, to love or to hate? and she tries to elucidate the question in a series of syllogisms and conceits:

> Que no me quiera Fabio al verse amado,
> es dolor sin igual, en mi sentido,
> mas que me quiera Sylvio aborrecido
> es menor mal, mas no menor enfado.
> ¿Qué sufrimiento no estará cansado
> si siempre le resuenan al oído,
> tras la vana arrogancia de un querido,
> el cansado gemir de un desdeñado?
> Si de Sylvio me cansa el rendimiento,
> a Fabio canso con estar rendida,
> si de éste busco el agradecimiento,
> a mí me busca el otro agradecida;

por activa y pasiva es mi tormento,
pues padezco en querer y en ser querida.[10]

Juana Inés penetrates gently the labyrinths of love; she explains its joys and its sadness, its deceptive appearances and its normal end:

Amor empieza por desasosiego,
solicitud, ardores y desvelos;
crece con riesgos, lances y recelos;
susténtase de llantos y de ruego.
Doctrínanle tibiezas y despego,
conserva el ser entre engañosos velos,
hasta que con agravios o con celos
apaga con sus lágrimas su fuego.
Su principio, su medio y fin es éste.
Pues ¿por qué, Alcino, sientes el desvío
de Celia que otro tiempo bien te quiso?
¿Qué razón hay de que dolor te cueste?
pues ni te engañó amor, Alcino mío,
sino que llegó el término preciso.[11]

Wandering along such involved paths, she seems to forget herself, opening her heart, as a flame to the wind, with such plenitude that we are prone to doubt her words in a sonnet that she "satisfies a misgiving with the rhetoric of tears." At times it seems that we see before us a woman in love, especially in such lines as the following:

Esta tarde, mi bien, cuando te hablaba,
como en tu rostro y tus acciones vía
que con palabras no te persuadía
que el corazón me vieses deseaba.
Y amor, que mis intentos ayudaba,
venció la que imposible parecía,
pues entre el llanto que el dolor vertía
el corazón deshecho destilaba.
Baste ya de rigores, mi bien, baste,
no te atormenten más celos tiranos,
ni el vil recelo tu quietud contraste
con sombras necias, con indicios vanos,
pues ya en líquido humor viste y tocaste
mi corazón deshecho entre tus manos.[12]

The loves of which Juana Inés sings bear the sweet appearance of dreams rather than the vibration and turmoil of real passions; and therefore, when the lover seems to withdraw physically, her feminine imagination imprisons his image and is satisfied with that triumph:

> Detente, sombra de mi bien esquivo,
> imagen del hechizo que más quiero,
> bella ilusión por quien alegre muero,
> dulce ficción por quien penosa vivo.
> Si al imán de tus gracias atractivo
> sirve mi pecho de obediente acero,
> ¿para qué me enamoras lisonjero
> si has de burlarme luego fugitivo?
> Mas blasonar no puedes satisfecho
> de que triunfa de mí tu tiranía;
> que aunque dejas burlado el lazo estrecho
> que tu forma fantástica ceñía,
> poco importa burlar brazos y pecho
> si te labra prisión mi fantasía.[13]

But one day the lover, real or fictitious, becomes only a sad memory, of which the mind must rid itself, for it is shameful to bear him still in fond remembrance:

> Sylvio, yo te aborrezco y aun condeno
> el que estés de esta suerte en mi sentido,
> que infama al hierro el escorpión herido,
> y a quien lo huella mancha inmundo el cieno.
> Eres como el mortífero veneno
> que daña a quien lo vierte inadvertido,
> y en fin eres tan malo y fementido
> que aun para aborrecido no eres bueno.
> Tu aspecto vil a mi memoria ofrezco,
> aunque con susto me lo contradice,
> por darme yo la pena que merezco,
> pues, cuando considero lo que hice,
> no sólo a ti, corrida, te aborrezco,
> pero a mí, por el tiempo que te quise.[14]

The last vestige of that love must disappear, erased by will, and that triumph will not be in forgetting; it will be more than mere forgetting, since in her memory her former love has no place whatever, not even as an object no longer recalled:

> Dices que yo te olvido, Celio, y mientes
> en decir que me acuerdo de olvidarte,
> pues no hay en mi memoria alguna parte
> en que, aun como olvidado, te presentes.
> Mis pensamientos son tan diferentes
> y en todo tan ajenos de tratarte,
> que no saben si pueden olvidarte,
> ni si te olvidan saben si lo sientes.
> Si tú fueras capaz de ser querido,
> fueras capaz de olvido; y ya era gloria
> al menos la potencia de haber sido;
> mas tan lejos estás de esa victoria,
> que aqueste no acordarme no es olvido
> sino una negación de la memoria.[15]

How can one see in these sonnets the trace of a great passion? Perhaps Juana Inés sought some Platonic love to satisfy the imperious desire for expression of her soul. Her temperament could not limit itself to the various forms of court gallantry. On the other hand, it was absolutely indispensable to write witty sonnets in which would be evident subtlety of conception, and further to deceive one's own heart with poetic adornments. As we have said, there are critics who see in these sonnets the reason for Juana's leaving the court. Actually, we do not know the real motive for that decision; she tells us that it was because of her aversion to marriage and her desire to devote herself more intensely to study. The fact is that Juana entered a convent in 1667. The most probable explanation is that the young girl longed for the peaceful, sheltered life that only the convent cell could afford to women of her time, and that her soul sought more elevated diversions than those offered by a group of affected courtiers.

Sor Juana knew that she would encounter in convent life difficulties, work, and distractions, which would necessarily disturb her meditation and serenity; nevertheless, she obeyed the advice of learned men, among whom the most persistent and exacting was her confessor, Padre Antonio Núñez, who urged her to "sacrifice to God those first fruits of her studies if she felt that they would be a hindrance to her spiritual perfection."

Dorothy Schons attributes Juana's decision to her desire to withdraw from so licentious a social environment. She says: "A careful study of contemporary writers shows that moral conditions in Mexico were very bad. The presence of many races, of adventurers, of loose women and worldly men, brought about conditions that were possibly unequaled elsewhere in the world."[16]

Be this as it may, Sor Juana was an exemplary nun, whether or not she was impelled by a true love for her calling. She divided her time between prayers and books. To her cell came a constant stream of scholars and nobles—even the viceroys themselves—to discuss literature, theology, and secular affairs. She could not escape the criticism of religious fanatics and the annoyances of the ignorant, but she always defended herself with discretion and tact. She remained in her cell for days on end to avoid the gossip of the servants and the insipid conversations of the other nuns.

But criticism was stronger than the will of Sor Juana. The Bishop of Puebla, Manuel Fernández de Santa Cruz, had reprimanded her for her famous refutation of the sermon of Padre Antonio de Vieira; he had told her, among other things: "I don't want you to change your nature by giving up your books; I desire only that you improve it, by reading occasionally the work of Christ. You have spent a great deal of time studying philosophers and poets."

An unfair criticism, indeed, since Sor Juana fulfilled properly her duties at the convent! Further, Padre Núñez constantly urged her to renounce her interest in secular letters and to dedicate herself entirely to God; however, having failed in his intent, he decided to cease being confessor to the nun. After her criticism of the sermon of Padre Vieira, the great Jesuit orator, the Order began a merciless persecution of Sor Juana, and even the Inquisition took part in the matter. The unfortunate nun, deeply grieved by these censures and attacks, saddened by the absence of several friends and by the death of others, began to doubt the wisdom of her own conduct. For the benefit of the poor she caused her books and her scientific and musical instruments to be sold, and signed her final renunciation with her own blood.

From then until the day of her death the life of the nun is buried in silence. Padre Calleja in his confused article on Sor Juana tells us that in 1695 "there entered the convent an epidemic so pestilential that of every ten nuns who became sick, hardly one recovered."[17] Without fearing for her own life, Sor Juana cared for the afflicted until finally she contracted the malady and died at four o'clock in the morning of Sunday, April 17, 1695.

She had interpreted faithfully the aesthetic sensibility of her times, and her work reflects the vibration of the world in which she lived. For this reason, her poetry, despite its conventional form, is admirably realistic. Her poem that begins:

> Hombres necios que acusáis
> a la mujer sin razón
> sin ver que sois la ocasión
> de lo mismo que culpáis...[18]

was the feminine indictment of the men of the seventeenth century, and could well be the protest of the woman of today. Her ideas on the education of women, on schools, free will, and on convent life are also notably modern. In our day she would probably have moved in university circles, as Pedro Salinas sees her. And perhaps, with her natural exuberance, she would have plunged into the feminist struggle against men "who by reason only of their gender think they are wise," and in favor of women, "those poor souls who are generally considered so inept."

The ideas of the nun on culture are rigorously realistic and characterized by sane pedagogy. For her, culture must be complete; otherwise, serious errors of interpretation and judgment are apt to be committed, "for there are many who study to be ignorant, especially those of arrogant, uneasy, haughty soul, very fond of any innovation in the established rule."

There are many who study to be ignorant!—a wise and very modern observation. Among them we find all the pedants and gossips, all those who disguise their ignorance with false syllogisms, the new Pharisees of life and art, the restless who try to assault glory and forcibly to divest beauty of its purity. To Sor Juana such people are extremely dangerous, and capable of any action in their attempts to appear original; in her own words, "they even utter a heresy just to say what no one had said before, and only in this way are they content. . . . A little learning is more harmful to them than complete ignorance would be." And the nun continues with the same wit that often characterizes her observations: "A wise man once said that anyone who does not know Latin is a total fool, but that he who does know it is well qualified for that very role." With a marvelous sense of realism and humor Sor Juana bares before us many "fools" of her time and of ours. We may note especially her incisive words on those who profess false erudition: "Acquiring a smattering of philosophy and theology, and achieving some idea of other languages, brings the fool to a state of perfection, for, with all that, he is a fool in many sciences and languages: because a really big fool does not fit into his native tongue alone."

Her great zeal for study did not blind the Mexican nun, for she recognized that knowledge in the hands of fools is a deadly weapon. "Study is dangerous to a dullard, for it merely places a sword in the hands of a brute; thus, education, that noble instrument of defense, becomes in his hands his own nemesis, and that of many others." Sor Juana applied to her reasoning so serene a critical sense and arrived at such sound conclusions on literature that they should be studied and considered as guide and model for writers of all times. Her humility parallels her discretion when she exclaims: "If all of us (and I first, for I am an ignoramus) took careful stock of our talent before studying, and even more so before writing with the greedy ambition of equaling and surpassing others, how little inclination to proceed would remain, how many errors we would avoid, and how many twisted minds that roam about here would not do so!" Her recommendation about measuring one's capacity before writing is merely urging upon us self-analysis of intellect, bravely facing one's own soul in the dramatic agony of the creative moment. How many people of yesterday and even of today have made this supreme gesture of sincerity? How many distorted intellects so common everywhere would be set aright, should they heed these wise words of the sage nun!

Let us glance now at the poetic technique of Sor Juana, whom I consider the greatest poetess of the Spanish language. She was so great a master of verse that it was as easy for her to write as for others to speak. It is interesting to recall here her complete surprise upon learning that this gift of poetic talent was not common to all mortals, and that there were people who could express themselves only in common prose. What a sad discovery this must have been for the poetess! It must have been similar to learning suddenly that there are people who cannot enjoy the sun, song, or love—a total negation of the faculty of perceiving and expressing the beauty of the world.

However, despite this natural faculty, Sor Juana confesses that she did not write for her own pleasure, but rather upon the requests of others. Only "that little paper that they call *El Sueño,*" she avows, was written of her own volition. Pedro Salinas seizes upon this statement to support his denial that Sor Juana wrote because of an absolute need of her soul, and points out to us the relative scantiness of her poetic production: "Three volumes, and not very large ones, strike us as being a rather limited quantitative result of a life totally dedicated to intellectual pursuits."[19]

But then, what shall we say of the two greatest poets of our language—the lofty San Juan de la Cruz, and the profound Fray

Luis de León, whose lyric work is inferior to that of Sor Juana in quantity? Do they also belong to the group of erring souls who have missed their calling? Was theirs a "frustrated vocation"? The life of these poets also was dedicated to intellectual pursuits and the scantiness of their work does not detract from their essential greatness.

Salinas insists on another assertedly negative aspect of Sor Juana's poetry. The critic asserts: "Her poetry also falls into the stream of the circumstantial." In my opinion, her best compositions, such as *El Sueño,* her ballads, dirges, lyric poems, and Christmas carols, are not circumstantial in the rather derogatory sense in which Pedro Salinas employs the concept. And even if they were, we must not forget that this very quality characterized also the major part of the poetry written by the masters of the Golden Age, without causing a subsequent loss of profundity in the work of Quevedo, or effecting a depreciation of aesthetic plenitude in that of Góngora. Lastly, we may recur to the well-founded platitude: it is not the theme that determines the worth of a literary work, but the talent of the writer. And, consequently, we shall have to agree that there is more beauty in Blake's *To a Fly* than in many grandiloquent odes with transcendental subjects.

In order to achieve the mastery of style evident in her best compositions, to perfect her technique, to discipline her thought, and even to understand religious doctrine fully, Sor Juana had to ascend patiently through the aid of science and art. She herself exclaims: "Without logic, how could I know the structure of the Holy Scripture? Without rhetoric, how could I understand its figures of speech, its tropes and phrases? Without physics, how could I comprehend so many scientific questions about the nature of sacrificial animals, in which so many manifest things and many other elements are symbolized? How could I decide to my satisfaction whether Saul's restoration to health by the sound of David's harp was due to the inherent virtue and natural power of music, or to some supernatural force that God had willed to place in

David?" And in this way she continues enumerating her reasons for studying arithmetic, geometry, architecture, history, law, and astrology. The nun adhered to a self-imposed educational discipline of extraordinary system and rigidity in order to acquire loftiness of spirit and a firm, basic culture, the first triumphs of genius along the path of intellectual pursuits. The next step was to purify the mind and to remain somewhat in a "state of perfect grace." Sor Juana bemoans the fact that she "never had a teacher, nor schoolmates with whom to discuss and put into practice the newly acquired knowledge; for a teacher, only a mute book; for a schoolmate, an inanimate inkwell, and instead of explanation and drill, many disturbances." She longed for human warmth, for the comradeship of others, but she had to live high above all, on a frigid, intellectual summit.

Despite all the inconveniences, obstacles, and warnings that constantly harassed her, Sor Juana bequeathed to us the exquisite, exalted verses of *El divino Narciso;* her carols, which rank among the best in the language; her sonnets; and her far-reaching poem, *El Sueño.* As for her sonnets, the themes are conventional. Many of them had served as means of diversion to the poetic fancy of Góngora and Calderón. The sonnets of the Mexican nun excel in their subtlety of ideas, in the charm of their expression, in their slightly euphuistic flavor, and in the tasteful procession of images and metaphors. Thus, the oft-used theme of time, enemy of youth and beauty, and of the fruition of the spring of life, embodied in the symbol of the rose, acquires singular charm in the verse of Sor Juana:

Rosa divina que, en gentil cultura,
eres con tu fragante sutileza
magisterio purpúreo en la belleza,
enseñanza nevada a la hermosura.

Amago de la humana arquitectura,
ejemplo de la vana gentileza,
en cuyo ser unió naturaleza
la cuna alegre y triste sepultura.

¡Cúan altiva en tu pompa presumida,
soberbia, el riesgo de morir desdeñas;
y luego, desmayada y encogida,

de tu caduco ser das mustias señas!
¡Conque, con docta muerte y necia vida,
viviendo engañas y muriendo enseñas![20]

Bearing in mind the incipient state of development of American poetry of that era, the prosaic sources of inspiration, the technical monotony of the poets, and the universal epidemic of exaggerated Gongorism, we must agree that Sor Juana's sonnets are truly exceptional compositions. Some of them equal fully the best Spanish sonnets of the Golden Age, in their color, sententious significance, and perfection of form. Sor Juana succeeded in maintaining this poetic form in its own terrain, imbuing it with the atmosphere and finished structure of classical artistry.

In her moral and religious ballads Sor Juana ranks with the greatest Spanish literary figures and seems to feel an especial predilection for the lyrical flights of Lope de Vega. In some of these ballads the virtuosity of the nun reveals a remarkably harmonious poetic facility without suffering in depth of feeling or in refinement of form. Furthermore, her *Redondillas,*[21] which describe rationally the very irrational effects of love, reveal an incomparably persuasive tenderness and melancholy.

How clearly we can visualize the soul of an enamored woman in these lines:

Este amoroso tormento
que en mi corazón se ve,
sé que lo siento y no sé
la causa por que lo siento.

Siento una grave agonía
por lograr un devaneo,
que empieza como deseo,
y para en melancolía.[22]

It is difficult to explain the subtle pain of love more charmingly than does the following quatrain:

Y cuando con más terneza
mi infeliz estado lloro,
sé que estoy triste e ignoro
la causa de mi tristeza.[23]

This prolonged game of reticences and confessions, this constant flitting between affection and disdain, of which Sor Juana was so fond, appears frequently in the ballad that begins:

Con poca causa ofendida
suelo, en mitad de mi amor,
negar un leve favor
a quien le diera la vida...[24]

Those well-known quatrains in which she accuses of inconsistency both the taste and the censure of men, who blame in women what they themselves cause, have been branded as superficial by more than one critic. Nevertheless, they are so full of provocative ideas and wise adages that they will always figure among the best poems of Sor Juana.

At times she becomes unnaturally embroiled in subtleties and precepts, and even develops in verse certain ideological formulae that disturb her continually. This is made manifest in the poem that begins:

Finjamos que soy feliz,
triste pensamiento, un rato;
quizás podréis persuadirme
aunque yo sé lo contrario.[25]

In this work she criticizes the mere accumulation of knowledge that is useless for wisdom and noxious in society, a subject which she had already broached in prose. Here she only develops her idea a bit further, but suddenly she bursts forth in a flood of beauty:

Si culta mano no impide
crecer al árbol copado,
quitan la sustancia al fruto
la locura de los ramos.

En amenidad inútil
¿qué importa al florido campo
si no halla fruto el otoño
que ostente flores el mayo?[26]

We may observe in her religious ballads the marked influence of Lope de Vega. Both she and the colossal figure of Golden Age drama dedicated sincere compositions to divine love, but neither felt an exaltation comparable to the flame of mystic love that lighted the heart of San Juan de la Cruz. The lyric poems of Sor Juana are of considerable merit, and her rondels reveal a jovial, frolicsome spirit. Nevertheless, of all her lesser works, the *villancicos* (carols) are the most exquisite. Several of them, composed in 1687, are worthy of inclusion in the most exacting anthology:

Aquella zagala
del mirar sereno,
hechizo del soto
y envidia del cielo...

La que al Mayoral
de la cumbre Excelso
hirió con un ojo,
prendió en un cabello...

A quien su querido
le fué mirra un tiempo,
dándole morada
sus cándidos pechos.

La que rico adorno
tiene por aseo,
cedrina la casa
y florido el lecho.

La que se alababa
que el color moreno
se lo iluminaron
los rayos febeos.

La por quien su Esposo
con galán desvelo
pasaba los valles,
saltaba los cerros.

La que preguntaba
con amante anhelo,
dónde de su Esposo
pacen los corderos.

A quien su querido,
liberal y tierno,
del Líbano llama
con dulces requiebros.

Por gozar los brazos
de su amante dueño,
trueca el valle humilde
por el monte excelso.

Los pastores sacros
del Olimpo eterno,
la gala le cantan
con dulces acentos.

Pero los del valle
su fuga siguiendo,
dicen presurosos
en confusos ecos:
  Estribillo:
Al monte, al monte, a la cumbre
corred, volad, zagales,
que se nos va María por los aires;
corred, corred, volad aprisa, aprisa,
que nos lleva robadas las almas y las vidas,
y llevando en sí misma nuestra riqueza
nos deja sin tesoros el aldea.[27]

In another of these songs Sor Juana appears at her most artistic, producing pure poetry radiant with conceits, images, and words rather removed from strictly conventional poetic or religious decorum, and presenting to us nature unadorned:

Las flores y las estrellas
tuvieron una cuestión.
¡Oh, qué discretas que son!
unas con voz de centellas
y otras con gritos de olores.
Oiganlas reñir, señores,
que ya dicen sus querellas.
1ª voz: Aquí de las estrellas.
2ª voz: Aquí de las flores.
Trop. Aquí de las estrellas,
aquí de las flores.[28]

The stars and flowers vie for the honor of bearing great similarity to the beauty of the Virgin. The first voice argues for the stars:

Las estrellas es patente
que María las honró
tanto, que las adornó
con sus ojos y su frente,
luego es claro y evidente
que éstas fueron las más bellas.
Coro: Aquí de las estrellas.

The second voice sings in crystalline verse the triumph of the flowers:

¿Qué flor en María no fué
de las estrellas agravios,
desde el clavel de los labios
a la azucena del pie?
Luego más claro se ve
que éstas fueron las mejores.
Coro: Aquí de las flores.

The first voice, in mystic tone, defends the purity of light:

Por lo más digno eligió
de lo que se coronó
y es su corona centellas.
Coro: Aquí de las estrellas.

The second, now in open, almost pagan form, speaks of the attraction of the colors:

Lo más hermoso y lucido
es su ropaje florido
y lo componen colores.
Coro: Aquí de las flores.

The two voices grow impassioned in praise of the Virgin. The first says:

Estrellas sube a pisar
y en ellas quiere reinar
coronándolas sus huellas.
Coro: Aquí de las estrellas.

The second:

Entre flores adquirió
esa gloria que alcanzó,
luego éstas son superiores.
Coro: Aquí de las flores.

The battle between the stars and the flowers continues in an exaltation of lyricism:

1ª voz: Fulmínense las estrellas.
Coro: Aquí de las estrellas.
2ª voz: Dispárense los ardores.
Coro: Aquí de las flores.
1ª voz: Aquí, aquí de las querellas.
2ª voz: Aquí, aquí de los clamores.
1ª voz: Batalla contra las flores.
2ª voz: Guerra contra las estrellas.
Coro 1º: Batalla contra las flores.
Coro 2º: Guerra contra las estrellas.

We behold here pure poetry, communicated to the reader through the elevated concept of aesthetic vision, through the repetition of rhythms and words, through the suggestion of colors and the impassioned movement. These songs have not been surpassed, and represent the highest artistic flight of this writer. And these are the poems that Salinas calls circumstantial!

Sor Juana declares that the only poem she wrote purely out of creative desire is the one entitled *El Sueño*. Let us pause to consider this composition for a moment. Sor Juana was very much given to investigation of the subconscious and at times found in dreaming the last refuge from grim reality. First, she devoted herself to direct observation of natural phenomena; next, she proceeded by mathematical deduction from cause to effect; following that, she engaged in abstract and metaphysical cogitation; and lastly, she entered into the realm of dreaming. Let her explain this to us in her own words:

> On one occasion when, because of a severe stomach illness, the doctors forbade me to study, I spent several days thus; and then I suggested to them that it was less harmful to allow me them [books], because my meditations were so strong and vehement that they consumed more energy in a quarter of an hour than would studying books for four days; and so they relented and allowed me to read: and what is more, my lady, not even sleep freed me of this constant activity of my imagination; rather, my mind generally functions through it even more free and unhampered, reviewing with greater clarity and ease the various events it has conserved from the daytime; reasoning, composing verse of which I could make you an enormous catalogue, poems of such meaning and subtle concepts that they are far superior to those I compose while awake; but I shall not continue further for fear of boring you, since what I have already said must suffice for one of your discretion and intelligence to understand perfectly and penetrate into my nature, and to the beginning, middle, and various stages of my studies.

All this brings us close to our own times, and following the course of our deductions we could consider Sor Juana a precursor of the most modern schools, with all the subtlety of neo-Gongorism and the complexities of Freudian analysis.

The direct result of this intense life and of her descent into the subconscious is her poem *El Sueño,* one of her most revealing compositions as an essay at aesthetic creation. In it Sor Juana gives us what could be called the anatomy of dreaming, basing her conclusions on the rudimentary scientific knowledge of her time. Because of its irregular movement, its arbitrarily wrought development, the apparent ideological chaos, the audacity of metaphors, and the flight of imagination *El Sueño* is the prime work of Sor Juana's poetic production. Karl Vossler says of it:

> Her own individual manner is best appreciated in the poem *Primero Sueño,* written, when she was between thirty-five and forty years old, not only to imitate and compete with Góngora, but, most essentially, to attract attention. The poem, consisting of 975 eleven- and seven-syllable lines in *silvas* (Italian strophes), unfolds without clearly defined steps, uninterrupted, very much like a real dream. The course of the ideas zigzags from one theme to another, with daring inversions, circumlocutions, and metaphors. The reader becomes so entangled in the ingenious web that, at times dashing ahead, other times glancing back, he comes and goes in every direction, in this labyrinth where he remains imprisoned, until, suddenly, the magic spell is broken, and nothing concrete remains in his hands—nothing but the rational outcome, like a mound of ashes.[29]

El Sueño begins with a description of night, full of strange visions and symbols. While man sleeps, his soul, like a butterfly, leaves his body and regains its independence. The body fulfills its natural functions, while fantasy and thoughts acquire their own life on the highest levels. The imagination gathers within itself the entire external world and ascends to the regions of the sky, arriving finally at the summit of the spiritual pyramid. The soul reaches the height happy and awed, with that divine amazement which Sor Juana feels before the marvels of the world. The soul is alert and tremulous, awaiting the miracle, while the mind withdraws. The brain, overwhelmed and confused by so enormous a quantity of phenomena and visions, remains empty amid this abundance, unobserving, undiscerning, and does not even recognize the parts of its own body. Now we are in the world of dreams, where the soul, once recovered from its ecstasy, tries to become oriented; there it attempts to coördinate its visions and to arrange things into ten metaphysical categories, to rise through the abstract from concept to concept: "Thus my mind tries to rise, methodically, from the inorganic to the humid flora, to the beings who feel and worry, and even to earth's most perfect creature, who reaches Heaven, and whose mouth is closed by dust, whose forehead is of gold, and whose foot is of clay. In this way I climb the steps of the staircase; then again, I stop, because I do not understand the smallest, the least handiwork of nature, nor the maze of the gushing, smiling fountain, nor the bays of the abyss, nor the fields of Ceres, nor the colored calyx, nor the perfume of the flower."

If reason cannot penetrate these simple phenomena of nature, it would be futile for it to try to explain the great machinery of creation. The ambitious spirit is daring; nevertheless, with such great effort, it succeeds only in consuming the nutriment within the person; the dream is ending; the body begins to recover its movement. It is dawn; the birds begin to sing, and the spires of the highest towers are tinged with red. "And tangible things are there once again, visibly colored; the senses turn decidedly outward, toward the earth now clearly bathed in light. I am awake."

Vossler, who has translated this poem into German, defines its central theme as a reflection of the awe inspired by the cosmic mystery of natural phenomena, of man, and of the world. This amazement is not childish, it is conscious; it contemplates everyday things, only too well known, through new sources of strength, turned toward exploration—but nevertheless insufficient.

The poem is not a scientific explanation of sleep, nor does it attain the mystic flight that seeks ultimate revelations. Sor Juana, transported by the analytical zeal and the feverish desire for knowledge that characterized her from childhood, tries to understand and explain her personal reactions. Despite the scientific shortcomings of the work, she has left us a profoundly sensitive portrayal of the poetic atmosphere of sleep, the impression of an exalted soul, and an insight into new worlds and widening poetic horizons. The poem reveals a tangible consciousness of beauty, expressed in plastic phrases and new images; there is a constant procession of visions, and of lights and shadows, as in the *Soledades* of Góngora. For these reasons, and for its genuine beauty and anticipation of forms which have been cultivated extensively only in our century,

El Sueño is one of the most outstanding attainments of Spanish literature.

Poetic expression becomes an infused gift in Sor Juana; for there we behold great poetry in the role of pure poetry. She transcends the lifeless religious poetry of the convents; she surpasses the epic genre, which is incapable of being classified as aesthetic matter; she supersedes courtly poetry, which usually is imitative and in bad taste. Her constant struggle for perfection gave forth its fruits, and today we are sure that Sor Juana Inés de la Cruz is a definitive force in Spanish and Hispanic American letters.

Chapter IV ◇ Independence and Romanticism

It has often been said that the Romantic Movement is merely one of a series of changes that took place in European society of the late eighteenth and early nineteenth centuries. Actually it could not be otherwise, since romanticism is a literary school severely limited in time and aesthetic motives, and hence should be considered as the product of a manner of feeling conditioned by the social context.

The English rationalist philosophy, as well as French thought of the eighteenth century, attacked a social structure supported by the solid substructure of centuries—one based on class privilege, the inequality of man, absolute rule of a centralized state, religious tyranny, and exploitation of the working classes. The spirit of free inquiry acted to destroy myth and superstition and to create in man a consciousness of his individual worth. Philosophy, goal and summation of all human knowledge, proved its importance as a concretive science, transforming radically all the political, religious, economic, and social concepts of the world.

Spanish America had been constituted until 1800 by a group completely united to the Spanish axis. Despite the enormous distances and the great difficulties involved in communication between the mother country and her colonies, the absolute regime stood unshakable for three centuries, aided by a church converted into an instrument of government. It is futile to insist upon the fact that there was some resistance to Spanish despotism on the part of certain missionaries and prelates. These isolated exceptions only emphasize the stern inflexibility of the state and the excessive power of the Inquisition. We need only glance at the campaign of slander directed against Padre las Casas, the effects of which are still utilized by historians who aspire to celebrity through the reinterpretation of the Spanish colonial system.

My purpose here is not to criticize the administration of the Indies, but merely to define a historic fact. The enslavement of Indians and Negroes, the social and political inferiority of the Creoles, the intervention of the clergy in government, and the gradual centralization of power are clear proofs of the intimate link between colony and mother country.

All the determining factors of the Spanish American movement for independence were in existence from the sixteenth century: commercial monopoly, political absolutism, discrimination against the Indians, mestizos, and Creoles, and interference of the Church in the administration of the colonies. Nevertheless, until 1800 the yoke of Spain, weighing heavily upon her New World subjects, was apparently tolerated uncomplainingly. In fact, I incline to believe that if a philosophic revolutionary consciousness had not existed in America, not even the conquest of Spain by Napoleon would have incited the struggle for independence on our continent. But that revolutionary consciousness did exist.

The distinguished Creoles who traveled through Europe toward the end of the eighteenth century were fully aware of the approach of a new era for humanity. The European scientists who alighted in America shortly thereafter, to measure meridians and to study the flora and fauna, wielded an enormous influence on Hispanic American political thought. In truth, even certain Spanish thinkers, such as Jovellanos and Padre Feijóo, prepared the ground in the mother country itself for the future revolt of the colonies. The spirit of the French encyclopedists was clearly manifest in all of them. As early as the mid-eighteenth century the Peruvian Pablo de Olavide, having settled in Spain, propagated the liberal creed of the French *philosophes,* of whom he was a friend ardent enough to merit written tributes from Diderot and Marmontel.

An Ecuadorian Indian, Francisco Javier Espejo, preached democratic ideas right in the midst of the colony and composed his

Nuevo Luciano (New Lucian), a work of daring criticism. Isaac Barrera says in his *Historia de la literatura hispanoamericana* (History of Spanish American Literature):

> But even more than in written works, the greater part of Espejo's political labor lay in the oral propagation of ideas substantiated by the undeniable prestige accruing from his learning and from his age. Students and men of wit and talent gathered about him, to read the books he would receive, to hear his discourse, and to discuss with him all questions, including public affairs. When the rebels were condemned in 1809, they were all accused of having been friends of Espejo, and a Spanish justice said of them that they were the "heirs to the seditious projects of one Espejo, an old inhabitant of the locality, who died several years ago in the capital [i.e., the capital of the colony]."[1]

Francisco José de Caldas, a Colombian scientist and disciple of Celestino Mutis, was saturated with the spirit of the encyclopedists. In his *Semanario de la Nueva Granada* (New Granada Weekly) there appeared liberal ideas which the Spanish authorities began to consider suspicious. And so Caldas was shot for those ideas. Francisco Antonio Zea introduced scientific methods of investigation into Colombia; Camilo Torres was the precursor of the revolutionary idea; Padre Varela disseminated in Cuba the principles of the sensationalism of Condillac. Later there appeared José Antonio Saco, Cuban scholar and encyclopedist; Simón Rodríguez, a faithful disciple of Rousseau, and teacher of Bolívar; and lastly, the great Francisco Miranda, a revolutionary in theory and action. *Le Contrat social* (The Social Contract) of Rousseau circulated among the cultured men of all the colonies; Montesquieu's *Esprit des lois* (Spirit of Law) was avidly read and studied; Diderot and Condillac had followers throughout the continent; Voltaire, despite the anathemas which he had hurled against the Church, succeeded in overcoming all obstacles, threats, and condemnations. The great wave of free thought could not be restrained, and so, after the theoricians, there surged forth the great men of action: Bolívar, Sucre, Hidalgo, San Martín, O'Hig-

[1] For notes to chapter iv see pages 222–224.

gins—men of pen and sword, liberals, philosophers, and warriors, who created twenty free American nations upon the ruins of the Spanish empire.

Spanish American independence found its source of inspiration in the principles of the French Revolution, and the movement spread throughout the entire continent, owing in great part to the first political periodicals and to literary societies. The struggle for independence was by no means the result of mere regional discontent, despite the opinion of many; for had it not been ventured upon an ideological base, it would have become only a succession of local revolts, without continental character. If the great leaders of the revolution had not been defeated and betrayed by the unscrupulous *caudillos* who succeeded them, America probably would have realized Bolívar's dream, a united continent. However, once independence had been achieved, the liberated countries fell into anarchy, which unfortunately, in certain areas, still prevails.

The political revolt inaugurated a reaction against all Spanish influence. It was not sufficient to repudiate the mother country politically. The American man did not want to be a *godo*[2] or a *gachupín*;[3] had it been feasible, he probably would have substituted French for the Castilian language. The American could not, therefore, remain faithful to a literature fettered with the myriad rules of classical doctrine: he disdained the enamored shepherd lad, the dove and the white lamb, the Arcadian visions of Meléndez Valdés, the placid, mediocre eclogue of Jovellanos; he despised the literary dictatorship of Luzán and of the Royal Academy as much as the tyrannical policies of Ferdinand VII.

Now he had other sources of inspiration, other models at hand. The nation that had given him the idea of liberty and its democratic republican concepts, offered him also new literary orientations. And America was then in that historic moment in which great transformations are imminent. The repressed colonies, the medieval isles, were about to become cosmopolitan nations, and their people were about to form societies European in character.

This is not the place to enter into a study of Hispanic America's philosophical formation, one determined almost exclusively by the theories of the French thinkers from Fontenelle to Rousseau. We shall limit ourselves to the literary aspects, emphasizing especially that formal evolution of prose which was taking place in France during the preromantic period of her literature.

It is only natural that the frenzied passions of civil war should engender an impassioned, violent, almost romantic poetic outburst, one which would not need models. This poetry forms what we may call our preromanticism, and is a historical literary movement that deserves more careful study in the future. To this school belong the Peruvian Mariano Melgar (1796–1814), a young poet who was shot, while yet an adolescent, by the Spaniards; José María Heredia (1803–1839), the civic poet of Cuba, who anticipates Spanish romanticism by more than ten years in his famous poems *En el Teocalli de Cholula* (1820) and *Canto al Niágara* (1824); and José Joaquín de Olmedo (1780–1847), the singer of Bolívar's glories.

Melgar deserves favorable recognition for having cultivated popular poetry, in the form of *yaravíes,* imitating the songs of the Quechua Indians, during an epoch of neoclassicism. José María Heredia is the first Hispanic American poet whose work is a series of subjective impressions, and thereby fundamentally romantic. In his two immortal compositions, *En el Teocalli de Cholula* and *Al Niágara,* he sings of the natural grandeur of his continent and reveals for the first time a spiritual approach to the beauties of the landscape. He could have been a great poet if his style had equaled his pronounced aesthetic enthusiasm and his impassioned emotion. He led an agitated and insecure existence, and hence could not cultivate at leisure his poetic technique. Nevertheless, his *Canto al Niágara* contains certain elements of greatness. From the initial verses, indications of genius are manifold:

> Templad mi lira, dádmela, que siento
> en mi alma estremecida y agitada
> arder la inspiración.[3]

Then, in a symphony of color, he follows the course of the torrent, comparing it with human destiny. Calmed finally, he watches the waters disappear in the distance, as the illusions of man vanish. Faced with the vastness of the spectacle, he laments his miserable forlornness, his lonely life as a poet, his solitude as a living man; he feels this torment deep within him in the form of a *saudade* (nostalgia), that is, in a definitely romantic form. In this place he can find no woman in whom to place his love; in this place he misses the palms of his beloved land; the poet is alone, very much alone, and thinks only of death—all this at twenty years of age! Heredia, exiled for political reasons, could not return to his native land, and therefore recalled with vivid anguish the tall palms which merged with the blue sky of his Cuban isle. He even lacked the consolation of the Brazilian poet enamored of the palms, Acevedo Diaz, who in similar circumstances said:

> Nao permita Deus que eu morra
> sem que eu volte para lá,
> sem qu'inda aviste as palmeiras
> onde canta o sabiá.[4]

José Joaquín de Olmedo laid claim to immortality with his *Canto a la victoria de Junín* (Song on the Occasion of the Victory of Junín), otherwise called his *Canto a Bolívar*. This is a descriptive, heroic poem in which we see the American patriots embroiled in fierce combat with the armies of Spain; Bolívar triumphs, and among the clouds appears the Inca Mancocapac, who salutes the conqueror in the name of his vanquished race. Olmedo employs a neoclassical technique, but his enthusiasm for the victory of Bolívar breaks all bounds and surrenders to a veritable poetic frenzy. In his opinion—and here is evident an anticipation of romanticism—Bolívar came to avenge the Quechua race, long oppressed by the Spaniards. We observe in Olmedo the typically romantic sympathy for the indigenous peoples, for that pure and innocent primitive man in whom Chateaubriand, Rousseau, and Fenimore Cooper believed so ardently. This noble savage figures constantly in the early colonial poets and historians: in Ercilla and in the *Historia* of Padre las Casas; in the Mexican Motolinía; in the Brazilians Basílio da Gama and Santa Rita Durão. In his *Confederação dos Tamoios,* Magalhaes maintains the theory that Brazil's struggle for independence prolongs until modern times the resistance of the Indian against the Portuguese conqueror, a position which corresponds exactly with that of Olmedo, who insists on the racial connection between Bolívar and the Peruvian Inca.

Olmedo was familiar with the work of Chateaubriand, and translated it; from this stems in part his romantic admiration for primitive man, for the Inca uncontaminated with Europeanism. But Indianism within the romantic school—as later cultivated by Magariños Cervantes, Juan León Mera, Zorrilla de San Martín, in verse, and by a great number of novelists and short story writers—is not exclusively a French importation, but already existed in the era of the chroniclers and in the epic poets of the sixteenth century. Magariños Cervantes in his novel *Caramurú,* Juan León Mera in his *Cumandá,* and lastly, Zorrilla de San Martín in his poem *Tabaré,* merely imitate the conventional interpretation of the Indian as presented in the epics and in some chronicles, just as *A Confederação dos Tamoios* is only an imitation of the colonial Brazilian poems *Caramurú* and *O Uraguay.* The idealization of the Indian is not a product of European romanticism; it already existed, and in a form even more emphatic, in the mind of the Spanish American. Chateaubriand merely removed old ashes, so that the fire hidden by a century of flat, colorless neoclassicism might shine forth once again. If the psychological portrayal of the American Indian is false in the great colonial epic poems and in the semihistorical narratives of the missionaries and chroniclers, it is equally inaccurate in the interpretations of the romantic novelists and poets, especially in the tales of Chateaubriand and Cooper.

Romanticism became acclimated in Spanish America with amazing ease. That was only natural. The grandeur of our panorama demanded the imaginative flights of the romantic poet. The setting of great forests, sprawling prairies, enormous boulders, lakes asleep in the moonlight, and primitive (therefore, as Chateaubriand would say, "noble") Indians was ideal for the introduction of the movement. Besides, romanticism is an easy school, which does not require classical discipline or knowledge of poetic technique. It is a school that believes in inspiration and in improvisation, both of which are comfortable, pleasing phenomena. Romanticism exaggerates sentiment and emotion, qualities very characteristic of the Hispanic American. That constant exaltation of the senses, that primitive enthusiasm, that constant external vitality lead the Nordic European and the North American to consider us "romantic." In short, we were awaiting the advent of a free, exalted tendency, and so, when romanticism appeared, we quickly adapted it to the setting. Further, romanticism because of its spontaneity and liberating fervor is much closer to the common people than classicism, and tends to blend into the popular soul. For that reason it is often difficult to determine whether a poem is the work of a romantic writer, or whether it is an anonymous composition kept alive for centuries in the memory of the people. The romanticist accepts as part of his creative process a great quantity of folklore and popular poetry, and in their turn the people accept romantic production with the greatest facility. At times, a song accompanied by the sound of a guitar recalls to us real romantic poetry, the work of some cultured bard whose name is drifting toward oblivion in the ample sweep of the popular domain. Upon hearing these verses:

Si hay algún césped blando
cubierto de rocío
en donde siempre se alce
dormida alguna flor,
y en donde siempre puedas
hallar, dulce bien mío,
violetas y jazmines
muriéndose de amor;

Yo quiero ser el césped
florido y matizado
donde se asienten, niña,
las huellas de tus pies;
yo quiero ser la brisa
tranquila de ese prado
para besar tus labios
y agonizar después[5]

few people would realize that they are listening to a poem of Manuel Acuña.

And how many know that the celebrated song *El Ciprés* which begins:

Si por mi tumba
pasas un día
y amante evocas
el alma mía,
verás un ave
sobre un ciprés;
habla con ella
que mi alma es[6]

was composed by a cultured romanticist, José Antonio Calcaño?

Besides offering these popular characteristics, romanticism reveals a marked inclination toward the interpretation of political sentiment. The most prominent European poets of this school—Byron, Victor Hugo, Lamartine, and Espronceda—engaged actively in political or revolutionary struggles. And Spanish America was undergoing those great political and social disturbances when romanticism made its appearance on the European scene. There is no doubt that we Spanish Americans imitated the Spanish romanticists, such as Larra, the Duque de Rivas, Espronceda, and Zorrilla, but we could not admit it then. We had broken definitively with Spain in political thinking. How could we maintain literary ties, at that time, with that nation? The ideal of independence had to be brought to its ultimate manifestations, and so romanticism necessarily became identified with political passion and with the revolutionary impulse.

But all this results in a contradiction of terms. On the one hand, in our desire to avoid all things Spanish, we had to resort to French culture in our search for models. Our intellectual life ceased being Spanish and approached with ardent devotion the French soul: painting, literature, music, education, sciences—all this and more did we expect from that marvelous culture. On the other hand, as I have already said, the exaltation of national sentiment carried us toward literary nationalism, of which the Indianist tendency and the return to popular poetry form an integral part. The penetrating Brazilian critic Sergio Buarque de Holanda observes: "The truth is that romanticism among us as in Portugal had a particularly important meaning when it contributed to the revival of a sensibility which had fallen into disfavor. . . . The correlation between the new sensibility and a manner of feeling which was already spontaneous in our people explains in large measure the attraction exercised immediately by these poets."[7]

The same may be said of all the Hispanic American poetry of the romantic period. Let us take as an example this school in Argentina. The first Argentinian romanticist was Esteban Echeverría (1805–1851). This poet, influenced by Chateaubriand and Byron, reveals the new aesthetic sensibility in style as well as in psychological interpretation of the landscape and the native theme, in his major work in verse, *La Cautiva*. The early romantic poet did not yet venture beyond the limits of cultured literature, since his form is painstakingly correct and elegant despite the more popular subject matter. Echeverría tends toward a spontaneity which he cannot quite achieve because of his cultural background and because of the poetic manner determined in him by the influence of Byron's romanticism.

But in other poets this quality of instinctive improvisation was more evident; literary formulae were abandoned before the absolute rule of the new sensibility, which admitted typically regional and popular expressions of all times. Thus, Argentina's literary production advanced toward that genre which is compounded of high poetic sensibility, free spontaneity, and popular theme and form, the poetry of the *gaucho*. Hernández, Ascasubi, and del Campo achieved much greater popularity than did the first Argentinian romanticist.

The struggle between the popular aspect of Hispanic American romanticism and the artistic sensibility imported from France was thus resolved on one side by the gauchesque genre and on the other by the postromantic school, which, utilizing all the new aesthetic discoveries, cultivated a simple poetry close to the soul of the people.

Despite the influence of French models, American romanticism displays clearly national characteristics. From 1820 on, Hispanic American literature manifests constant progress toward more authentic formulae of expression. It is more difficult to note marked divergences in those countries which still moved within the orbit of the Spanish empire. For example, in Cuba, which remained a colony throughout the entire nineteenth century, only the landscape could lend local color to the work of Gertrudis Gómez de Avellaneda, who otherwise preferred the life of Madrid to that of her native island. In the mulatto poets, such as Plácido, the only discernible American note is the brilliance and grandiloquence of form, what we would call "tropicalism"; but on the other hand the Spanish poet José Zorrilla could be designated "tropical" in this sense. A curious case is that of the Negro poet, Juan Francisco Manzano, who managed to cultivate the poetic muse in spite of his condition of servitude. Strangely enough, his work is purely conventional, and in vain do we seek in him revelation, not of the poet of his time or nation, but of his race. In 1837 the Cuban writers purchased Manzano's freedom, and during the last seventeen years of his life the former slave was able to devote himself to a more independent lyricism. This Negro poet had at his disposal a considerable fund of folkloric elements which, if he had employed it, would have injected a new color into his poetry. Instead of adapting the *rumbas, sones,* funeral dirges, the airs of the *com-*

parsa, snake charmers' chants, and council songs, he chose to imitate the Spanish poets, and left us a poetry filled with commonplaces and empty words.

Juan Clemente Zenea is the most clearly defined urban romanticist. His is a disconsolate, intimate, melancholy poetry whose elegiac tone precedes Bécquer in Spanish poetry. Zenea was a forerunner of the type of "ineffable" poetry written by Juan Ramón Jiménez, but he failed to attain his most profound aesthetic expression, despite the guidance of Lamartine and Musset. In Plácido and in Zenea, romanticism drew already from the fount of popular poetry, adapting itself to that creole modality which is so typically American. Zenea abandoned grandiloquence and the frenzied note so characteristic of his contemporaries, and his verse flows with the soft purity of a popular couplet. The transition from European romanticism to the authentically Hispano-American version was now effected.

It would be a long and futile task to attempt to describe in detail the birth and progress of romanticism in each country of South America; for we find first in all the poets of this school the cult of nature, and then, a delicate elegiac note. To cite the works of all these writers in an anthology would be an offense against aesthetics, since one could hardly travel a more monotonous path. The romantic theme, already identified with the temperament of the poet, can offer no surprises to the reader. It treats always of despairing love; of a noble Indianism reminiscent of the novel of chivalry; of romantic reverence before the greatness of the landscape; of the bitter religious skepticism so characteristic of the group. Its poetry invariably contains long series of "ah's" and "oh's," direct invocations to the muse, apostrophes to the sun, the moon, to God, and to the sea, imprecations Biblical in tone, eternal rhymes of *mundo* with *profundo,* of *Andes* with *grandes.* Never does there once appear the daring metaphor introduced by the modernist; never the word of humble derivation, ushered into the romantic idiom by Victor Hugo. The exaltation of the school is due almost always to its repetition and movement, and never to originality of approach, which cannot be expressed except by change in style. Histories of literature generally list the names of numerous romantic poets, some of whom are worthy of recollection: Julio Arboleda, José Eusebio Caro, Gutiérrez González in Colombia; Maitín, Lozano, Pérez Bonalde in Venezuela; Zaldumbide, Mera in Ecuador; Calderón, Altamirano in Mexico; Salaverry and Ricardo Palma in Peru; Ricardo Bustamante, Adela Zamudio, and Néstor Galindo in Bolivia; Salvador Sanfuentes, Blest Gana, and Guillermo Matta in Chile; Juan Zorrilla de San Martín in Uruguay; Echeverría, Mármol, and Olegario Andrade in Argentina. Almost all these poets had their day of glory, were consigned to anthologies, and now are victims of historical research. Some of them were elected to literary academies, and others merited a monument or commemorative plaque. Certain more fortunate ones are still defying the sentence of history; they defend themselves anecdotically. Ricardo Palma is remembered for his great prose work, *Tradiciones peruanas;* Adelia Zamudio, because she was a woman poet; Echeverría, for having been the first American romanticist officially accepted as such; José Mármol, for his fiery strophes against the tyranny of Rosas. Time, the supreme critic, has already destroyed some who in their own epoch were Olympian gods; it has passed harsh judgment on others; very few have escaped its censure.

For reasons of pure sentiment, Manuel Acuña, the Mexican poet who committed suicide at the age of twenty-four, still remains alive in anthologies and in the hearts of romantically inclined young ladies. Especially famous are his verses *A Rosario,* which begin:

Pues bien yo necesito
decirte que te quiero,
decirte que te adoro,
con todo el corazón;
que es mucho lo que sufro
que es mucho lo que lloro,

que ya no puedo tanto,
y al grito que te imploro,
te imploro y te hablo en nombre
de mi última ilusión...[8]

On the other hand, the shadows of oblivion tend to enfold an erotic poet who merits serious consideration, since no American writer surpasses him in the so-called "essence of romanticism." He is remembered constantly by the people, especially by poetry-loving women, in the lyric song of the guitar, in the love billet, in the amorous confidence. That poet, also Mexican, is Manuel Flores; and I may say here that I consider him one of the best in the Spanish American romantic movement.

But their glory is ephemeral, and Acuña and Flores too will fade into oblivion, as did all those worthy Spanish poets of the eighteenth century—such worthy, yet such fleeting figures. The reason for this decline is clear. Hispanic American romanticism, which boasted so many poets, such noble, ardent devotees of the muse, had not yet produced the great bard whom the continent awaited.

In the last thirty years of the nineteenth century, romanticism was transformed; it no longer contained the elements which had given it vitality about 1850. Remote influences of measure and form had acted upon it for many years. The exuberance and spontaneous exaltation of Hugo yielded before the polished, rhythmic elegance of Théophile Gautier and the stoic purity of Alfred de Vigny. Unfortunately, some of the best romantic poets are unknown even to the literary historians, whereas others, acclaimed for other than artistic reasons, appear prominently everywhere. Among those neglected writers, we find Luis G. Ortiz (1835–1894), an excellent Mexican poet, who, abandoning the frenzy of romanticism, limited the bounds of his inspiration, stressing formal perfection and anticipating the Parnassian reform. The sonnets of his *Boda pastoril* (Pastoral Wedding) equal and surpass the aggregate of many fiery, heroic works of his contemporaries.

La Boda pastoril

I. LA ALDEA

Azul el cielo está, y es la montaña
toda flores, verdor, trinos y aroma,
y finge el aura arrullos de paloma
y se mira en las fuentes la espadaña.
Apolo, en tanto, fulgurante baña
el valle hermoso en cuya verde loma
como cisne entre mirtos, blanco asoma
el sacro templo, abajo la campaña.
La Inocencia que vive entre pastores,
feliz habita la apacible aldea,
donde entre acacias, rosas y verdores
besa en la noche, cándida Febea,
dos chozas en que viven con las flores
Mirtilo en una, en otra Galatea.

II. LA CITA

Como el lirio que nace con la aurora
de nieve el manto y salpicado de oro,
sale al oír el matutino coro,
suelto el cabello, la gentil pastora.
Mirtilo el boquirrubio, en esa hora
la espera al pie del verde sicomoro;
zagal enamorado que un tesoro
de amor guarda a la virgen que le adora.
Ella dichosa sus ovejas guía,
y él sus inquietas cabras al enhiesto
peñón cercano de la fresca umbría;
y uniéndose a la vez en el recuesto
se ven, se hablan, se besan, y decía
ella: «¿Cuándo, mi bien?» Y él: «Presto, presto.»

III. HIMENEO

Saltó el Héspero ya: su cabellera
de azules llamas, perfumada agita
la antorcha que en el templo dulce imita
la luz de Venus que en el cielo impera.

Sobre el altar la ofrenda, sólo espera
a los amantes en la sacra cita;
a ella cual blanca y pura margarita,
a él como nardo en su estación primera.
La multitud en entusiasta grito
«ellos,» prorrumpe, y el pastor Alfeo
dirige el coro en el sencillo mito;
Amor realiza el férvido deseo,
y entre el perfume del sagrado rito
canta el coro tres veces: «¡Himeneo!»

IV. EL TÁLAMO

Llega la esposa al tálamo que en flores
Placer y Amor en competencia ornaron,
mustios los dulces ojos que cerraron
los besos de la madre en sus amores.
Virginidad llorando, los primores
que a la blanca doncella engalanaron,
ve bajar de sus hombros que temblaron
desnudos cual sus senos seductores.
Huye la diosa; al lecho misterioso
Venus conduce a la beldad divina
que mal esconde el susto fatigoso.
Mirtilo, hablando quedo, a ella se inclina,
y se oye un ¡ay! Mas el Pudor cuidoso
cierra del lecho la nupcial cortina.[9]

From yet other directions came the influence of two poets of vigorous personality and pure lyricism: a Spaniard, Gustavo Adolfo Bécquer, and an American, Edgar Allan Poe. With the former, the simple, elegiac note of Heine (whose *Book of Songs* was translated into Spanish by the Venezuelan poet Pérez Bonalde) entered into Castilian poetry. With the latter, the essentially rhythmic, suggestive, mysterious verse, which exercised such great influence on the poetic formation of Baudelaire and Mallarmé, found ample field in our continent.

The romantic movement was approaching its end around 1875. New schools arose, always under the shade of the French. Leconte de Lisle, Flaubert, that great poet in prose, and Heredia were the emulated masters of the Parnassian formula; Verlaine, Baudelaire, and Samain contributed notably toward the formation of the symbolist school. Thus, with the intimate combination of these two tendencies, we Hispanic Americans created the first great poetic school of our history—modernism, initiated officially in 1888 with the publication of *Azul,* by Rubén Darío.

Impassioned, orgiastic, completely subjective romanticism had ended; and with it disappeared the exalted lyricism, crowded with invocations to the muses, with interjections, shouts, and blasphemy. Poets no longer could—or would—speak of the "roaring sandbank," of the "tenebrous abyss," of the "seas of sympathy," of the "waves of lyric harmony." Rather, in token of humility, they became simple, contemplative. Silently, they penetrated into the recesses of the heart. The transition is easy from Zenea, Luisa Pérez de Zambrana, Pérez Bonalde, and Gutiérrez González, to the entirely transfigured poetry of Manuel González Prada, José Martí, and Gutiérrez Nájera.

The great Peruvian anarchist González Prada conserves much of the romantic, but the intimate refinement of his poetry, evident in the following excerpt, raises it into new spheres of artistic expression:

Suspira, ¡oh corazón! tan silencioso
que nadie sienta el eco del suspiro.
Por no turbar los sueños del dichoso,
suspira, ¡oh corazón! tan silencioso.
Fingiendo la alegría y el reposo
en la quietud y sombra de un retiro,
suspira, ¡oh corazón! tan silencioso
que nadie sienta el eco del suspiro.[10]

Clearly, we are here in the presence not only of a tenderly emotional poetry, but of a perfected technique, the work of a true artist. We note the same process in the verse of Martí:

Cultivo una rosa blanca
en Mayo como en Enero
para el amigo sincero
que me da su mano franca.

Y para el cruel que me arranca
la placidez con que vivo:
cardo ni ortiga cultivo:
cultivo una rosa blanca.[11]

We remark the emotional expression of an inherent romanticist, Gutiérrez Nájera, who wrote, fortunately, during the height of the modernist impulse. Listening to Schubert's "Serenade," he exclaims:

¡Oh, qué dulce canción! Límpida brota
esparciendo sus blandas armonías.
Y parece que lleva en cada nota
muchas tristezas y ternuras mías...

¿De quién es esa voz? Parece alzarse
junto del lago azul, en noche quieta,
subir por el espacio y desgranarse
al tocar el cristal de la ventana
que entreabre la novia del poeta...

¡Cuántos cisnes jugando en la laguna!
¡Qué azules brincan las traviesas olas!
En el sereno ambiente ¡cuánta luna!
Mas las almas ¡qué tristes y qué solas![12]

And this, which would be the summit of the prosaic and awkward in a poet of 1845, is redeemed in Gutiérrez Nájera by the technical skill manifest in his verse, and the simplicity of his vocabulary and images.

Thus we approach the ineffably profound, tormented author of the *Nocturnos* (Nocturnes), the Colombian José Asunción Silva, the last romanticist, and also the first true modernist of our continent. Silva committed suicide at the age of thirty-one, depriving Spanish America of its greatest poet. If Silva had lived longer, our modernism would have become something else. His tragic concept of life, his deep respect for art, his marvelous lyrical sensibility would have led us toward aesthetic forms infinitely more elevated than those we have followed under the modernist and vanguard movements. The position of José Asunción Silva before art is one of true mastery; his zeal for pure aesthetic interpretation enabled him to avoid the demagogical gesture of certain poets of the vanguard and the exuberance of decorative elements so characteristic of all the modernists. But Silva died before reaching full artistic maturity, and for this reason the history of our poetic development is necessarily different. His sense of rhythm, his instinctive choice of the pure word, the subtle image, and his personal interpretation of life rank him high among our most celebrated men of letters.

His famous *Nocturno* can well figure among the most definitive compositions in our language:

Una noche,
una noche toda llena de murmullos, de perfumes, y de música de alas;
una noche
en que ardían en la sombra nupcial y húmeda las luciérnagas fantásticas,
a mi lado, lentamente, contra mí ceñida toda, muda y pálida,
como si un presentimiento de amarguras infinitas
hasta el más secreto fondo de las fibras te agitara,
por la senda florecida que atraviesa la llanura
caminabas;
y la luna llena,
por los cielos azulosos, infinitos y profundos esparcía su luz blanca;
y tu sombra
fina y lánguida,
y mi sombra,
por los rayos de la luna proyectadas
sobre las arenas tristes
de la senda se juntaban;
y eran una,
y eran una,
y eran una sola sombra larga,
y eran una sola sombra larga,
y eran una sola sombra larga.

Esta noche solo,
el alma llena de las infinitas amarguras y agonías de tu muerte,
separado de ti misma por el tiempo, por la tumba y la distancia,

por el infinito negro
donde nuestra voz no alcanza,
mudo y solo
por la senda caminaba;
y se oían los ladridos de los perros a la luna,
a la luna pálida,
y el chirrido
de las ranas.
Sentí frío. Era el frío que tenían en tu alcoba
tus mejillas y tus sienes y tus manos adoradas,
entre las blancuras níveas
de las mortuorias sábanas.
Era el frío del sepulcro, era el hielo de la muerte, era el frío de la nada.
Y mi sombra
por los rayos de la luna proyectada,
iba sola
iba sola por la estepa solitaria;
y tu sombra esbelta y ágil,
fina y lánguida,
como en esa noche tibia de la muerta primavera,
como en esa noche llena de murmullos, de perfumes y de música de alas,
se acercó y marchó con ella,
se acercó y marchó con ella,
se acercó y marchó con ella... ¡Oh las sombras enlazadas!
¡Oh las sombras de los cuerpos que se juntan con las sombras de las almas!
¡Oh las sombras que se buscan en las noches de tristezas y de lágrimas![13]

This poetry is intimately romantic, but the stylistic evolution demands the mark of a new classification: we are at the beginning of the modernist movement, that impulse which was to give to the Spanish language some of its most outstanding poets—Guillermo Valencia, Amado Nervo, José Santos Chocano, Julio Herrera y Reissig, Leopoldo Lugones, Ricardo Jaimes Freyre and Rubén Darío. And although our romanticism did not produce a single genius, it did succeed in creating a new poetic idiom, one which was to be utilized by later poets, one which made possible the formation of our first literary school: modernism.

Chapter V ◇ Martín Fierro

In 1872, Buenos Aires witnessed the appearance of the first part of a book that was destined to exert a transcendental influence on Argentinian literature, and to create a great stir throughout all Spanish America. The work bore the title *Martín Fierro* and represented the apogee of a poetic cycle devoted to the life and deeds of the gauchos. The year 1872 was especially appropriate for the publication of the most representative gauchesque poem, because it marks, in a sense, the disappearance of that type of American man. In effect, the civilization that had already reached Argentina's pampas could accept neither the completely freedom-loving nature of the gaucho nor his nomadic existence on the open plains. *Martín Fierro* depicts the birth and death of the gaucho: the birth of a symbolic type of man; the death of the human, real, historical type. The gaucho, through the work and the charm of José Hernández, acquires a poetic character; he becomes a legendary figure. It is for this reason that I say the time was exactly right for the publication of the poem; *Martín Fierro* could not have appeared either before or after 1872.

We must always keep in mind the dual source of Argentinian literature and of Hispanic American literature in general: on the one hand the folkloric forms of expression, and on the other the academic tendency which inclines toward precise imitation of European models. In Argentina both genres attained a noteworthy degree of development. The popular forms have been evident ever since the days of the struggle for independence, in songs accompanied on the guitar, in patriotic dialogues, in the poems that the soldiers of liberty once sang in the long nights on the pampas. Drawing upon this material, on his direct observation of the atmosphere, and on his knowledge of history, Domingo Faustino Sarmiento was able to produce his great book, *Facundo*. But, contemporary with Sarmiento, was José Mármol, of the European school, an imitator of the French. Even in his novel *Amalia,* which attacks bitterly the regime of the Argentinian dictator Rosas, Mármol follows the cult of French romanticism. Similar to him in ideals was the young disciple of Musset and Byron, Echeverría, who essays an interpretation of the soul of his land in the heroic and clearly romantic poem *La Cautiva* (The Captive Woman). These two tendencies appear until 1872. However, Hernández, himself a man of the plains,[1] wished to introduce into fiction the fading figure of the gaucho, and he chose to consign him to history, with his own moral credo and his own linguistic expression.

That degree of literary differentiation is due, in some degree, to two ways of interpreting life: one concentrated in the city, with its European institutions; the other in the country, in the limitless Argentinian desert. In fact, ever since 1850, Buenos Aires has given clear evidence of its great future. It has always looked toward Europe, indifferent to the offerings of the seeming desert that was to become the granary of the world. Buenos Aires is in a sense anti-Argentinian, conscious of its strength, defying the past, disavowing the gaucho.

On the other hand, the pampa is America—the rusticity and the authentic life, the plenteous udder and the wheatfield. From the clash of these two concepts of life, one agrarian, the other bureaucratic, industrial, arises the great Argentinian conflict which Sarmiento termed the "struggle between civilization and barbarism." Those differences, already manifest among the first Argentinian leaders, such as Rivadavia and Moreno, and the first *caudillos,* such as Rosas and Facundo Quiroga, continue today, although the power of Mendoza, San Juan, and Entreríos is diminishing as the cities progress. Nevertheless, even in the literature of today these contrary positions are clearly defined in the gauchesque character of the work of Benito Lynch and Juan Carlos Dávalos, and in the Europeanism of Victoria Ocampo and Mallea.

[1] For notes to chapter v see pages 225–229.

That picturesque type of man whom history knows as the gaucho inhabited the vast expanse of the pampas. He lived free from all physical and moral bonds, undisputed master of his soul. Amid the loneliness of the prairie nights his heart was tempered by the elements. Errant on the desert, without other company than that of his horse, without other weapon than his *facón* (knife), his figure has reached Herculean proportions in poetry and in popular balladry. In reality, his physical appearance is the complete negation of his literary image: ridiculous in his *chiripá* and *bombachas,*[2] unkempt and coarse, lacking in the indispensable elements of daily grooming, with long hair and thick beard, ever on his faithful mount of the pampas. But in gauchesque poetry he is gallant, witty, heroic, and of cultured tongue. In the *payada,*[3] his skill as a singer and guitarist shines forth; in the novel, he displays indomitable valor in his fights with the police; in what is called the gauchesque epic, he is the "hero par excellence." In this form he passes also to the Argentinian theater, and even later is stylized in the symbolic figure of Don Segundo Sombra. The tendency which I have previously called *mester de gauchería*[4] forms an entire literature, from the Andalusian type of couplet, amorous and simple, to the most complicated dramatic plots of the school of Ibsen, in the work of that dramatist so genuinely American, Florencio Sánchez.

The *payadas* and the *diálogos,* the *cielitos* and the *tristes* are the most rudimentary aspects of this poetry. They were sung to the accompaniment of a guitar, in the sheds and in the *pulperías.*[5] A song of love, and at times of melancholy, a song at times bantering and subtly intentioned, it turns up now in popular anthologies and songbooks, errant as the Andalusian couplet, lost in the oblivion of time. In its most completely evolved form this primary poetry acquires consistency of narrative material, the body of the Spanish ballad. In the three outstanding poems of the gaucho school there is such great variety of aspects and of expression that we can well assert that all three form an intimately fused cycle, a rather complete revelation of the soul of a people. *Fausto,* by Estanislao del Campo, reveals the humorous side, the deformation of an aesthetic reality as it passes before the ingenuous eyes of the gaucho. The figures of Dr. Faust and Marguerite are transformed, as if by reflection in concave mirrors, into comic, absurd beings. The *Santos Vega* of Rafael Obligado is the lyric poem in which we hear the sobbing voice of an entire race of guitarists; the disillusioned soul of the gauchos laments in tender elegy the defeat of its last interpreter, the legendary Santos Vega, who is overcome in the tourney of *contrapunto* (improvisation) by the Devil himself! The *Santos Vega* of Hilario Ascasubi is a gauchesque poem with exceptional lyric elements and numerous dramatic episodes, which afford it the external movement that differentiates it from the other poems of its kind. *Martín Fierro,* the pinnacle of gauchesque expression, exalts the dramatic moments of the hero. It is the culmination of all the poetic efforts of the *payadores;* it marks the apogee of a poetic school. If one of these works were lacking, we would have an imperfect view of the soul of the gaucho. Therefore, the study of *Martín Fierro* should be preceded by a knowledge of *Fausto* and of *Santos Vega.*

The story of the principal poem of this genre is as follows.

At the outset, Martín Fierro is living happily, devoted to the labors of the field and to the pleasures of domestic life:

> Yo he conocido esta tierra
> en que el paisano vivía;
> y su ranchito tenía,
> y sus hijos y mujer...
> Era una delicia ver
> como pasaba los días.
>
> Entonces—cuando el lucero
> brillaba en el cielo santo,
> y los gallos con su canto
> nos decían que el día llegaba,
> a la cocina rumbiaba
> el gaucho que era un encanto.

Y apenas la madrugada
empezaba a coloriar,
los pájaros a cantar,
y las gallinas a apiarse,
era cosa de largarse
cada cual a trabajar.[6]

From time to time, in order to break the monotony of his existence, he goes to the *pulpería* to intone some *payadas.*

Mi gala en las pulperías
era cuando había mas gente,
ponerme medio caliente,
pues, cuando puntiao me encuentro
me salen coplas de adentro
como agua de la vertiente.[7]

But one day the local magistrate appears there and arrests the gauchos and *gringos* who are present. Most of them, including Martín Fierro, are sent to a frontier army regiment. The gaucho describes the miseries of army life, his suffering, and the constant threat of attack by the Indians. After three years of this unfortunate existence Martín Fierro is impelled to desert, but on returning to his home, he finds that it has been totally destroyed.

No hallé ni rastro del rancho.
Sólo estaba la tapera:
¡Por Cristo! Si aquello era
pa enlutar el corazón
yo juré en esa ocasión
ser más malo que una fiera.[8]

Here begin his adventures. Martín Fierro becomes an outlaw gaucho; he engages in furious quarrels in dance halls and *pulperías;* he kills a Negro and is forced to leave his native district precipitately.

Limpié el facón en los pastos,
desaté mi redomón;
monté despacio y salí
al tranco pa el cañadón.[9]

Now Martín Fierro, trusting only in his steadfast arm, treads alone the infinite prairies.

Vamos suerte... Vamos juntos
dende que juntos nacimos.
Y ya que juntos vivimos
sin podernos dividir,
yo abriré con mi cuchillo
el camino pa seguir.[10]

But the police are on his trail, and finally find him. A veritable pitched battle ensues. One of the soldiers, admiring the valor of the outlaw, abandons his companions to fight at the side of the fugitive. The rebels are at last victorious.

Yo junté las osamentas
me hinqué y les recé un bendito;
y pedí a mi Dios clemente
me perdonara el delito
de haber muerto tanta gente.[11]

Martín's new friend, Cruz, narrates his own story, the tale of another life filled with sadness and unjust persecution. His wife had deceived him in favor of the commandant. The gaucho, having taken manly vengeance, fled to the pampas. On one occasion, he had killed a singer; but later, he had come to an agreement with the judge, turned his attention to maintaining the political position of his patron, and obtained a post on the police force.

Martín Fierro again takes up the narrative, saying:

Ya veo que somos los dos
astillas del mesmo palo;
yo paso por gaucho malo
y usté anda del mesmo modo.
Y yo, pa acabarlo todo
a los indios me refalo.[12]

His decision signifies the death of the gaucho *cantor* and the beginning of the gaucho outlaw. Hence Fierro breaks his guitar, which to him is the last symbol of civilization.

En este punto el cantor
buscó un porrón pa consuelo,
echó un trago como un cielo,
dando fin a su argumento,
y de un golpe el instrumento
lo hizo astillas en el suelo.
«Ruempo, dijo, la guitarra,
pa no volverla a templar,
ninguno la ha de tocar
por siguro tenganló:
pues naides ha de cantar
cuando este gaucho cantó.»[13]

The first part of the work ends with their entrance into the desert. At the first light of dawn the two friends draw away definitely from civilization.

Y cuando la habían pasao
una madrugada clara,
le dijo Cruz que mirara
las últimas poblaciones.
Y a Fierro dos lagrimones
le rodaron por la cara.[14]

In the second part, Martín Fierro continues his narrative. The two gauchos arrive at an Indian camp, where they are imprisoned as hostages, to be exchanged for Indian captives in the hands of the white men. They undergo great trials among the savages. After two years of captivity, Cruz dies of smallpox, entrusting to Martín Fierro the search for his son. Fierro rescues a white woman who has been taken by the Indians, and the two escape together. After a trip of extreme hardship, they finally arrive at the old farms, where Fierro finds his two sons and the young gaucho Picardía, who turns out to be the son of Cruz. A Negro challenges Martín Fierro to a match of *contrapunto*. The challenger, who is the brother of the first victim of Fierro, is defeated by the gaucho hero. Finally, the wretchedness of their state forces Martín, his two sons, and

Picardía to separate. And so they roam the bypaths of the world, guided by the wholesome moral advice that Fierro has given them. Martín Fierro has now become somewhat of a philosopher, with an exact knowledge of life and of man.

The immediate success that greeted the first part of *Martín Fierro* encouraged Hernández to compose the second part, which was published in 1879. Within six years there appeared eleven editions of the poem, and fifty thousand copies were sold. There are marked differences between what has been called *La Ida* (The Departure) and *La Vuelta de Martín Fierro* (The Return of Martin Fierro). It may be said that there is an abrupt change of tone, a new poetic atmosphere; in the first part, the narrative is dramatic and direct, and in the second, less rapid, and dotted with frequent interruptions and parenthetical remarks. The number of characters in the second part is considerably increased, and there is excessive repetition in the relation of their adventures, which actually are always the same. The author has by now acquired a poetic technique that is no longer wholly suitable to the theme. Furthermore, the moralizing air of the second part of the poem is inappropriate to the characters of the story. The only variety offered in the sequel is the introduction of a type clearly distinct from the previous figures, old Viscacha, a sort of Sancho Panza of the pampa, whose occasional proverbs, though always commonplaces, are often of notable wit.

El primer cuidao del hombre
es defender el pellejo.

...

El diablo sabe por diablo
pero más sabe por viejo.[15]

No andes cambiando de cueva.
Hace las que hace el ratón—
Consérvate en el rincón
en que empezó tu existencia—
Vaca que cambia querencia
se atrasa en la parición.[16]

El hombre no debe creer
en lágrimas de mujer
ni en la renguera del perro.[17]

El cerdo vive tan gordo
y se come hasta los hijos.[18]

La vaca que más rumbea
es la que da mejor leche.[19]

Cada lechón en su teta
es el modo de mamar.[20]

Es un bicho la mujer
que yo aquí no lo destapo.
Siempre quiere al hombre guapo,
mas fíjate en la elección:
porque tiene el corazón
como barriga de sapo...[21]

Los que no saben guardar
son pobres aunque trabajen.
Nunca, por más que se atajen
se librarán del cimbrón,
al que nace barrigón
es al ñudo que lo fajen.

Donde los vientos me llevan
allí estoy como en mi centro.
Cuando una tristeza encuentro
tomo un trago pa alegrarme;
a mí me gusta mojarme
por ajuera y por adentro.[22]

Further, the vivacity of the tourney of *contrapunto* between Martín Fierro and the colored *cantor* serves to relieve the monotony of the second part. It is probable that the lyric tone becomes excessive in these strophes, especially when a philosophical tinge colors his inspiration. The two guitar players are seated face to face. Martín Fierro challenges with this question:

—Decime, ¿cuál en el mundo
es el canto de la tierra?—[23]

The Negro answers him forthwith:

Forman un canto en la tierra
El dolor de tanta madre,
el gemir de los que mueren
y el llorar de los que nacen.[24]

Martín Fierro again questions:

—Es preciso que me expliques
¿cuál es el canto del mar?—[25]

The colored *cantor* replies:

Cuando la tormenta brama,
el mar que todo lo encierra
canta de un modo que aterra
como si el mundo temblara,
parece que se quejara
de que lo estrecha la tierra.[26]

Martín Fierro then wishes to know the meaning of the song of the night. The Negro explains that:

Son los secretos misterios
que las tinieblas esconden.
Son los ecos que responden
a la voz del que da un grito,
como un lamento infinito
que viene no sé de dónde.[27]

Martín Fierro is desirous of knowing his rival's definition of love, and the latter sings:

Ama en el fondo del mar
el pez de lindo color.
Ama el hombre con ardor,

ama todo cuanto vive.
De Dios vida se recibe
y donde hay vida hay amor.[28]

Satisfied of the ingenuity and skill of his opponent, Martín Fierro offers him a chance to take over the interrogation. The Negro asks concrete questions about quantity, measure, weight, time and its divisions. Fierro replies with wit and even a bit of malice. Finally, the challenger admits his defeat.

From the foregoing excerpts we may easily note that the originally martial, characteristically regional nature of the poem has been supplanted by a series of abstractions and recitatives. The reader feels that the poet, finding his heroic material exhausted, wished to sustain his fame as a lyricist by adding elements completely alien to the principal motive. And in this sense the second part, if not a fiasco, is at least inferior to the first.

I believe that calling *Martín Fierro* an epic poem implies a confusion of genres. An epic is generally objective in tendency; it celebrates the great deeds of a mythological or historical hero, aspires to the sublime, and generally presents a perfect unit. Its expression is highly noble in form, not only in the Renaissance epic, but also in the popular one.

It has been said that Homer does not maintain the epic tone throughout the *Iliad,* and that he frequently falls into a certain vulgarity of expression; that he has dressed his gods in excessively mundane garb, and that the moral sentiments of his heroes are scarcely edifying. Of course, many objections may well be leveled against the works of Homer, as against those of Virgil, Dante, Ariosto, Tasso, Camões, and Voltaire; but the grandiose, truly epic character of all these poems, and the elevated aesthetic purpose of their authors, cannot be denied. Even in the eminently popular epic, the most genuine example of which is probably the *Cantar de mío Cid,* which does not in the least maintain classical precepts, there is a harmonious fusion of human elements, coarse and vulgar at times, with a robust poetic inspiration, which on many occasions attains true greatness. It seems that the author, very Spanish in character, and therefore inherently realistic, deliberately introduced comic, familiar, popular, even ridiculous episodes to offset the exceedingly noble form of the work. But its loftiness, as well as its essential unity, effected through the heroic actions of the Cid Campeador, remains everywhere apparent.

On the contrary, none of the elements which determine the epic appears in *Martín Fierro*. The hero is neither grandiose nor awe-inspiring; he does not represent a race, nor even a people in a critical moment of its evolution; it would be absurd to pretend that the gaucho symbolizes the genesis of the Argentinian nation, especially if we judge it from the viewpoint of Buenos Aires, heart and head of that country. *Martín Fierro* is lacking in epic spirit, not because its action is unheroic, but because it does not denote a philosophy of heroic existence. In general, Martín Fierro is the most absolute negation of that spirit, since he always bewails his sufferings, the hardships of life, the daily dangers, the absence of comfort. At the end of his varied career he suddenly becomes a mixture of the parochial moralist and the evangelist.

Aside from his love for the rustic tasks, his primary ideal is expressed at the beginning of the poem in these words:

> Y sentao junto al jogón
> a esperar que venga el día;
> al cimarrón le prendía
> hasta ponerse rechoncho,
> mientras su china dormía
> tapadita con su poncho.[29]

Martín Fierro drifts into the life of adventure unconsciously, almost against his will, carried along like an inert form by the abuses of the authorities and by the economic conditions of his time; he is filled with an absolute pessimism that makes of him, far from an epic hero, a poor victim of an anarchical society. His great desire is the elimination of magistrates, enemy Indians, and police, so that he may devote himself unhampered to the placid life of the ranch and the *pulpería*. The hard life of the cattle driver and the cowboy, which for Don Segundo Sombra was the most virile of professions, is for Fierro something of a sport, although, as a sport, it rates second to rest and abundant food:

> Y con el buche bien lleno
> era cosa superior
> irse en brazos del amor
> a dormir como la gente
> pa empezar al día siguiente
> las fainas del día anterior.[30]

Martín Fierro lacks unity. Since the principal hero has neither a heroic philosophy nor a great human mission to fulfill, he falls into innumerable repetitions of external events effected exclusively by chance. He then has to come into contact with other individuals, who in turn repeat the same adventures and acquire an importance equal to that of Fierro in the poem. In the second part, the poet, at a loss for new material, merely denounces the same abuses of the civil magistrates and of the police which he had described in the first part. Here the hero disintegrates. His two sons, Picardía, the old Viscacha, and the Negro *cantor* make their appearance, depriving Fierro of his preëminent position in the work. Critics have praised in Martín Fierro his loyal friendship with Cruz; his chivalry in rescuing a captive white woman; his chastity in not taking advantage of the services rendered her, and so on; but these characteristics are not in the least heroic or original, being generally accepted as the duty of every member of modern civilization. He who lacks such attributes is considered in our current society a coarse and inhuman fellow.

It is interesting to note that geography and landscape play no part whatever in the poem. It would be difficult for a person intimately acquainted with the pampas to determine the region in which the action of *Martín Fierro* takes place. The landscape, in fact, is so little present that the author might well have written his masterpiece far from the places that had inspired it.

A great deal has been said about the usage of the gaucho dialect of *Martín Fierro*—a great deal of nonsense.[31] A simple glossary of infrequently used terms would solve the problem, which actually does not exist. I should like to cite here, as opposite, the opinion of Ricardo Rojas:

> If the poetic technique of the *payador* was already completely created and defined when *Martín Fierro* appeared, so was that interesting philological formation which has been called gauchesque language. Hernández needed to invent nothing—and he did *not* invent anything—not in meters, vocabulary, syntax, nor the art of poetic composition in order to narrate the life of his protagonist. He who studies the technique of *Martín Fierro* will therewith have studied in its unities and types all the fragmentary forms of couplets and *payadas* that preceded it, and that previously had been integrated into *Santos Vega* or *La Cautiva,* to generate a poetic cycle; in other words, *Martín Fierro* is a synthesis of the gaucho genre, both in its versification and in its vocabulary.[32]

Granting that Hernández employs the authentic speech of the gauchos—and even this is not proven,—I would venture to deny the importance of that language. The fact that today the Argentinians do not speak that jargon is ample proof that gaucho expression was not the genesis of a new idiom. Nowadays, when gaucho syntax or words appear, emphasis is placed on their regional, picturesque value. And that is all!

There exists in the language of *Martín Fierro* a goodly number of archaisms, Indianisms, neologisms, and vulgarisms, formed frequently by metathesis and defective assimilations. However, these linguistic varieties are not exclusive to the *Martín Fierro* but are found in Spain as well and in other Spanish American countries. Within the geographical area of the Castilian tongue the gauchesque dialect is merely a regional form comparable with hundreds of variants scattered throughout the world, from Salonica and Manila to the towns of Arizona and New Mexico. What is of importance is that this localism has produced a style of poetry, a special literary atmosphere that lends novelty to poems such as *Fausto, Santos Vega,* and *Martín Fierro;* to novels such as *Don*

Segundo Sombra and *Los Caranchos de la Florida;* and to dramas such as *Barranca abajo* and *M'Hijo el Dotor* of Florencio Sánchez.

The gauchesque style has been compared to the more popular forms of Spanish balladry. This is a grave error which serious literary criticism should avoid. The language of the ballads is vigorous, abounding in hidden, indefinable energy. It represents philologically the formation of a new language and politically the reconstruction of an entire race. On the other hand, the gauchesque idiom marks the disappearance, the death, of an isolated group of men, and the degeneration of a language already formed. We must reject the gauchesque style as unsuitable for epic.

The poetry of *Martín Fierro* at no time reaches epic heights. The images of the poem are excessively common; the use of metaphors descends to the most objective form and never achieves a poetic abstraction. There do not appear in the poem the profound symbols of *Paradise Lost* or of the *Divine Comedy,* the strong, virile verse of the *Cantar de mío Cid,* the dazzling comparisons or the ardent lyricism of *Os Lusiadas.* The vocabulary is of a simplicity bordering on the trivial, and the poetic vision of the whole simply does not exist. So then, if we choose not to classify *Martín Fierro* as an epic, preferring to associate it with the primary sources of popular poetry, and if, instead of granting it lofty heroic conception, we place it on the more limited plane of folkloric excellence, we may be assigning to it its just merits.

José Hernández himself knew that his work was of relative importance only in its spontaneous improvisation and simplicity. Never did he think of vying with the great literary figures of the world, nor even with the cultured poets of his own country. Martín Fierro was born a gaucho *cantor:*

> Cantando me he de morir,
> cantando me han de enterrar,
> y cantando he de llegar
> al pie del Eterno Padre.
> Dende el vientre de mi madre
> Vine a este mundo a cantar.[33]

Hernández was familiar with other poetry, with the cultured production of the *letraos* (the learned), as Fierro would say:

> Yo no soy cantor letrao,
> mas si me pongo a cantar
> no tengo cuando acabar
> y me envejezco cantando.
> Las coplas me van brotando
> como agua de manantial...[34]

But he was a bard of the people, a guitarist proud of his art, no matter how limited that might be:

> Con la guitarra en la mano
> ni las moscas se me arriman,
> naides me pone el pie encima,
> y cuando el pecho se entona
> hago gemir a la prima
> y llorar a la bordona.[35]

The style is well adapted to the theme, and expresses a series of idiomatic shades of positive merit. The humor of the situations and of several of the characters is sterling; and the proverbs, which the author employs abundantly, have true provincial charm. Within the somewhat maladroit taste of the poet there is a certain naïveté of genuine rustic flavor. To compare *Martín Fierro* with the *Odyssey* or even with the *Araucana* is like placing a Mexican curio shop on a par with the Prado Museum or the Louvre. But we cannot deny that in a well-stocked shop there is often a goodly number of small articles of beauty and novelty.

Further, I have read several commentaries on the moral loftiness of the hero, Martín Fierro. Actually, I can perceive that nowhere, but this may be due to my own incapacity to attribute moral significance to simple actions characteristic of any man in any part of the globe.

Martín Fierro has had an enormous influence on the literature of Argentina; it has been a source of inspiration to poets, novelists, and dramatists. This is a historic merit that no one can dispute, and that even by itself would be sufficient to consecrate a literary work. Its fame has been celebrated by many eminent critics, including Menéndez Pelayo, Miguel de Unamuno, Azorín, and Vossler. There are translations of *Martín Fierro* in several languages, and I believe that at this very moment in our literary history it is one of our most esteemed works abroad.

I think that *Martín Fierro* must be rescued from that overly generous critical evaluation which sees masterpieces at every turn, and which, for puerile reasons, places at a vertiginous height certain works that are aesthetically limited. Under the classification of the epic, *Martín Fierro* loses the primal charm of its lyric poetry and autobiography—"autobiography" because the elegy upon the death of the gaucho is little other than the individual elegy of Fierro, the man whose life is basically a tragedy of maladjustment, the elegy of a man yet alive, but suffering, dying, "agonizing," as Miguel de Unamuno would say.

Another classification that would suggest a new point of departure for the study of this poem is that of the picaresque novel. The only possible sources of unity in the work are that series of adventures through which the hero comes into contact with the few aspects of the society in which he lives; his bantering, festive nature; and the consistant moral atmosphere created by the narrative. The various personages who appear in the poem represent many other phases of everyday existence, of modes of living. Picardía is a new Lazarillo; old Viscacha seems torn from the pages of *Guzmán de Alfarache;* Fierro is a squire in an environment of simplicity and barbarity. The constant protest against governmental abuses bears great similarity to the moral tone of the picaresque novels of the sixteenth century. If *Martín Fierro* were a prose work, its approximation to the picaresque genre would be absolute.

Today the book appears in the dusky hands of the peasants of Mendoza, San Luis, and Córdoba. But it is also found, in elegant English editions, in the classrooms of North American universities.

Its great human vigor reaches out to all, and this is the greatest homage that can be accorded to any work of art. *Martín Fierro* immortalizes a type of man who no longer exists, fixes in its historical moment a language now extinct, and perpetuates in ideal a vanished race. It is only right that Buenos Aires should reject Martín Fierro, because civilization has the supreme power to destroy—in order to construct once more.

Chapter VI ◇ The Influence of French Culture

FRANCE has wielded an influence of indescribable magnitude on the systematic evolution of aesthetic ideas in Hispanic America. First was the example of the Encyclopedists, which determined a new political philosophy in a continent still of colonial mentality. We should not forget, moreover, that the French spirit had already made itself felt in Spain, in such writers as Torres de Villarroel, Padre Feijóo, and Jovellanos, and that these in their turn were known and imitated in the colonies.

In strictly literary spheres the predominance of French taste was absolute. The fact that a scholar of such purely Spanish inclination as Andrés Bello should accept romantic poetry affords ample proof of the complete Gallicization of a whole generation of writers. When Bello wrote his famous *Oración por todos* (Prayer for All), he was already far removed from Spanish lyricism; clearly, this poetry is of pure French sensibility. How can it be denied that Rousseau and Chateaubriand are the preceptors whose example inspired in America a new prose of musical elegance and vague melancholy? Early in the century the *Noches tristes* (Sad Nights) of Fernández de Lizardi, called *El Pensador mexicano* (The Mexican Thinker), indulges in imitation of the preromantic French style and gives a new impression of nature, as viewed subjectively by the author. Heredia, Echeverría, Mármol, indeed all of our early romanticists, mark a clear withdrawal from Spain, an alienation that turned to contempt and a complete negation of all peninsular values in the massive prose of Domingo Faustino Sarmiento. Just as the Spaniards Larra, Espronceda, and the Duque de Rivas tried to Europeanize Spanish literature, so did our romanticists, imbued with the desire for aesthetic liberty, cling to the French pattern.

We must read Sarmiento many times if we would comprehend fully the profound hatred that existed in the first half of the nineteenth century toward everything Spanish. Sarmiento conceded nothing of merit to that culture, which in large measure was ours; in the opinion of the great Argentinian polemist, Spain could boast neither mathematics, physics, history, nor philosophy. He would deny any trace of Spanish genius, be it in poetic or other expression, and even dared to condemn the language as incapable of expressing modern thought. Of course, not all the thinkers of his time carried their hatred so far, but the attitude of Sarmiento facilitates the understanding of our vassalage to French culture. After a study of his works, we know why Juan Bautista Alberdi, Bilbao, and Echeverría resorted to French sources in order to express their ideas of democratic government; why Bolívar, Miranda, and Rodríguez shared such overwhelming admiration for the French Revolution; why Spanish American philosophical thought was oriented definitively toward the French genius; and why the scientific, historical, and literary texts used for the first time in our schools were written in the language of Voltaire.

And that was only the beginning. French intellectual dictatorship was later absolute. Lamartine and Musset were read and imitated throughout an entire century; Victor Hugo was for the bards of our continent emperor of the realm of poesy; Balzac was for our first novelists undisputed master, for they had not yet discovered the genius of Stendhal; Théophile Gautier revealed to us a world of exotic beauty. Bibliographies and adequate critical works are notoriously lacking, but a chronological study of French translations would give us a fairly precise idea of all we owe to French romanticism. It is axiomatic that Hispanic American literature begins about 1825, and that even then it is not Spanish in type. Poetic enterprise is directed away from the pseudo-classical, pseudo-philosophical, pseudo-artistic ode, from pastoral exercises in verse, from anacreontics, from moral epistles and elegies. Rather, we find the beginning of the poetry of primordial, untamed nature, the hymns to the sun, to the sea, to volcanoes and tropical tempests; there appears, like a crimson javelin, the ardent verse hurled against the military chieftains and political tyrants; civic, heroic song worthy of the great continental heroes; poetry that reflects the suffering of the American romanticists, the subjectivity of the sentimental, erotic man—the sensuous, violent, solitary man of a primitive, semibarbarous race. Thus America, immersed in the French pattern, began to create a new poetry, the product of a changed soul; an ardent poetry, full of primitive impurities, obscure instincts, generous aspirations. If it had followed its own impetus, this poetry would have degenerated into an orgy of intimate confessions, a constantly anarchical, individual form; but fortunately the French masters channeled our ebullient lyricism. Romantic disorder, the spectacle of mad young poets and frenzied suicides and the bohemian artists of the first half of the nineteenth century, was displaced by the restraint and polish of the French Parnassian school. The poet, no longer the spontaneous improviser inspired by the Muses, was transformed into a technician in his art; his mournful wail, his self-compassion, his amorous accusations, his grief before the ravages of death, faded into oblivion as he assumed a new objective position, one of analysis, historical investigation, aesthetic rationalism. Under the renewed influence of the French, the Spanish American poet acquired a cultural consciousness.

The Parnassian frequently may not have been a poet—neither, at times, was the romanticist,—but he never failed to be an artist. Leconte de Lisle, Heredia, and Baudelaire taught us how to employ a poetic idiom, how to manipulate a language as the artist his brush or the sculptor his chisel. The Parnassian movement was of capital importance for the development of our poetry, which tended toward abruptness in manner and was poor in technical resources. The instruments of artistic creation supplanted devotion to inherent quality in the art of the poet. Aesthetic evaluation yielded to technical analysis. As a result, the Parnassian artist was less concerned with the comparative merits of Olavo Bilac and Castro Alves than with the unique literary value of the work of the former. The same may be said of Díaz Mirón in Mexico, Leopoldo Díaz in Argentina, and González Prada in Peru. All these are creators of a kind of classical poetry, of metallic rhythm, of Olympian aristocracy. It is probable that none of them is a great poet, but that is irrelevant to the topic under discussion. French Parnassian influence is notable in almost all the modernists of Spanish America: in the *Lascas* (Chips from a Stone) of Salvador Díaz Mirón, in the *Hojas al viento* (Leaves in the Wind) of Julián del Casal, in the best works of Gutiérrez Nájera, in the exquisite *Nocturnos* of José Asunción Silva, and especially in the *Prosas profanas* of Rubén Darío. It appears later in the *Sonetos vascos* of Julio Herrera y Reissig, in *Alma América* of José Santos Chocano, in the *Ritos* of Guillermo Valencia, in the *Perlas negras* of Amado Nervo. When Leopoldo Lugones and Jaimes Freyre abandon free verse, they are almost always Parnassians, as are also José Juan Tablada and Luis Urbina. Parnassian poetry, with its decorative elements, sculptural images, and martial rhythm, even today exercises an influence on several Hispanic American poets.

I should like to remark here, parenthetically, the symbolic fact that José María Heredia, one of the greatest poets of French Parnassianism, was of Cuban origin. And Nicanor de la Roca de Vergallo, whose *Livre des Incas* introduces a special form of free verse into French poetry, was by birth a Peruvian. Later, there arose other Hispanic American poets, such as Laforgue and Supervielle, who were to lend a new note to French poetic production.

When symbolist poetry appeared in France, poets in Spanish America were adhering to Parnassian formulae; consequently, their assimilation of symbolism was slow, and at times it only modified their work superficially. Darío may serve as an example. In his *Prosas profanas* (1896) he is the perfect Parnassian; in his next volume, *Cantos de vida y esperanza* (Songs of Life and Hope, which appeared in 1905), the symbolist technique is evident in a few poems, but in his compositions of greater depth he still reveals the influence of classical form, of pictorial, sculptural effects, and of precise rhythm. And to the end of his life Darío remained fascinated by light and rhythm, by decorativeness and brilliance of expression, qualities more characteristic of the Parnassian mode than of the symbolist.

But French symbolism (that of Verlaine more than that of Baudelaire or Mallarmé) penetrates deeply into our aesthetic sensibility. Its atmosphere of vague confines, its quality of fantasy and metaphysics, its undulating, subtle rhythm, its emphasis on musical expression find easy access to the soul of the Spanish American. It is difficult to determine the exact extent of the influence of this tendency on the modernists, because, as we noted above, along with the soft, musical, delicately obscure tones of one poem, there appear in the same author moments of objective, brilliant composition. For example, this is evident in such poets of the Verlaine school as Amado Nervo, Julio Herrera y Reissig, Leopoldo Lugones, José Juan Tablada, and Rubén Darío. It is easier to observe the symbolist influence in postmodernist poets, among whom Parnassianism no longer carries weight. Among them may be glimpsed in all its exquisiteness the soaring, suggestive poetry of the author of *Fêtes galantes;* as also in Manuel Magallanes Moure, in Enrique Banchs, Delmira Agustini, Juan Guzmán Cruchaga, and in many others.

It is interesting to note that Spanish America affords no representative symbolist poet such as Cruz e Souza or Alphonsus de Guimaraens in Brazil. Rather, the combination of symbolism and Parnassianism gave birth to our modernism, the death of which, about 1914, was followed directly by the vanguard schools. The evolution from Parnassianism to symbolism took place within the same poet. In other words, both schools lost their individual character upon reaching our continent, and became instead only two aspects of a revolutionary aesthetic attitude. Modernism, therefore, is not blind imitation; rather, it is an assimilation, a combination of foreign elements in which a genuinely Hispanic American sensibility is expressed.

With modernism, we could have become entirely independent of French tutelage, and in fact we did so, partially. We have had highly original, extremely American poets, such as Luis Carlos López in Colombia, and López Velarde in Mexico, for whom it would be impossible to specify European models; we have had others who run the complete gamut of tendencies and whose sources would be difficult to ascertain, poets such as Gabriela Mistral, Juana de Ibarbourou, Alfonsina Storni, Ricardo Arenales, Alfonso Reyes, and José María Eguren. But the "militant poets"—if I may use that term—remain faithful to the French norms. About 1920 they instituted that series of revolutionary schools which proceed from dadaism to surrealism. Some taught us poetic geometry, the infantile distribution of verses in the shape of pyramids and rectangles; others inaugurated a reform that was of transcendent significance to them, the abolition of periods and commas; many adopted the novelty of baby talk, and most merely indulged in a system of images and symbols drawn from the mechanical sciences. They had declared war on the two great French poets of the late nineteenth century: Verlaine and Baudelaire. Of the "ancients"—as they called them—they respected somewhat Rimbaud and Mallarmé, but their current masters were others: Cocteau, Apollinaire, Valéry, and Supervielle. It cannot be denied that the poetic revolution was useful, since by 1914 modernism had aged noticeably and such poets as Guillermo Valencia, Leopoldo Lugones, and Santos Chocano were merely repeating themselves. Clearly, the numerous manifestoes proclaimed between 1918 and 1930—for, in truth, there were more manifestoes than real poems—left in their wake such utter confusion that even the poets themselves, I suspect, did not fully comprehend their own chaotic theories. Nevertheless, there remained also the desire to create individual art and to exceed the bounds of prescribed, fixed expression.

Those reform movements of Spanish America find their counterpart in Brazil in the Paulist modernism of 1922, which also, in spite of its nationalistic formula, reveals a strong French ancestry. But although in Brazil the names of its initiators, such as Bandeira, Mário de Andrade, and Oswald de Andrade, have remained alive, and their poetry revolutionary, in the Spanish-speaking countries the originators of these schools—for example, Huidobro, Oribe, Hidalgo, Borges—have noticeably declined and poetry turns constantly toward greater simplicity, as is revealed in Barbieri, Barrenechea, Neruda, Villaurrutia, Ballagas, and in the great Uruguayan poetess Sara Ibáñez.

It is hardly necessary to speak of the influence of French prose on that of Hispanic America. Rousseau and Chateaubriand made us aware of artistry in style. The colorless, academic, cold, pedantic prose of the colonial period was supplanted by the new style of refined sensibility, of rhythm conditioned to animistic movements, of appropriate images and modern color. The eighteenth century in Spain, a period characterized by a crocodile-like lethargy, had been rich in academicians, and in "medalhões" (pompous figureheads), as the Brazilians say so meaningly, the leader of whom was the soporific Ignacio Luzán. But let us not think for one moment that the Spaniards lacked literary talent, for the examples of Santa Teresa, Quevedo, and Cervantes alone are ample proof to the contrary. It was merely that the oppressive weight of libraries and academies, of didacticism, and of the political and domestic economy had temporarily stifled creative expression. We should be deeply grateful, then, to the authors of the *Nouvelle Héloïse* and *Atala*. After them come Balzac, source of inspiration to the early American novelists; Dumas, father of the writers of adventure serials; Hugo, whose *Les Misérables* was the first "best seller" in America, model for authors who would philosophize on social problems; Flaubert, master of a whole generation of Hispanic American writers, author of the provocative *Madame Bovary, Education sentimentale,* and *Salammbô*. Flaubert wielded as much influence on Spanish American prose writers as did Heredia, Verlaine, and Baudelaire together, since he is the great master of poetic style, as revealed in *Salammbô,* and the psychologist of the modern soul, maladjusted and tormented. I am reviewing here those authors whose influence has been general among our novelists, and so do not pause for such distinguished figures as the Goncourts, Daudet, Paul Adams, Barbey d'Aurevilly, and Huysmans, who also had disciples on our continent.

Emile Zola, whose protesting voice echoed through his strong novels, provided our great social inspiration. There is no Spanish American country that does not have its critical reformer. Some denounce the immorality of bourgeois women; others, political venality; a goodly number, the exploitation of the miners; yet others, the hypocrisy of false patriots. Zola's *Nana* initiated a series of novels in which the heroines are poor, exploited, pitiful creatures; this genre reached its apogee on our continent with the *Santa* of Federico Gamboa. The naturalistic novel is easily acclimated in countries such as ours, where every aspect of poverty finds its abode and every kind of discrimination its lair. Thus, for us, Zola was not only a great writer, but also an exemplary man, and it is highly probable that he has more admirers today in America than in his native land.

After Zola, Proust is the most esteemed French novelist in Spanish America, despite the fact that the slow movement of his works and the complicated net of his internal plot are not easily adapted to the psychology of our readers. He has disciples throughout the Hispanic world, although at times it is difficult to discern absolutely whether his influence is direct, or whether it has reached us through some English or North American writer.

I should like to say once more that the French authors I have mentioned were sources of definite literary schools among us. Other influences, such as that of Anatole France, for example, were superficial and transitory; those of André Gide, Aragon, and Malraux are at present evident in certain of our authors, and it would be hazardous to attempt definition of their radius of action.

In the field of literary criticism the masters of the past century were Brunetière, Sainte-Beuve, Taine, and Renan. Further, we must not forget the profound influence, in aesthetic ideas as well as in remarkable style, that Rémy de Gourmont exercised on the criticism of modernism. We owe him a debt of gratitude for his interest in Spanish American letters and his admiration for our greatest poet, Rubén Darío. Several contemporary French critics, such as André Gide, Paul Valéry, and Valéry Larbaud, are widely known, but since our current theories of criticism are somewhat confused, their teachings almost invariably fall on barren ground. However, the outstanding Mexican critic, Alfonso Reyes, has drawn a great deal from them.

At this point it would be appropriate to ask: To what extent has the influence of French literature been beneficial to us? What turn would our letters have taken if deprived of the constant guidance of French models? The answer is obvious. During the entire nineteenth century, France boasted a magnificent lyrical poetry, superior in artistic sensibility and in formal distinction, if not in profundity, to that of all the other European nations; her novelists, from Stendhal to Proust, were masters in their genre; her critics combined classical culture with an extraordinary artistic intuition. Not all these admirable qualities passed into our literature, but on occasion the disciple was truly worthy of his teachers, as, for example, were José Enrique Rodó, Rubén Darío, Alfonso Reyes, and Eduardo Mallea.

French taste offered us a noble standard of measure and refinement. It is not difficult to imagine what our fine arts would have become, had they been subjected to the popular common taste and to the anarchy of the individual temperament. We need only remark the example of two prose writers who were impervious to the teachings of cultured literature. First, consider Vargas Vila, a Colombian novelist who poisoned the taste of an entire generation with pornographic works, written in a style of repugnant vulgarity. Vargas Vila had thousands of readers—and still has!—especially among adolescent girls, which indicates all too clearly the danger of his influence. The other, Hugo Wast, is an Argentinian novelist whose works are published in editions of two hundred thousand copies; yet despite this enormous popularity his style is of the utmost indelicacy, his narrations are pitiful in their mock simplicity, and the psychology of his characters is always and absolutely false. If Vargas Vila had been even slightly influenced by the self-control and discretion of the French, his novels would have borne at least a resemblance to literary production; and if Hugo Wast had read the French novelists of his time, his style would have undergone some alteration and his works would contain at least a spark of talent.

French literature has served also to counterbalance the disproportionate enthusiasm that exists on our continent for popular and folkloric literature. Mistakenly enough, we have believed that the strictly popular is necessarily the most strictly American. However, if this were true, we would classify ourselves as peoples of an essentially primitive culture. We cannot persist in that state of elementary literary development in which folkloric tales, the rudimentary epic, *tonadas, coplas,* or gauchesque *payadas* suffice to represent our entire production. Indeed we may employ this material creatively, as have Ricardo Güiraldes in Argentina, Rómulo Gallegos in Venezuela, and Rubén Romero in Mexico. Even the indigenous legends may pass into refined literature, as certain Peruvian and Mexican novelists and writers of short stories have amply proved.

On the one hand, then, without the orientation afforded by French models, our literature would have remained chiefly popular, and on the other, it would have turned inevitably to the most current forms cultivated on the Iberian peninsula. However, we must bear in mind that during the first half of the nineteenth century the greatest literary activity of Spain as well found inspiration in French sources: the outstanding essayist of his time, Mariano José de Larra; the foremost romantic poet, José de Espronceda; and the leading dramatist of the period, the Duque de Rivas, all reveal strong Gallic influence. Thus, at best, we would have discovered in secondary sources what in actuality we took from the primary.

During the second half of the nineteenth century Spanish literature notoriously lacked unity; it may be said that instead of a literary current there was only a group of individual writers, who express merely a series of strictly personal conceptions rather than a national aesthetic movement.

It would be difficult to find two poets more unlike than Bécquer and Núñez de Arce, unless they be Campoamor and Rosalía de Castro. Galdós' concept of the purpose and goal of the novel is the direct antithesis of that of his contemporary, Juan Valera. The regionalism of Fernán Caballero, of Pereda, or of Countess Emilia Pardo Bazán, similarly cannot be reconciled with the skepticism of the author of *Pepita Jiménez* nor with the reforming zeal of the author of *La Familia de León Roch* (The Family of Leon Roch). Neither did the regionalism of the majority of Spanish writers exercise much influence on those of distant Hispanic America; and if there do appear on our continent occasional reminiscences of the Spanish authors, it is almost always in the external elements of the novelistic genre.

To account for these wide divergences, we should recall that the Spanish American sees the world from a viewpoint greatly divergent from that of his Iberian forebears. The Spaniard, a tenacious regionalist within Europe, exalts the characteristics peculiar to his racial make-up. With reason does Unamuno affirm that Spain is situated in the north of Africa! Spanish America, on the contrary, ever since the early days of its independence, has tried to place itself in contact with all the cultures of the world and to profit from the best elements of each. This cosmopolitanism has given a special tinge to our culture, forbidding forever its return to the old Spanish forms. This attitude has drawn us closer to France, whose type of culture, eminently cosmopolitan, has been welcomed throughout the world.

It may be said, then, that we approached the universal through French culture and that we continued in that eclectic position during the entire nineteenth century, and still retain it today despite the apparent temporary eclipse of French civilization. The defining elements of our personality have already been fused into a new whole. No one can deny that the Spaniard and the Spanish American are different men. The Spaniard is dogmatic, simple, severe, sober, impassioned, carved of a single block; the Spanish American is less decisive, less assured, more flexible, elegant, pliant, superficial, sensitive. He offers in opposition to the virile austerity of the Spaniard the courtesy of the Frenchman. Even the language, spoken and written, has undergone modification in America. Our manner of speaking is less declamatory, less emphatic than that of the Spaniard; rather it is softer, more intimate; the Spaniard is more dramatic, we are more lyrical. Hardly can our expression convey the violence of Spanish emphasis. We soften the consonants where the Spaniard intensifies them or suppresses them with harsh effect. For example, our final "s" is at times almost completely lost, or at most becomes a very fine sibilant; in Spain, on the other hand, it is almost sonorous. In the past participles of the first conjugation the intervocalic "d" is among us a vague, undecided sound, whereas in the pronunciation of Madrid it disappears entirely, leaving two strong vowels in vigorous contrast. The same phenomenon may be observed also in the final "d": the Spaniard omits it, ending the word with a stressed vowel, while the Spanish American forms at least the beginning of the sound.

There are basic differences also in the written language. The typically Spanish period of great sweep, constructed with numerous relative pronouns and conjunctions, is broken by the Spanish American into independent sentences. Spanish style, even that of such authors as Unamuno and Baroja, who are so little inclined toward purism, gives evidence of strong racial flavor, inherent in the structure of the sentence and in countless archaisms. Spanish style breathes of harsh landscape, of austere nobility. When a

Spanish American writer tries to imitate it, as for example Rodríguez Larreta in *La Gloria de don Ramiro* (The Glory of Don Ramiro), the result is an obviously un-Spanish concoction that gives us the impression of a French stylist trying to imitate the prose of Santa Teresa.

The harmonious, musical, colorful, sensitively vibrant style of such writers as Díaz Rodríguez, José Enrique Rodó, Ventura García Calderón, and Carlos Reyles approximates far more closely the work of any French author of our century than that of any Spanish author. The sensibility of our modernist prose is essentially French and is best adapted to the complicated mechanism of our psychology, now constantly undergoing transformation. To illustrate further the differences between Spanish and Spanish American style, we may note that where the Spanish American would employ a Gallicism as the logical solution to a minor linguistic problem, the Spanish writer would prefer to reconstruct his entire sentence so as to avoid the Gallicism. This phenomenon is truly indicative of what is happening to a language and to the soul of two peoples.

When a Spanish poet wishes to introduce a new aesthetic orientation in his time, he reverts to the old national models; thus, for example, García Lorca sought inspiration in Góngora, in the old songbooks and ballad collections, and in the dramatic works of the Golden Age. On the other hand, when a Spanish American poet seeks to create a new literary school, he resorts directly to French sources. Rubén Darío, Herrera y Reissig, González Martínez, José María Eguren, Vicente Huidobro, Pablo Neruda, Xavier Villaurrutia—in effect, all the poets desirous of innovation—have scrupulously avoided the Spanish tradition, adopting rather the Gallic intellectual attitude, target of the criticism of Juan Valera.

If the influence of French culture is at an end on our continent, we should lament an irreparable loss. I have great faith in the permanence of French genius; I hope that Hispanic America will continue faithful to certain dictates of its spirit and that it will maintain that democratic conscience which was created for our good by the *philosophes* of the *Encyclopédie*. We are now just at the dawn of our existence and must not allow ourselves to be blinded by dazzling but adequate formulae for life. Very often, when I think of the future of our continent, I recall the words offered by José Vasconcelos as the motto of the University of Mexico: "Por mi raza hablará el espíritu (The soul will speak for my race)."

Chapter VII ◇ A Reëvaluation of Rubén Darío

I

TODAY, the thirty years that have passed since the death of Rubén Darío afford a perspective through which we may view his poetry afresh. I have always maintained that Darío is *the* great poet of our continent and one of the most eminent in the Spanish language. But since recent criticism of him has been increasingly adverse I should like to examine, in this chapter, the reasons for it.

I believe that, as a general rule, every writer who is not a man of genius diminishes in esteem with the course of time. It cannot even be said that each generation produces a literary genius in any language. Hence the writers who compose the greater part of a nation's literary tradition are consigned to virtual oblivion; although their names recur in histories, anthologies, and even in conversation, their works do not command permanently the interest of readers. They are dying souls, who, though lingering on the brink, are nevertheless condemned without hope of reprieve.

Take, for example, the Spanish, Spanish American, and Brazilian romanticists. The names of Espronceda, the Duque de Rivas, Zorrilla, Echeverría, Mármol, Gonçalves de Magalhães, Gonçalves Dias, and Castro Alves are known by all, but rare nowadays is the person of refined literary taste who will seek spiritual solace in the works of these poets. The bedside companion of yesterday graces the forsaken library shelf today. They are all drifting away on the stream of oblivion; some are still in sight, others already so far distant as almost to have disappeared. Time will carry them all from view; and when on occasion they are recalled in the future, it will be for reasons other than their purely poetic value.

Already this is beginning to happen to the Hispanic American modernists. In Mexico, for example, present-day critics are repudiating Gutiérrez Nájera and Amado Nervo, two poets who very recently were considered great; in Chile, the modernist Pedro Antonio González has been buried definitively; José Santos Chocano, who was once called the foremost poet of the continent, is now accused of superficiality and prosaism; Leopoldo Lugones faced disavowal even before his death; Herrera y Reissig is termed a verbalist; and so on down the list. Only Darío has remained erect on his pedestal; but already that eminence is challenged.

It would be pertinent to ask here: What type of poetry does the reader of today prefer, and which of the required poetic qualities are absent in Rubén Darío?

The reading public from 1890 to 1915 was accustomed to a type of poetry the prime elements of which were romantic sentiment and euphuistic style, mingled with an Oriental sensuousness of images and a warm French intonation. The romanticists had already popularized such melancholy, despairing poems as Lamartine's *Le Lac* (The Lake) and Musset's *Nuits* (Nights); José de Espronceda had written his *Canto a Teresa* (Song to Theresa); Bécquer, his intimately despondent verse; Manuel Acuña, his tormented *Nocturno a Rosario;* Gutiérrez Nájera, his familiarly nostalgic *Serenata de Schubert;* and José Asunción Silva, his voluptuous, mournful *Nocturnos.* Thus, when there appeared such works as Darío's *Sonatina, Marcha triunfal* (Triumphal March), *Era un aire suave* (It was a Gentle Breeze), and *El Reino interior* (The Inner Kingdom), poems rich in color, resplendent with dazzling images, exquisite elegance of diction, and rhythm linked with purpose and idea, the Nicaraguan bard was acclaimed as the interpreter of the aesthetic sensibility of the time. No poet of his period surpasses him in brilliance or in refinement. For nearly thirty years he reigned, from Paris and Madrid, over the kingdom of decorative poetry, Parnassian-symbolistic in theme and expression. His celebrated *Marcha triunfal*[1] is illustrative of the enthusiastic energy which captivated the American continent.

[1] For notes to chapter vii see pages 229–233.

When González Martínez composed his famous sonnet, *Tuércele el cuello al cisne* (Wring the Swan's Neck),[2] in which he condemns the baroque poetry of modernism and advocates instead the interpretation of the mysteries of life and nature, he revealed the birth of a new aesthetic sensibility; he proved that devotees of poetry were already tired of princesses, swans, winged steeds, nightingales, and roses. Rather, they were turning to a more intense poetry, to expression more akin to the suffering and struggle of life, to composition more daring in form. They were beginning to prefer free verse to the Alexandrine,[3] brusque rhythm to monotonous cadence, social themes of vibrant import to Greek friezes and eighteenth-century drawings. In a word, they demanded that the poet be a man of his time and environment. If we had had a virile lover of democracy as was Walt Whitman, we would have turned toward him after the First World War.

To the generation of 1920, Rubén Darío was an artificial, courtly, Gallicized poet, totally alien to the life of his continent. His metrical reforms did not interest those new writers who proclaimed the destruction of poetic form; his verbal refinement sounded hollow in the ears of the revolutionary followers of Marinetti and Cocteau; the anachronism of his themes was interpreted as an evasion of reality.

I do not know what kind of poetry the cultured Spanish American reader of today prefers. It is highly probable that there exist as many tastes as there are cultural divisions. Besides, taste is often conditioned by elements foreign to creative production. For example, the poets of social themes—Vallejo, Neruda, Guillén León Felipe—are read frequently just because they are of the left, even though their comrades may not understand their works. Further, there is a group of people who sympathize with everything new, with all vanguard and leftist movements; and especially evident among them are students, those firm believers in social and racial revindications. If they could express themselves in verse, they would be social or political poets; this, in my opinion, constitutes, even as a doctrine, a serious menace to poetry.

Rubén Darío was not a social poet; he did not cultivate the Negro theme; he was not a Catholic poet, though he was a Catholic man; he was not even a democratic poet. Moreover, I am certain that these characteristics have nothing to do with poetry. But the public demands such elements nowadays; literature of the moment is in vogue, and therefore Darío is not the favorite poet of Spanish Americans today.

Curiously enough, we have let ourselves be lured by García Lorca's poetry, which is really as superficial as the most shallow moments of Darío; actually, García Lorca presents a mixture of Spanish classicism with a waggish touch of the Madrilenian dandy. His is poetry for recitation, a characteristic from which the Spanish American seemed to flee in 1930, at least in the poetry of Rubén Darío. Within another twenty years all the poems of the *Romancero gitano* (Gypsy Ballads) of García Lorca will seem to us merely another literary fad. The admittance of the surrealist poetry of a Villaurrutia or of a Neruda would be more logical, since that mode is currently the most accepted in Europe and since its psychological significance invades the fields of sculpture and painting.

Rubén Darío does not meet fully the demands of today's reader, but part of the fault belongs to that reader and not to the poet. I have already stated that Darío is known essentially for his most superficial poems, for those in which there is more external luster than profound sensibility, more beauty of form than vital vibration. For example, we may recall *La Bailerina de los pies desnudos* (The Barefoot Dancer), *El Clavicordio de la abuela* (Grandmother's Clavichord), *Cyrano en España* (Cyrano in Spain), *El Faisán* (The Pheasant), *La Marcha triunfal, La Sonatina, Margarita Debayle, El Reino interior* (The Inner Kingdom)—all very beautiful poems, but lacking in the anguish, the tremors of life.

But Darío was much more than this. Like Verlaine, he succeeded at times in penetrating the innermost recesses of the soul, in revealing the most intimate, most subtle emotions, and in expressing them without rhetoric, in the simple communication of sentiment. He created poetry of enduring beauty; even as early as in his *Prosas profanas* he gives evidence of that type of composition:

DICE MÍA

Mi pobre alma pálida
era una crisálida.
Luego mariposa
de color de rosa.
Un céfiro inquieto
dijo mi secreto...
«¿Has sabido tu secreto un día?
¡Oh Mía!
Tu secreto es una
melodía de un rayo de luna...»
«¿Una melodía?»[4]

Darío sought an interpretation of the designs of God in natural manifestations, approaching thus a kind of modern mysticism. He was always the exponent of the cultivation of internal rhythm as opposed to profane clamor. In fact, he was the profound, philosophical, carefully scrutinizing poet that González Martínez (who himself imitated Darío) demanded in his *Tuércele el cuello al cisne* (Wring the Swan's Neck); for Darío in the following sonnet reaches the same serene heights as the Mexican poet:

Ama tu ritmo y rima tus acciones
bajo tu ley, así como tus versos:
eres un universo de universos,
y tu alma una fuente de canciones.
La celeste unidad que presupones
hará brotar en ti mundos diversos,
y al resonar tus números dispersos
pitagoriza en tus constelaciones.
Escucha la retórica divina
del pájaro del aire y la nocturna
irradiación geométrica adivina;
mata la indiferencia taciturna
y engarza perla y perla cristalina
en donde la verdad vuelca su urna.[5]

Dissatisfied with the gaudy brilliance of his *Prosas profanas,* Darío, in despair before the apparent impossibility of finding a definitive form of expression, attempts to analyze himself, and writes the following:

> Yo persigo una forma que no encuentra mi estilo,
> botón de pensamiento que busca ser la rosa;
> se anuncia con un beso que en mis labios se posa
> al abrazo imposible de la Venus de Milo.
> Adornan verdes palmas el blanco peristilo;
> los astros me han predicho la visión de la Diosa;
> y en mi alma reposa la luz como reposa
> el ave de la luna sobre un lago tranquilo.
> Y no hallo sino la palabra que huye,
> la iniciación melódica que de la flauta fluye
> y la barca del sueño que en el espacio boga;
> y bajo la ventana de mi Bella-Durmiente,
> el sollozo continuo del chorro de la fuente
> y el cuello del gran cisne blanco que me interroga.[6]

With the appearance of his *Cantos de vida y esperanza* (Songs of Life and Hope), in 1905, Darío became a social poet in the high sense of the word. He gives voice to the inner uneasiness of his continent in *Salutación del optimista* (The Optimist's Salutation) and *A Roosevelt* (To Roosevelt), and no longer can it be said that he is not the poet of America.

But it is in the constant probing into his soul that he displays best his greatness as a poet. Wounded to the core by the challenge hurled at him by José Enrique Rodó, he attempts not only to be the poet of his race, but also to reflect intensely all humanity.

> En mi jardín se vió una estatua bella;
> se juzgó mármol y era carne viva;
> un alma joven habitaba en ella;
> sentimental, sensible, sensitiva.[7]

The poet, keenly aware of the tragedy of his life, sums up his suffering in the words: "a vast pain, and minor cares." And he finds strength for resignation before his great doubts in the beauty of the world and in a vague mysticism:

La Dulzura del angelus

La dulzura del ángelus matinal y divino
que diluyen ingenuas campanas provinciales,
en un aire inocente a fuerza de rosales,
de plegaria, de ensueño de virgen y de trino
de ruiseñor, opuesto todo al rudo destino
que no cree en Dios... El aureo ovillo vespertino
que la tarde devana tras opacos cristales
por tejer la inconsútil tela de nuestros males
todos hechos de carne y aromados de vino...
Y esta atroz amargura de no gustar de nada,
de no saber adónde dirigir nuestra prora
mientras el pobre esquife en la noche cerrada
va en las hostiles olas huérfano de la aurora...
(¡Oh, suaves campanas entre la madrugada!)[8]

He had already spoken of his frustrated youth, of the bitter defloration of his existence, of the falsity of bohemian life: he had felt the terror of stumbling gropingly toward the unknown, the horror of the human slough, of feeling himself ephemeral in the world, of the terrible nightmare of the thought of death. But he does not want to know the answer to these enigmas, and, with the humility of a monk, he says:

Saluda al sol, araña, no seas rencorosa.
Da tus gracias a Dios, ¡oh sapo! pues que eres.
El peludo cangrejo tiene espinas de rosa
y los moluscos reminiscencias de mujeres.
Saber ser lo que sois, enigmas siendo formas;
deja la responsabilidad a las Normas
que a su vez la enviarán al Todopoderoso...
(Toca, grillo, a la luz de la luna; y dance el oso.)[9]

The innately Christian poet that Darío always was could well understand what he terms "the hopeless despair, the utter futility of a struggle with the infinite, in which the efforts of man are as fragile as butterfly wings, and the rhythm of his heart as potent as the descent of a snowflake." The simple soul redeems man, whereas the covetous, envious nature harbors a nest of burrowing moles. Imbued with a delightful pantheism, the lofty soul may discern the turbulent music of the world in the twilight, or even in the pupil of a cow's eye.

Cleopompo y Heliodemo

Cleopompo y Heliodemo, cuya filosofía
es idéntica, gustan dialogar bajo el verde
palio del platanar. Allí Cleopompo muerde
la manzana epicúrea y Heliodemo fía
al aire su confianza en la eterna armonía.
Malhaya quien las Parcas inhumano recuerde:
Si una sonora perla de la clepsidra pierde,
no volverá a ofrecerla la mano que la envía.
Una vaca aparece, crepuscular. Es hora
en que el grillo en su lira hace halagos a Flora,
y en el azul florece un diamante supremo:
Y en la pupila enorme de la bestia apacible
miran como que rueda en un ritmo visible
la música del mundo, Cleopompo y Heliodemo.[10]

The simple soul of man should ever remain in an attitude of ineffable repose before the wondrous phenomena of nature; wrapped in a mystic quietism, sheltered in Franciscan retirement, it should blend inseparably with the beauties of the world. This mystic pantheism boasts a long history among Spanish peoples; it appeared among Spain's earliest poets as an instinctive exaltation of the motivating forces which failed of expression in words and ideas. Witness these lines of Diego Hurtado de Mendoza, one of our early bards:

A aquel árbol, que mueve la foxa,
algo se le antoxa.
Aquel árbol del bel mirar
façe de manyera flores quiere dar,
algo se le antoxa...[11]

Later, this pantheism became Spanish mysticism, which made itself felt widely in European thought. In Darío, this philosophy is tinged with Oriental fatalism:

> Ay, triste del que un día en su esfinge interior
> pone los ojos e interroga. Está perdido.
> Ay, del que pide eurekas al placer o al dolor.
> Dos dioses hay, y son Ignorancia y Olvido.
> Lo que el árbol desea decir y dice al viento
> y lo que el animal manifiesta en su instinto,
> cristalizamos en palabra y pensamiento.
> Nada más que maneras expresan lo distinto.[12]

But actually, he was the first to forget his philosophy, for neither through this pantheism nor through his orthodox Catholicism did he ever achieve the tranquillity or the confidence of the mystics. His consciousness of original sin, his desire to encounter the living God, almost the human God, his absurd persistence in attempting to penetrate the ultimate mysteries of life, and his terror of death never gave him peace. His existence was one of inner torment, and upon giving expression to the fearful turmoil that reigned within him he rose to great poetic heights. Few poems can equal the following in dramatic intensity and aesthetic vision.

Lo Fatal

> Dichoso el árbol que es apenas sensitivo,
> y más la piedra dura porque ésa ya no siente,
> pues no hay dolor más grande que el dolor de ser vivo,
> ni mayor pesadumbre que la vida consciente.
> Ser, y no saber nada, y ser sin rumbo cierto,
> y el temor de haber sido y un futuro terror...
> Y el espanto seguro de estar mañana muerto,
> y sufrir por la vida y por la sombra y por
> lo que no conocemos y apenas sospechamos,
> y la carne que tienta con sus frescos racimos,
> y la tumba que aguarda con sus fúnebres ramos,
> ¡y no saber adónde vamos,
> ni de dónde venimos!...[13]

Darío's excellent *Poema del otoño* (Poem of Autumn), published in 1907, revealed such dexterity of employment of the poetic idiom that he could well be considered our classic poet. This work may be compared favorably with the *Rubáiyát* of Omar Khayyám; it is a song of pagan optimism, an appeal to eternal youth and love. Lapidary strophes of exceptional lyricism succeed each other in amazing profusion. Forgetful of his old sorrows, the poet exclaims jovially:

Y no obstante la vida es bella,
por poseer
la perla, la rosa, la estrella,
y la mujer.[14]

The overwhelming beauty of life makes him remark in an exaltation of crystalline purity:

Y sentimos la vida pura,
clara, real,
cuando la envuelve la dulzura
primaveral.

The Bacchic fervor of these words of Darío recalls to us Anacreon and Omar Khayyám:

Gozad de la carne, ese bien
que hoy nos hechiza
y después se tornará en
polvo y ceniza.
Gozad del sol, de la pagana
luz de sus fuegos;
gozad del sol porque mañana
estaréis ciegos.
Gozad de la dulce armonía
que Apolo invoca:
gozad del canto, porque un día
no tendréis boca.
Gozad de la tierra, que un
bien cierto encierra;
gozad, porque no estáis aún
bajo la tierra.

We seem to catch glimpses of this modern poet of almost pagan sensuousness in a context of idyllic Grecian woodlands; we see him surrounded by nymphs and centaurs, oblivious of the Sphinx, yet heading fatally toward death, crowned with the laurel wreath and bearing the dove of Venus on his shoulder:

En nosotros la vida vierte
fuerza y calor.
¡Vamos al reino de la Muerte
por el camino del Amor!

The day will yet come when we shall realize that this poem is worthy of comparison with the best in any literature, and that Darío was not only the superficial artisan of *Prosas profanas*, but the poet of depth, representative of the desires, the joys, and the anguish of his century. His *Poema del otoño* will remain the loftiest contribution of aesthetic sensibility from a continent which has inherited a great deal of the pagan temperament of Greece.

Only Góngora, that incomparable master of the lyric muse, equaled the great Nicaraguan poet in artistic agility in the Spanish language. It would seem impossible that the vigorous author of the *Canto a Argentina* should be able to refine his poetic instrument, purify his prodigious wealth of expression, and sharpen his vision so ineffably; but in his *Canción otoñal* (Autumn Song) Darío's multiple gift, that capacity for emotional artistic adjustment which gives to his poetry its great variety, is clearly manifest; and we must confess that in purity of diction, in lightness of treatment, and in intimate harmony this poem is definitive.

En occidente húndese
el sol crepuscular;
vestido de oro y púrpura
mañana volverá.
En la vida hay crepúsculos
que nos hacen llorar,
porque hay soles que pártense
y no vuelven jamás.

Vuela la mágica ilusión
en un ocaso de pasión,
y la acompaña una canción
del corazón.

Este era un rey de Cólquida
o quizá de Thulé;
un rey de ensueños líricos
que sonrió una vez.
De su sonrisa hermética
jamás se supo bien
si fué doliente o pálida
o si fué de placer.

Vuela la mágica ilusión
en un ocaso de pasión,
y la acompaña una canción
del corazón.

La tarde melancólica
solloza sobre el mar.
Brilla en el cielo Véspero
en su divina paz.
Y hay en el aire trémulo
ansias de suspirar
porque pasa con Céfiro
como el alma otoñal.

Vuela la mágica ilusión
en un ocaso de pasión,
y la acompaña una canción
del corazón.[15]

II

When Darío died in 1916, González Martínez had already proclaimed his defiance of the master; French iconoclastic poets were already known in America, and literary reform was clearly under way. In Spain, Juan Ramón Jiménez and Antonio Machado tried to forget the teachings of modernism and to create poetry reflecting their own lives. Miguel de Unamuno had given impetus to the reaction with his dry, tormented poetry, totally lacking in elegance and melody. José María Eguren had published some beautiful poems devoid of eloquence and of the superficial enhancement of music and color. Lugones was attempting by every means within his power to find a new literary orientation. José Juan Tablada almost accomplished this goal with his "hai kais" and his Japanese forms.

But after the death of Darío it was no longer a question of desire. Rather, the old masters were forced to yield their position to the renovators of the language and of poesy, to those who had never contracted the modernist vogue. And the field is dominated now by the Mexican López Velarde, by the Chilean Vicente Huidobro, the Peruvian Valdelomar, the Argentinian Borges, and the Uruguayan Sabat Ercasty. In these writers, rebellion and originality are defining qualities—their reason for existence.

Synthesizing genius that he was, Darío could have been the leader of a new school if only he had not died exactly at the moment in which the great change was in process of formation. His last poems already give evidence of that zeal for novelty in which he had gloried during his youth. In his poem *Caminos* (Roads), for example, he approaches a patternless simplicity:

¿Qué vereda se indica,
cuál es la vía santa,
cuando Jesús predica
o cuando Nietzsche canta?
¿La vía de querer,
o la vía de obrar?
¿La vía de poder,
o la vía de amar?
Embriagarse en el opio
que las tristezas calma.
Ser el mártir de su alma
o ser el héroe propio.
Martirizar la vida
en perjuicio del juicio,

y hacerla decidida
para ir al sacrificio.
Tener la voluntad
hecha de acero y oro:
tener la honestidad
como íntimo tesoro.
O bien ser el tirano
que surge de repente,
con la idea en la mente
o la espada en la mano.[16]
En la tierra o el mar
ser el conquistador,
que lleva su esplendor
a matar y a aplastar.
Pues nuestro hombre de barro
es en todo país
o Francisco Pizarro,
o Francisco de Asís.
Juntas almas fervientes
han tenido igual vuelo:
conquistar continentes
o conquistar el cielo.
Santidad y heroísmo
tienen el propio vuelo
con el genio que vuela entre los dos:
los Santos y los Héroes
tienen el propio cielo.
Y todos ellos buscan la dirección de Dios.

In his last years Darío was intensely interested in Dante and especially devoted to the Bible. Attempting to express his apocalyptic visions, he veered toward the poetry of dreams. Rare combinations of images and reminiscences imbue it with the tone of mystery, the constant fluctuation between the visible world and the metaphysical, so essential to all great poetry. Here he ceases to be the diverse, sensational, voluptuous poet, fond of rapid shifts of sentimental states. Now he has found his source of moral and aesthetic unity, the former in an orthodox Catholicism, the latter in a bare form of rhetoric.

I recall here the words of the Spanish thinker Ramiro de Maeztu on Rubén Darío: "If, as he felt the dualism of pure form as opposed to impure, he had felt with the same perspicuity that of the pure life as opposed to the impure, Rubén would not be merely one of the greatest poets of our language, but another Milton (in my opinion, the greatest poet that the world has known), and his verses would reveal to men from now till the end of time the fount of life."[17]

Actually, Rubén Darío was not far from that state of exaltation in which one goes through the world conscious of good and evil, of virtue and sin. He felt with absolute certainty the duality of life, and he expressed it in many poems. Nevertheless, only at the end of his life did he prefer the difficult road toward God, and then he followed it with fanatical ardor. In his poem *Peregrinaciones* (Peregrinations) he embarks on a long journey through the desolate shades of death:

En un momento crepuscular
pensé cantar una canción
en que toda la esencia mía
se exprimiría por mi voz:
predicaciones de San Pablo
o lamentaciones de Job,
de versículos evangélicos
o preceptos de Salomón,
¡Oh, Dios!

¿Hacia qué vaga Compostela
iba yo en peregrinación?
Con Valle Inclán o con San Roque,
¿adónde íbamos, Señor?
El perrillo que nos seguía
¿no sería acaso un león?
Ibamos siguiendo una vasta
muchedumbre de todos los
puntos del mundo, que llegaba
a la gran peregrinación.

Era una noche negra, negra,
porque se había muerto el sol:
nos entendíamos con gestos,
porque había muerto la voz.
Reinaba en todo una espantosa
y profunda desolación.
¡Oh, Dios![18]

¿Y adónde íbamos aquéllos
de aquella larga procesión,
donde no se hablaba ni oía,
ni se sentía la impresión
de estar en la vida carnal,
y sí en el reinado del ¡ay!
y en la perpetuidad del ¡oh!
¡Oh, Dios!

At the end of that road the pilgrim finds the revelation of the miracle of Christianity. Like a modern Dante, he feels there the pleasure of the supreme harmony, in the presence of Our Lord Jesus Christ:

Las torres de la catedral
aparecieron. Las divinas
horas de la mañana pura,
las sedas de la madrugada
saludaron nuestra llegada
con campanas y golondrinas.
¡Oh, Dios![19]

Y jamás habíamos visto
envuelto en oro y albor
emperador de aire y de mar,
que aquel Señor Jesucristo
sobre la custodia del sol
¡Oh, Dios!
para tu querer y tu amar.
Visión fué de los peregrinos,
mas brotaron todas las flores
en roca dura y campo magro;
y por los prodigios divinos,

tuvimos pájaros cantores
cantando el verso del milagro.
Por la calle de los difuntos
vi a Nietzsche y Heine en sangre tintos;
parecía que estaban juntos
e iban por caminos distintos.
La ruta tenía su fin,
y dividimos un pan duro
en el rincón de un quicio oscuro
con el marqués de Bradomín.

The last important poem of Darío was *Pax* (Peace), written in New York when the poet was in the last stage of his voyage toward death. It is the magnificent invocation of a Catholic poet:

Io vo gridando pace, pace, pace...[20]

He hurls an imprecation upon Pallas:

odiosa a las dulces mejillas
puesto que das las flechas y las balas,
abominada seas...[21]

Men in their madness do not want to understand the future miracle of the coming of Christ. They shout "Holy war!" but:

acercando el puñal a la garganta
o sacando la espada de la vaina;
y en el nombre de Dios
casas de Dios de Reims y de Lovaina
las derrumba el obús cuarenta y dos.[22]

The poet vibrates with the tragedy of his times, that tragedy which has been repeated in our days and for which there seems to be no cure in this world of ours—so small and yet so haughty. The Catholic poet knows the solution which will end wars:

Que la guerra es infernal, es cierto;
cierto que duerme un lobo
en el alma fatal del adanida;
mas también Jesucristo no está muerto,
y contra el homicidio, el odio, el robo,
él es la Luz, el Camino y la Vida.[23]

We have seen that the decorative, baroque style of Rubén Darío yielded before the sincerity of his poetic vision, becoming transformed into expression of perfect clarity. The monotonous rhythm based on regularity of accents effects the brusque movement inherent in the theme. His very concept of poetry marks a definitive evolution, for Darío here abandons French or exotic themes in order to interpret his own suffering, his maladjustment, his ultimate faith in Christ, his constant awareness of the presence of death.

At the time of Darío's death that revolution in world literature the repercussions of which resounded among us in the Week of Modern Art celebrated at São Paulo, and in the multiple vanguardist tendencies, was already evident. Darío was neither the assailant of those new theories nor the defender of an obsolete aesthetic sensibility; on the contrary, more than one revolutionary poet was encouraged by the master.

Some critics assert that the true precursor of the lyrical vanguard was the Uruguayan poet Julio Herrera y Reissig. This belief implies an error in vision. Herrera cultivated a form original to America but too close to the French model. Darío, on the other hand, possessed a formula of his own, developed in accord with his intimate artistic sense. He himself tells us: "My poetry is mine, within me." And that is why he once asked the young poets of America not to try to imitate him.

I have presented here a Darío whom few people know. The harmonious but cold poet of *Prosas profanas* has his well-defined place in our letters; the interpreter of the Spanish soul has been recognized by critics of the Iberian peninsula; Darío, composer of civic songs, has been called the "poet of America"; he has been studied as a classicist, as a romanticist, and as a modernist. The new Darío, whom I analyze here, though generally unknown in this aspect, may still be considered the greatest poet of the Spanish American continent.

Chapter VIII ◇ José Enrique Rodó

THE DEVELOPMENT of literary criticism denotes in a certain sense the maturity of a literature, the moment when one passes from the impulsive or emotional creative gesture to an attitude of repose in which the intelligence establishes standards, analyzes, and opens new paths. A culture in which criticism does not exist has not achieved its full growth; it is still in the formative stage.

The man who chooses so serious a profession as criticism must be well versed in arts and sciences, and in languages both living and dead. He must also subject himself to a rigid mental and moral discipline. His task must be one of orientation, definition of values, and encouragement of well-directed effort, as well as denunciation of mediocrity; in a word, he should be the teacher of a generation. The development of such a mentor represents a distant, almost unachievable goal in countries of limited cultural heritage, young nations lacking in broad university programs and historic cultural tradition.

For these reasons it is safe to affirm that throughout the entire colonial period true literary criticism did not exist, despite the laudable attempts of Espinosa Medrano, Sor Juana Inés de la Cruz, Carlos Sigüenza y Góngora, and Peralta Barnuevo. The efforts of these writers to analyze their own works and those of others are truly praiseworthy, though their approach is always purely subjective, without solid basis for the formation of definitive opinions and without the scientific method of the contemporary critic. Nor has criticism been cultivated sufficiently in Spain. During the nineteenth century it was notably below poetry and imaginative prose. The first half of the century can boast, in the field of noteworthy criticism, only the excessively impressionistic articles of Mariano José de Larra, and unfortunately the turbulent and extraordinarily brief life of the author of *Macías* prevented his more intensive cultivation of this genre. The production of other serious writers of that epoch (almost all of whom were disciples of Luzán) is too didactic to merit our sustained attention.

Later, when literary criticism in Germany, France, and England laid the foundation for a genre of artistic as well as scientific worth, Spain, wrapped in its garb of sterile nationalism, refused to heed the new voices. Even the monumental and varied work of Marcelino Menéndez Pelayo must be judged as historical criticism if it is to be appreciated in all its greatness. The penetrating, keen essays of *Clarín* (Leopoldo Alas) lack ideological substance; Juan Valera, who possessed fine artistic taste, was a dilettante in criticism; and the Countess Pardo Bazán always maintained a didactic attitude toward the genre.

Only in the generation of 1898 do we find true internal analysis of a work of art, explanation of the creative process, and definition of aesthetic values. The new novel of Ganivet and Valle Inclán and the poetry of Antonio Machado and Juan Ramón Jiménez find their parallel in the criticism of Miguel de Unamuno, and soon thereafter in that of *Azorín* (José Martínez Ruiz) and Diez Canedo. We observe, then, the following phenomenon: the Spanish American desirous of dedicating himself to criticism could find neither teachers nor models in Hispanic America or in Spain of the nineteenth century. Only the great Menéndez Pelayo offered an example at all worthy of imitation; and such great scholars as García Icazbalceta, José Toribio Medina, and A. Gómez Restrepo followed in the steps of the Spanish master, producing works of historical synthesis. On the other hand, French literature offered to Hispanic American youth evaluative norms as well as stylistic innovations in such craftsmen of form as Huysmans, Flaubert, and the Goncourt brothers.

French criticism, cyclic and historical, became more philosophical and aesthetic as the end of the century came into view. Rémy de Gourmont was the great theorist of symbolism and the true source of inspiration of Spanish American critics, who often applied the French critic's theories in their study of the modernist movement.

The work of Rodó is the product of that criticism. He marks in prose, as positively as Rubén Darío in poetry, the constant orientation toward the French spirit. But Rodó, with his profound philosophical culture, offered no new values in thought. At the outset he studied the Spanish thinkers and writers enthusiastically; but he could not share their stoicism or their sobriety of expression, and so he gradually approached the sources of French culture. There, he learned many things alien to the Spanish temperament: intellectual tolerance, which affected his taste and all his opinions; gracious skepticism, which never culminated in the definitive negation of values; a just zeal for raising literary production to the highest plane of aesthetic realization; theories of criticism which rest on scientific pillars; an intimate comprehension of the history of art, which served him only in formulating relative, subtle judgments; and a style of pure transparency, undulating and musical, until then unknown to Spanish prose. To Rodó, criticism was a work of artistic creation, spiritual understanding, and re-creation of beauty, rather than an enumeration of classifying elements, as until his advent it had been. Although it is true that Rodó sometimes applies the determinist theory of Taine (as in the study on Juan María Gutiérrez), at other times he relies more on his intuition, applying his knowledge of symbolist criticism, with its interchanges, suggestions, and divinations, as in his essay on Rubén Darío.

Rodó then abandoned the type of Spanish criticism to enter wholly into the currents of the European, thus continuing a general process of artistic orientation. We could apply to Rodó the same words with which he defined Rubén Darío: "He is not the critic of America"—that is, we could use those words if we did not believe that the genius of the Hispanic American resides precisely in that facility of adaptation, in that malleability, in that very attitude of acceptance.

We cannot but esteem this generous contribution to aesthetic evaluation, this new manifestation of poetic style applied to a discipline of rigid concepts and cold formulae. We cannot but recognize that José Enrique Rodó is the creator of a new technique, in which exact judgment is merged with artistic flight.

In his zeal for definition of the essence of art, in internal analysis, and in modernist nuances he anticipated José Martínez Ruiz (*Azorín*); and in some degree, Rodó is a precursor of Ortega y Gasset, although the Spanish critic also reveals the influence of German philosophical method. All Hispanic American criticism was influenced by the technique of the Uruguayan master; for Rodó effected a new stylistic orientation in the literature of an entire continent, as Darío had done in poetry.

José Enrique Rodó, born in Montevideo in 1872, led a life devoid of the brilliance, adventure, and glamour so typical of many Spanish American men of importance. Rather, he lived always in the midst of a placid mediocrity, and were it not for the richness, the nobility of his inner life, he would have been lost among the multitude of commonplace folk. He never had a great amorous passion, nor, I dare say, even a minor love affair. He never made a major error or committed a mortal sin. In fact, so moderate was he in everything that even in his polemic writings he appears more as a teacher than as a disputant. He could well have been an exemplary Protestant minister, a persevering, colorless Y.M.C.A. secretary, or a model American college professor. It is indeed a pity that he never suffered a serious illness as a child, that he never knew hunger, that he never was the victim of a grave injustice, nor of disillusion in love, that he never became entangled with the police during his youth—in short, that he never had to come face to face with personal sorrow nor with the anguish of his fellow men.

He was a good pupil in elementary school, a good pupil in high school, a good student at the university. He was a college professor, placidly professorial. He was a liberal, a moderate one; a moderate representative in Congress; a moderate editor of a moderate newspaper.

In 1916 he felt disillusioned with life and forthwith decided to take a trip through Europe. He arrived in Lisbon, but, not caring to visit Portugal, crossed directly into Spain. Apparently uninterested in that land of artistic treasures, he continued rapidly on to Italy. He visited Rome and other Italian cities, and then arrived in Palermo, where, stricken with abdominal typhus, he died on May 10, 1917, in the same hotel, according to his critics, "in which Wagner had written the last act of *Parsifal.*"

A strange life indeed was this for one who had preached that the first duty of every human being is to achieve the greatest plenitude of existence. In effect, much to the contrary of his avowed beliefs, Rodó retreated totally into his inner world, disdaining, or avoiding, certain of those vital aspects which are indispensable to the full life. Wrapped in his role of a teacher, he tried to "harmonize life with thought." Attentive only to the serenity of his spirit, he withdrew from all strife, from the joys of life, from smiling, from hearty laughter. He was puritanical in the externals of daily living, although he always maintained, in theory, that moral independence is an absolute necessity. He passes into history as a perfect teacher, an apostolic figure, without any slips, without any defects, without any flaws, but also without that aura of poetic greatness that pervades the life of a José Martí or a Lord Byron.

The first two critical essays of Rodó, *El que vendrá* (He Who Will Come), and *La Novela nueva* (The New Novel), were published in 1897. From that very moment we may note his desire to form a kind of literary Americanism, without forgetting the purely Spanish roots of our culture. In these works he casts a scrutinizing glance toward his own soul, wherein he discovers the solution to his problems and an inner tranquillity which he maintained throughout his life. *El que vendrá* heralds the arrival of the great orientator of diverse efforts, the Master, who is to guide the spirit of a whole generation. In *La Novela nueva,* Rodó demands of novelists conformity with the present, realism, and the true artistic expression of the heart. It may be said that, to a degree, he announced the novel of today, with its historical background, its social preoccupation, and its vast panorama of nature.

In 1899 appeared his *Rubén Darío,* an essay in aesthetic and scientific criticism, and in 1900 his masterpiece, *Ariel.* For several years Rodó seemed to be gathering forces for new intellectual ventures, and finally, in 1906, he brought forth his polemic work, *Liberalismo y Jacobinismo* (Liberalism and Jacobinism), which is pervaded by a noble spirit of religious tolerance. Three years later his now famous *Los Motivos de Proteo* (The Motives of Proteus) reached the press, to be followed in 1913 by *El Mirador de Próspero* (The Gallery of Próspero), which contains the well-documented study *Juan María Gutiérrez y sus tiempos* (Juan María Gutiérrez and His Times), of great value to our understanding of Rodó's determinist theory and his exalted literary Americanism. After his death his brothers edited the *Ultimos Motivos de Proteo* (Last Motives of Proteus). He had taken it with him on his journey to Europe, and unfortunately, it had been lost. However, employing several manuscripts which he had left on his desk, they succeeded in putting together this new volume, which presents at least partially the content of the original work.

Above all, we must consider Rodó as a literary critic. In *El que vendrá* and *La Novela nueva* he looks into the future and affords a sage example of nobility of thought. In the essay on Gutiérrez he sets down with admirable effect the bases of a deterministic criticism, drawn from Taine. We note throughout all his works a seriousness of purpose, a skill in exposition, and a clarity of definition hitherto unknown on our continent, and a desire to reveal his author through images and metaphors, which give a poetic atmosphere to all his commentaries. It may be said of him that he criticized by beautifying, and that the writer studied by him always gained by it, even when the criticism was negative. Furthermore, there was established an intimate unity among all the creative elements, and complete harmony of vision reigned between the commentator and the author under discussion. Rodó's critical writings create a magnificent fresco of the world, its people, and their temporal aspect, all illumined by a light soft in tone, and remarkable for its synthesis of comprehension. Although chiefly concerned with the conception of beauty, the Uruguayan did not neglect the secondary elements of every work of art.

The appearance of Rubén Darío's *Prosas profanas* in 1896 provoked a storm of criticism, applause, generous gestures of admiration, and coarse attacks. Indeed, it was an extraordinary book for its time; it denoted a poetic revolution such as occurs among a people but once in a century. But the significance of that revolution needed explanation, and Rodó was its masterly interpreter. His *Rubén Darío* is unprecedented in our literature. It marks a date which might well have been the beginning of a great philosophic-critical movement, but which unfortunately was lost in the vast cultural lacuna of the times.

In phrases of exceptional beauty Rodó explains the innovations and virtues of *Prosas profanas,* its soaring rhythm, the exquisite selection of vocabulary, the images, the motifs, the quintessence of form, and the background of exotic themes. In prose worthy of the verse of Darío, Rodó makes observations of striking originality, and ends by remarking the animistic impassivity of so refined a poet. For under that array of brilliant lights, precious stones, fireworks, roses, and tinfoil there lay a "soul wrapped in Swedish fur." Darío was not the poet whom America awaited. He was a master in the assimilation of French poetry; but although his value as a craftsman was unquestionably great, he did not interpret the soul of his continent.

And Rodó was not mistaken in his evaluation. For Darío, in that volume, was indeed not the poet of a primitive, unmannered continent, but a talented and audacious imitator of the French. He was a great poet in form, but he lacked the vibrating, savage energy that his race demanded. Later, the poet sought to defend himself, saying:

> En mi jardín se vió una estatua bella;
> se juzgó mármol y era carne viva;
> un alma joven habitaba en ella,
> sentimental, sensible, sensitiva.[1]

Nevertheless, that young soul was not the soul of our America.

Rodó's essay, written in an undulating style, slow in movement, dazzling in color, serene in judgment, and profound in thought, soon became known throughout the Spanish-speaking world and carried the fame of Rubén Darío from Buenos Aires to Madrid. Never before had the Castilian tongue known so intimate a fusion of definitive ideas and artistic form. For the first time there appeared in our lands a phenomenon not rare in France, the combination in one person of the thinker and the poet. Such was Rodó then—philosopher and aesthete; and thus he continued to the end of his days.

With his analysis of the principal work of the movement perfected by Rubén Darío, the Uruguayan writer became the recognized critic of modernism. In effect, his essay notes carefully all the salient points of that movement. Rodó, who was familiar with the French Parnassian and symbolist schools, found little difficulty in observing the repetition of the French poetic phenomenon in America. Thus he could well conclude that the volume of the Nicaraguan bard represented little else than a transplantation of aesthetic forms. Despite the fact that almost every Spanish American critic has discussed the question of the degree of French influence in the work of Darío, the germ of all that has been said may be found in Rodó's essay. I shall go even further, and say that, in my opinion, a study of the other modernist poets—Santos Chocano, Herrera y Reissig, Lugones, Valencia, and the others—must

[1] For notes to chapter viii see page 234.

of necessity be preceded by an intimate knowledge of the Uruguan's essay on Rubén Darío.

No contemporary critic has surpassed Rodó in psychological penetration, in literary culture, in serenity, or in fairness of critical judgment. For these reasons, today, when we may speak of modernism as a thing of the past, I would assert that no one has a more valid claim to be considered the essential critic of that movement.

We turn now to Rodó's masterpiece, *Ariel,* a spiritual message dedicated to the youth of America. At its outset, the old Master, Próspero, is taking leave of his disciples. Bidding them farewell, he remarks upon the significance of a little bronze statue that seems to preside over the affairs of his desk. The figure is that of the Ariel of Shakespeare's *Tempest.*

> ... For Ariel embodies the mastery of reason and of sentiment over the baser impulses of unreason. He is the generous zeal, the lofty and disinterested motive in action, the spirituality of civilization, and the vivacity and grace of the intelligence;—the ideal end to which human selection aspires; that superman in whom has disappeared, under the persistent chisel of life, the last stubborn trace of the Caliban, symbol of sensuality and stupidity.[2]

Próspero speaks of the duties of youth, the cultivation of the individual will, the noble effort to achieve liberty and life. He repeats with Renan: "Youth is the discovery of an immense horizon, which is life." Youth was once the privilege of a race, the attribute of a nation—Greece. And Greece "did great things because its youth afforded it joy, which provides the atmosphere for action, and enthusiasm, the omnipotent impulse." From that youthful culture, art, philosophy, free thought, intellectual curiosity, and the consciousness of human dignity were born.

Próspero speaks of the great spiritual movements of humanity: of the Christian idea, which at the outset was an inspiration essentially youthful, of the glorious times when young souls offered models for the brilliant dialogues of Plato, in the brief spring of our world. The young Spanish American should dedicate himself to that spiritual life which exalted the ancient cultures, and should strive for the fullest expression of his being, since "there is, according to Guyau, a universal profession—that of being a man." Accordingly, youth should avoid soul-deforming specialization and the automatism, the opprobrious servitude, of materialistic activity.

> "I demand of you," says Próspero, "that in the battle of life you defend your souls against the mutilation of them by the tyranny of a single and self-interested object. Never give, to either passion or self-interest, but a small part of what is *you*. For even in material servitude there is a way to keep free one's inner self, the self of reason and of feeling. So never do you try to justify, by your absorption in labour, in conflict, the enslaving of your soul."[3]

Youth should work with hope; with unbridled optimism it should cultivate the kingdom within, should think and dream; and it should admire and defend beauty against the attacks of the Philistines. It should propagate the cult of beauty because "making loveliness felt is a work of mercy."

Good taste is a restraint imposed by rational standards and ethics. But the utilitarian conception is the constant opponent of the contemplation of beauty. Modern science and democracy are two leveling forces which favor the triumph of utilitarianism over the most noble idealism. The interest of science in the microorganism is beginning to create a new world composed of humble, anonymous beings; the rise of the masses is a serious menace to the élite, to whom is entrusted the preservation and progress of lofty culture. The United States represents most faithfully that leveling democratic society which fosters material well-being, the success of audacious men, and scorn of all spiritual and artistic manifestation. There, everything has a utilitarian purpose. Hispanic America must not let itself be conquered by North American pragmatism, for in that way we would lose our racial personality. On the contrary, we should drink from our sources and cultivate the heritage bequeathed to us by the Mediterranean people. We should cherish the ideality of beauty and thought for its own sake.

Old Próspero finishes his discourse, and his young disciples bid him farewell. Ennobled and optimistic, they go out into the stillness of a summer night.

I do not pretend that Rodó is an original philosopher. He himself realized his own limitations, and accordingly was content with applying his knowledge to only a few cultural problems. His entire work, but especially *Ariel,* is distinguished by its impassioned idealism. The idealistic philosophy which Rodó would have Spanish Americans adopt is based, not on a new ideological theory, but on a new spiritual attitude. His scorn for machinery, science, material well-being, and democracy had been expressed previously in the works of Renan, Guyau, Carlyle, and Boutroux. In this sense, then, Rodó can claim only the merit of having given a new tone to these concepts.

Actually, the teachers and thinkers prior to Rodó had been more inclined toward an English type of positivism. No one had dared speak to youth of the road toward the fulfillment of inner desires, for fear of being accused of anachronistic mysticism. No one had been concerned with pointing out the path of personal vocation; no one had praised the noble endowments of youth or had so cherished the ideal. Two mutually contradictory forces pervade the philosophy of Rodó: on the one hand, a strong sense of discipline, born of his respect for already established values—in a word, his boundless optimism; on the other hand, the influence of French models, especially Renan, almost all of whom were skeptics. However, of undeniable merit in the work of Rodó is the importance which he attributes to beauty in the formation of every society. In this respect, Rodó is more the poet than the thinker. It is a pity that he did not realize that, in order to disseminate the cult of beauty in a society, one must first eliminate economic inequality and other social ills, and that this can be achieved much more easily in a democracy than under an authoritarian regime. His reasoning is imperfect in this sense. His analysis of the United States was not accurate, because by 1900 there were beginning to appear the vigorous artistic manifestations of that nation which Rodó neither knew nor would have wished to acknowledge. He praises the noble idealism of the Greek people, but he heeds not the tormented cry of their slaves. He is ecstatic confronting the gentle fields of Galilee, but he casts not a single glance upon the multitude of lepers and the lame; he assigns marvels to intellectual France, without remarking the slow degeneration of a noble people. In the United States, on the contrary, he saw only vulgarity, spiritual deformation, and moral pettiness, and so did not consider that nation a proper example for a continent in which he desired to effect a hybrid culture, one composed of the merciful spirit of Christianity and the aesthetic bases of Greek civilization. However, all his errors stem from his shortness of vision. He could not understand the beauty of machinery, of dynamism, of the heroic contemporary spirit. Like the French thinkers of his time, Rodó is imbued with a concept of ecstatic beauty. However, whereas among the French this attitude constitutes a defense of their culture against a new aesthetic orientation based upon the North American civilization, in Rodó it is pure imitation, since his America, *our* Latin America, has so little to offer that is attractive to an idealistic approach. We may admire, then, the beauty of his program, but let us realize too that his theories are both impractical and dangerous for a continent yet in formation, as is ours. I say "impractical" because the realism and democratic spirit of today do not permit certain quintessential luxuries; I say "dangerous," because, if a continent remains placidly playing the flute or wielding the brush or sculptor's chisel on top of its petroleum reserves, copper mines, and immeasurable riches, it is easy prey for the more dynamic nations, those more alive—in the double significance of this word.

Rodó's hostility toward the United States is basically unjustified, for he knew nothing about the North American culture of his time. His ignorance even of its literature is absolute. Knowing only the works of Longfellow, Emerson, and Poe, and these but slightly, he concedes to them an importance far in excess of their worth. He was totally unaware of Thoreau, Melville, Hawthorne, and of the most outstanding American poet, Walt Whitman. Rodó believed that democracy is a force that levels downward; he never imagined that the masses could raise their cultural plane indefinitely, even to the point of reaching that of the élite. Blinded by French aristocratic tradition, he never thought that an entire mass of men could enjoy intellectual life. Today there are still those in Spanish America who hold the same view, despite the notable advancement of the masses in the United States and in Russia. Those pseudo-aristocrats are defending not an ideological theory but a program of economic exploitation! They still dare to speak of the North American "Caliban," and to consider themselves Arielists by temperament, by culture, and, especially, through convenience.

For all these reasons Rodó was an antirealist. It seems that common sense would hardly penetrate his aestheticism and find lodgment there. His judgment of the United States was European rather than Spanish American. Otherwise he would have realized that much of that nation's progress was perfectly adaptable to a Hispanic American cultural program, without any danger ensuing of the submergence of our racial idiosyncrasy. His continental patriotism, nevertheless, is undeniable; he loved his America, and even his last days were filled with anxiety for its present and future. As Gonzalo Zaldumbide says:

> Day by day, his thoughts turned more exclusively, more affectionately toward America. As he was walking up the steps of the Capitol one day—the last day of the year, it was—and meditating on what would be the greatest votive message he could send to his beloved lands across the sea, he decided that the only valid watchword would be, "Consolidate the feeling of America; try to establish firmly in the conscience of our peoples the idea of *our* America, as a common force, an indivisible soul, a single nation." "The whole future lies in that work," he affirmed with perfect faith, and then added: "All that tends in any way to oppose that work or to retard its definitive fulfillment is wrong and the seed of evil."[4]

We should not, then, criticize Rodó too severely for his erroneous conceptions, because they were those of an entire generation of writers, who found their inspiration in French culture.

Rodó's prose inaugurated a brusque change in Spanish style. True, it was the epoch of marked French influence—in such poets as Gutiérrez Nájera, Silva, and Darío. But it would be an oversimplification to believe that Rodó was merely one of this group. On the contrary, his style, characterized by long, undulating periods, with regularly recurring clauses and a sustained, vaguely musical rhythm, is essentially in the best Spanish classical tradition, of the type of Cervantes. But Rodó is also the product of his century, and, despite his denials, a modern spirit. Hence his purity of tradition is rejuvenated by the order and harmonic distribution of elements in the sentence, taken from the best French form.

He is classical for yet another reason. He always tries to harmonize the rhythm of his word with the intention of the idea. Thus, when he treats of profound or transcendental matters his style is serious, almost heavy. In the description of an idyllic scene his sentence unfolds limpidly transparent and crystalline. His impassioned thoughts are expressed in terse, abrupt, incisive tones. Without becoming excessively ornamental, he possesses an elegance truly rare in our language. His images tend to assume parabolic form, and give evidence of remote Biblical influence. He carves his sentence *con amore* and with a plastic sense, but nevertheless remains objective, impersonal. In spite of his preference for the long sentence filled with extensive interpolations and abounding in references and repetitions, he has nothing of the monotony of the new-classical authors. On the contrary, no contemporary prose writer has surpassed him in purity of diction or in the lightness of sweeping sentences embellished with a profusion of adjectives. Let us glance at a paragraph drawn at random from his *Ariel:*

New-born Christianity was, in the interpretation of Renan—which I hold only the more true that it is the more poetic,—a picture of youth unsullied. Of the youth of the soul, or, which is the same thing, of a living dream of grace and purity, is made that divine fragrance which floats over the slow journeyings of the Master across the fields of Galilee; over his sermons, which are developed, free from any penitent sadness, hard by a lovely lake, in valleys full of fruit; heard by the birds of heaven and the "lilies of the field," which thus adorn his parables; preaching the happiness of the "Kingdom of God" to a sweetly smiling nature.[5]

His prose bears a certain resemblance to the poetry of Emerson, in that the main idea moves in ascending circles, resting on lesser points, growing in hierarchy (if we may use the analogy) before the vassalage rendered it by adjectives, symbols, images, gerunds, and conjunctions. The idea begins to whirl spirally, and, with the very intensity of the accelerated movement, keeps rising, like a perforated metal plate spinning about a rod, until it is thrown off to lofty zones of harmony and violent energy.

His style bears the brand mark of his genius; it is unique and unmistakable. His ideological poverty is redeemed by his indisputable mastery of expression; and thus Rodó is a stylist rather than a philosopher, critic, or thinker, and, being a stylist, was destined to a life of brief duration in literary history.

And in effect Rodó has died. Spanish American youth today, dynamic and conscious of its immediate duties, rejects his idealistic but unfeasible credo. Our primary desire as free peoples is to live—I should say, survive—in this moment of history. We cannot heed his noble message. But the fault is ours, and not his, for his kingdom was for better men than we are, for societies of a higher degree of evolution than ours. His idealistic attitude cannot die. And when there appear political leaders, statesmen, teachers, writers, and poets less corrupt than those of today, we shall hear again the noble voice of this man who dared to preach on the barren desert of our culture; and with profound respect we shall follow once more the rhythm of his thought and of his seed-scattering hands.

To deny Rodó totally denotes a lack of taste, ill-befitting the select soul. There is a tendency in our America to destroy values rather than to reduce them to their proper level, a trend toward suicidal negation of moral and aesthetic norms. On the other hand, we find everywhere that spirit of blind imitation against which this master had preached so forcefully; we discover a continuous process of approximation to the United States, not in the noble aspects of that great people, but in the most trivial, the most vulgar facets of its culture.

We must recall this noble thinker to mind, so that his symbol may again assume its rightful meaning; lest, in the transmutation of his philosophical formula, we come to represent the image of Caliban while the United States possesses the attributes of the Ariel of his legend.

Chapter IX ◇ Social Poetry

It is axiomatic that poetry, to remain alive, must undergo a total renovation at least every twenty-five years. A single poetic formula is not tolerated longer than that. A century ago, a generation of Brazilian readers was enraptured with the lines:

> Minha terra tem palmeiras
> onde canta o sabiá...[1]

But today this very verse is used only in schools, in anthologies, or as a lesson in patriotism. In other words, it has ceased to hold interest purely as poetry.

Half a century ago, Rubén Darío sang:

> La princesa está triste;
> ¿Qué tendrá la princesa?[2]

And all Spanish America echoed his words. Nowadays we are not in the least concerned with the maladies of the princess, and for many reasons. First, we must consider the factor of changing times: no longer are we interested in princesses in their role of socially privileged beings, distinct and apart from all other women. In these days of rampant feminism it would be fantastic to envision a princess, prisoner in a marble cage, surrounded by luxuries, yet fading away by reason of melancholy unrelieved and unrelievable. The second reason is an aesthetic one. We reject the too slow movement of poetic expression. It is for this reason, I believe, that opera has been losing much of its charm. We are living in a rapid, direct epoch, the very essence of which is economy of elements. We are bored by the overly decorative, the baroque. We no longer accept the Alexandrine, the monotony of rhythmic clauses, the arbitrary rhyme, the cloistered, strictly "poetic" vocabulary, the picturesque employment of adjectives, the carefully chosen image,

[1] For notes to chapter ix see pages 234–240.

which characterize Darío's *Sonatina,* a poem which only thirty years ago the Countess Emilia Pardo Bazán thought one of the most beautiful in the Spanish language. Darío applied a poetic formula to a theme of transitory significance; now, both theme and form are antiquated.

But every great poet is a reformer in his time, and we must so consider Rubén Darío and Gonçalves Dias. As a further example, these words of Machado de Assis:

Era uma môsca azul, asas de ouro e granada,
Filha da China ou do Indostão,
Que entre as fôlhas brotou de uma rosa encarnada,
Em certa noite de verão,[3]

give clear evidence of greater technical skill than is shown by Gonçalves Dias in the lines:

Nosso ceu tem mais estrêlas,
Nossas várzeas têem mais flores,
Nossos bosques têem mais vida,
Nossa vida mais amores...[4]

But Machado de Assis is more limited in time, because his formula is more artificial. Neither he nor Gonçalves Dias achieves the direct communication of a subjective experience, such as Murilo Mendes effects in the strophe:

É doce o pensamento da morte
Quando o corpo exausto de prazer ou de dor
Sofre os seus limites,
É doce o pensamento da morte.[5]

Murilo Mendes, like Drummond de Andrade, Jorge de Lima, Mário de Andrade, and Manuel Bandeira, has broken with the poetic tradition of romanticists, Parnassians, and symbolists. His poetry, in common with that of almost all the Brazilian modernists, disdains the usual rhythms, obligatory rhymes, and poetic vocabulary. Any verse of Drummond de Andrade would strike harshly upon the ears of Olavo Bilac. And now I shall make a statement that to many may seem absurd, but that to me bears infinite truth: Drummond would not be a poet if he resembled Olavo Bilac or Machado de Assis! In effect, his merit lies in his very dissimilarity to these masters. Let us call to witness the stanza:

Bôca que nunca beijarei
bôca de outro que ri de mim,
no milímetro que nos separa
cabem todos os abismos.[6]

Here, Drummond sets before us a simple, objective, yet poetic revelation. It seems to be poesy without poetry—without poetry's decorative elements, without poetic emphasis, without poetic vision: it seems to be more than poetry, as that form is generally understood.

On the other hand, Olavo Bilac, who belonged to an epoch which required that poetry be distinctly poetic, or dramatic, but never simple, would say:

Eu, com o frio a crescer no coração—tão cheio
De ti, até no horror do derradeiro anseio!
Tu, vendo retorcer-se amarguradamente
A bôca que beijava a tua bôca ardente,
A bôca que foi tua![7]

The attitude of the two poets is essentially different. Both have a common background of vital experiences: love, suffering, joy, triumph. Both draw upon a common fund of artistic knowledge (from earlier poets, from Brazilian, Portuguese, and French literature, from painting, music, and other arts). Both had at their disposition the same poetic idiom. Nevertheless, they are separated by half a century. I do not know—and I do not care to know—which of the two poets is the greater; but I cannot help seeing that, although their poetry is different in type, the artistic process is greater in Drummond de Andrade, because he has the mentality of his epoch and nation and because his poetry does not stem from human emotion, but—most important of all—from a true sentiment of poetry.

One of the characteristics which most distinguish the poet of today from the poet of yesterday is the absence of emotion, the impersonalization, or, in the words of Ortega, "the dehumanization of art." The Spanish romanticist José de Espronceda makes of his *Canto a Teresa* (Song to Theresa) a veritable deluge, a fantastic waste, of emotion. The poet suffers, shouts, curses, implores, and sheds abundant tears; but his work itself is a series of repetitions, infantile phrases, and skillful artifices. The emotion is in the poet, not in his poetry!

I should like to offer the foregoing as proof of the fact that the poet desirous of recognition must always present something new. He must transform poetry; he must make it a novel means of communication between himself and his contemporaries. He should be the heart of his times, so that some day his epoch may live again in his work;—so that he may be its perpetuator.

The average man of culture accepts progress in every field except art. He believes in vitamins, allergies, and penicillin, but he does not accept Picasso; he travels by air, but he detests Stravinsky; he admits the theory of relativity, but will not read James Joyce; he finds Communism plausible, but he refuses to understand Alfaro Siqueiros. The fault is not his. At school he has been taught to paint—by a man who knows nothing about painting, an enemy of Portinari, of Diego Rivera, and of Picasso. He has been made to memorize meaningless verses—by an opponent of Rafael Alberti, of Valéry, and of T. S. Eliot. He has been accustomed to military music and motion-picture scores—by the antagonists of Stravinsky and Schoenberg.

The artist, then, has a dual mission to fulfill. Not only must he interpret his times; he must also convey that interpretation to the common man. He must not allow himself to be captured by facile aesthetic formulae—by obvious means of apparently spontaneous communication. His instrument must be fine, precise, and he must master it. Only in this way can he improve himself and create a better public. He must invade the schools, the press, the town square, the salon. He must not allow the schoolteacher, the reciter, the composer of tangos to corrupt his public. That public, like a child, in its state of primitive innocence knew nothing at all; it had neither bad taste nor good. If today its taste is bad, we may attribute the fault to our schools. If the average man reads trash, it is because the novels thrust into his hand are indescribably base; if he prefers the tango, it is because the tango is offered him at every hour of the day; if he goes to the movies, it is because movies abound. Give him high tragedy, symphonies, the music of Villalobos, the paintings of Orozco, and he will enjoy them; and his pleasure will be more cultivated, more noble.

How often have we heard the complaint: "I can't stand Beethoven. Bach bores me to death. The modern composers drive me to despair. The artists are laughing at us all, and the poets are frauds!" Why should we expect otherwise? The victim has been taught only waltzes, marches, and tangos; to paint cows that look like cows and chairs that look like chairs; to read patriotic little poems, puerile, moralizing stanzas written by the assassins of poetry! We must take the man who does not dare to deny the advances of chemistry, biology, and electricity (of which he knows precious little!) and say to him: "No, you don't have bad taste. You are merely ignorant of what art is. You are disrespectful of what you don't understand." And there is another who is far more difficult to overcome, the man who *thinks* he knows it all. His is a very common species. We find him everywhere under the guise of a professor, academician, politician, general, doctor, lawyer. He wants to have everything explained, rationally and in minute detail. "Look at that thing in this picture!" he exclaims; "I can't tell whether it is a cow, a poplar tree, or a fireplace." When he appeals to me, I cannot explain it; nor do I wish to do so. And the self-styled fount of learning, seizing upon my reluctance to reply, shouts: "You see? You don't understand it, either. And I—doubtless you have heard of me, in the medical profession,—I don't understand it. It is just a piece of nonsense!"

Or he comes along all prepared with a poem. "Look at what I found! Here is a poet who says to the ocean:

> Si tu desnudo aparecido y verde,
> si tu manzana desmedida, si
> en las tinieblas tu mazurca ¿dónde
> está tu origen?[8]

"Now, could you put this within range of my feeble intelligence?"

"No, I can't," I tell him, "for then it would no longer be the poem, but something else; the explanation of the poem. You don't have to understand every word to derive a sensation of beauty." Exultant then, he hurries to exclaim: "What did I tell you? You, a critic, can't understand the poet. Now I—and of course you know who I am, in politics,—I emphatically declare that this has no rhyme or reason; it is just a lot of silliness!"

Such men are already beyond recall, where aesthetic comprehension is concerned. They have placed their arrogance, and their ignorance, between themselves and the artist. Among them we find the omnipotent critic, the one who advises the young writer: "Live a bit more intensely, my boy, and you will write better." And notorious among them is the pedant, who feels morally obliged to quote Aristotle, Vico, Taine, Valéry, and Gide, in order to compose a simple little book of say a hundred pages! All these men are dangerous, and I am at a loss to recommend an effective method of nullifying their influence.

Now we are aproaching our designated topic, social poetry. By that term I mean poetry that is objectively concerned with social problems, especially with matters relating to all who are economically and socially oppressed. But here we encounter the usual misconception. Does the fact that a work deals with the Indian, with a strike, or with Communist doctrine, classify it automatically as social poetry? The answer is "No," because oftentimes it is propaganda and not poetry. Aside from content, the only prerequisite demanded is that the composition have the necessary aesthetic characteristics. Of course, it may contain other elements incidentally. Social poetry varies, then, with its epoch, and disappears without trace. Poetry remains.

Of course, it is to be assumed that every artist injects propaganda into his work; for he lives in a society, and he is atheistic or devout, reactionary or radical, or, as they say today, aristocratic or bourgeois. The artist has a very definite conception of the world, and his work must reflect that viewpoint. How can we deny that Cervantes was a propagandist in his descriptions of an epoch in which the idea of "mine and thine" was nonexistent? The intellectuals of the Spanish Republic unearthed Lope de Vega's drama *Fuente ovejuna* just because they considered it a work of social protest. And the enormous popularity of García Lorca is due to the fusion of aesthetic elements and social attitudes in his poems. The reader, nevertheless, does not have to conform to the social or political opinions of the author. I have read Santa Teresa and San Juan de la Cruz quite thoroughly, and with the greatest of pleasure, but I am not therefore a mystic; nor do I believe that I am in a "state of grace"; I enjoy reading T. S. Eliot, though I do not sympathize in the least with his neo-Catholicism; I am charmed with the novels of Malraux and Sender, and with the poetry of Alberti, yet I am not a Communist. In other words, I am able to distinguish between the poetic sentiment of the work and the vital ideas of the author.

Even in poems as subjective as the *Vida retirada* (Life in Reclusion) of Fray Luis de León there is a goodly proportion of propaganda. The poet sings of the superiority of country life and condemns the courtiers and mariners, the powerful and the rich. To us who are city-bred, rustic life is the ultimate impossibility and we cannot accompany the poet in his predilections. But Fray Luis does not exact proselytic faith, and we are unfailingly overcome by the magic of his verse.

Many critics fall into the error of attacking a poet's work because it does not accord with their own religious, political, and social ideas. In Brazil, for example, certain critical writings have condemned the Catholicism of Jorge de Lima and of Murilo Mendes. When I read their poetry, however, I am not at all concerned with their opinions on Marx or Christ. Rather, I am interested only in whether or not their poetry is good. When one reads *The Magic Mountain* of Thomas Mann, one marvels at so much beauty, without troubling to learn whether Mr. Mann is reactionary or liberal. I have often denounced reactionary writers, but I have fought them because they were poor authors and not because they were reactionaries. It would be difficult to exclude from literature such luminaries as Dante, St. Francis of Assisi, and Santa Teresa de Jesús because we do not accept their religious credo, just as it would be absurd for the devout believer to assert that they were great writers only because they were Catholics!

Of course, our times have seen great ideological movements for which we feel sympathy or aversion. It is only natural, then, that as men of our epoch we should tend to accept a poet of our own inclinations so long as he meets the requisites of a good poet. On the other hand, we are instinctively dubious of the poet who represents a contrary ideology, and at times we choose not to read him but to form our judgments *a priori.* Obviously, this attitude contains an impure element wholly foreign to aesthetic appreciation.

But let us return to contemporary poetry. The poet who most nearly approaches the masses and a great many intellectuals is the bard of Communism, or at least the sympathizer with that doctrine. The majority of such poets are not Communists; but, as modern men who do not live in a vacuum, they feel a strong attraction towards the Communist philosophy. Their poetry is rather an aesthetic justification of Communism; the universality of the idea, quite evidently, is of prime importance to the poet.

The bards of German Nazism and Italian Fascism, limited by their all-pervading nationalism, were not accepted outside of their own countries; and none of them is a great poet. Let us then consider it established that, directly or indirectly, a poet is the reflection of his times. These words of the poet Cecília Meireles, serve to substantiate my view: "It is notable that, in any period, a literature may be characterized by tendencies which clearly define the epoch in which it is produced, or, diversely, by self-projection into the recent past, or into a magically divined future."[9] Here, Mrs. Meireles merely determines the characteristics of literary evolution. In another passage she seems to define all Hispanic American literature: "When a literature prolongs events just completed, it is more easily appreciated since it is governed by well-known formulae, and it can be understood without surprise or difficulty. However, when one evaluates a literature thus, one must not overlook the cost of the transition from a previous state of affairs when it too was considered 'new,' before its precepts had been sufficiently discussed, opposed, and denied until they finally prevailed, becoming after that familiar, comfortable, and normal."[10]

Here is clearly defined our Spanish American modernism of 1888. Rubén Darío was the leader of the new poetry; he bore the fury of uncomprehending critics; he was the first victim of his school. But modernism triumphed, and what his hostile critics had attacked in him they applauded enthusiastically in his disciples, José Santos Chocano, Amado Nervo, and Leopoldo Lugones. The modernist formula had lost its mystery and could be understood by even those of the lowest literary culture. These poets, then, mark the beginning of the disintegration of the movement, the beginning of the end of modernism. If Spanish American poetry of the first quarter of the twentieth century had continued in that state, it would surely have died.

But poetry is like a flame; before a school dies out, a last spark springs forth to ignite the next bit of fuel. And thus, from the ashes of our modernism, arose the new poets: López Velarde in Mexico, José María Eguren in Peru, Ricardo Arenales in Colombia, Gabriela Mistral in Chile, Juana de Ibarbourou in Uruguay, Alfonsina Storni in Argentina.

This second period evokes the following commentary from

Cecília Meireles: "When, however, it is a contemporaneous reflection of an artist who is disturbed by his own problems, sorrows, and hopes, perhaps from lack of distance for proper perspective, a literature cannot be easily understood by the public which hesitates to acknowledge and accept it, dubious concerning what is being offered, suspicious of the intentions, seriousness, or soundness of the artist."[11] But at last the new school gained recognition—to be challenged once more by a group even more daring in expression. Meanwhile, the poor public is almost never in complete communion with its best artists: "When the precursor goes beyond the present and takes on aspects of the future, exceeding the most advanced of his own period, no one wants to give ear to his predictions. Not only do we disbelieve what has not yet been observed: we are possessed by a kind of rage against whoever dares to say that he is already seeing what we have not yet glimpsed."[12]

So were regarded Cervantes, Beethoven, Victor Hugo, Picasso, and many others. And so now are regarded our progressive poets, termed the "vanguard," whose most salient figures are Rafael Alberti, Pedro Salinas, Pablo Neruda, César Vallejo, and Jules Supervielle. Actually, the greatest difficulty lies not in the creative process but in the communication of its product; and since in poetry of a social character its communication is almost as important as its essence there results a marked conflict between purpose and outcome.

If the communication of social poetry is of the utmost importance, its cultivation should be obligatory for our young poets. Only the most strident cries can awaken impassive man to the existence of the countless injustices and the terrible misery that surround him. It seems cowardice, defeatism, at times, to remain eternally introspective while people are suffering, while man is exploited, while the Indian is bled of his rightful possessions and deprived even of his soul, while the world is being ravaged of its beauty. It is impossible to remain silent. And the poet of America must not be, as Rabindranath Tagore desired, "a flute through which passes the harmony of the world," but rather a hammer which strikes the lips of the demagogue and the grasping fingers of the trafficker in national honor.

The Spanish American poet did not betray his continent. José Martí dedicated his genius to the service of his oppressed Cuba; José Mármol and González Prada systematically attacked tyranny; Juan Montalvo wished to write an essay on the Indian "that would arouse even the inanimate to tears"; Rubén Darío sang about his race menaced by potential conquest; Castro Alves placed his faith in the violent sea of the masses; and beyond, to the north, the genius of Walt Whitman, like a fiery steed, raced across the American plains.

New themes have come to the fore in our times. In Cuba, Venezuela, and Brazil, Negro poetry has made notable strides; in Ecuador and Peru, the Indianist tendency appears with remarkable strength; in Chile, the social struggle assumes lyrical form; in Argentina, new Catholic poets have surged forward; in Mexico, revolutionary poetry has acquired militant recognition. Poets today affiliate themselves with civic factions as in the glorious days of our struggle for independence.

The impulse toward social poetry, toward the epic, had long existed among our young poets, but they could not find the motivating impulse in an epoch of economic and social change. They did not witness the terrible drama of the Negro in slavery; the tragedy of the Indian took place far from their urban centers. The epic poet needs heroic actions, great human movements. Without the Trojan wars, there would be no *Iliad* or *Odyssey;* without the Spanish reconquest, no *Poema de mío Cid;* without the wars in Chile, we should have no *Araucana;* without the maritime adventures of Portugal, there would exist no *Lúsiadas.* Gauchesque poetry, so well represented by *Martín Fierro,* would have been limited to the *contrapunto,* had it not been for the constant clash between the gauchos and the government's armed forces, between the latter and the hordes of Indians of the pampas.

At the outset, then, the indigenous material afforded inspiration for a lyrico-dramatic poetry, in which the Indian appears as the victim of the white boss; these compositions never achieved true greatness, because their authors are excessively literary, rather than human, in approach. Some of these poets, however, such as the Venezuelan poet Fombona Pachano, reveal far greater sincerity. Nevertheless, the poet who bears the Indian most deeply in his soul is the Peruvian, César Vallejo.

The Negro theme has followed a similar course of development. It was born in Cuba, essentially as poetry for North and South American tourists. It consisted of numerous Afro-Cuban words, and many *rumbas, sones,* and *sambas,* similar in essence to American jazz. Only two poets, Nicolás Guillén and Emilio Ballagas, manifest true dramatic vigor. The social theme appears at times in the compositions of the Chilean poet Pablo Neruda. Revolutionary zeal is evident on occasion also in the works of the Spanish-Mexican poet León Felipe.

The truth is that these poets lacked the inspiration of a vital drama. But at last this presented itself in the form of the Spanish civil war, which left us all horror-stricken and filled with rending anguish. The poet was there, in the trenches, with rifle poised—or in the desolation of his soul, with the searing flame of his song.

The Cuban Nicolás Guillén is a mulatto writer whose Negro poetry was at first merely picturesque and folkloric. But later, influenced by the work of García Lorca, it acquired a gypsy audacity. The social themes peculiar to the Negro are introduced even in Guillén's earliest poetic efforts; but there they are treated with charming lightness, rather than in transcendental form:

> Ayé me dijeron negro
> pa que me fajara yo;
> pero e que me lo desía
> era un negro como yo.
> Tan blanco come te ve
> y tu abuela sé quién e.[13]

Confronted with the North American established on the island, or with the tourist, Guillén presents the dual aspect of the defender of his continent against the millionaire invader, and of the sarcastic, apparently carefree poet:

> Con tanto inglé que tú sabía,
> Bito Manué,
> con tanto inglé, no sabe ahora
> desí: ye.
> La americana te buca
> y tú le tiene que huí;
> tu inglé era de etrai guan,
> de etrai guan y guan-tu-tri.
> Bito Manué, tú no sabe inglé,
> tú no sabe inglé,
> tú no sabe inglé.
> No te enamore ma nunca,
> Bito Manué,
> si no sabe inglé,
> si no sabe inglé.[14]

But he does not always smile thus at the Americans. Rather, at times, he expresses tersely a controlled uneasiness in the presence of certain representatives of that nation:

> Con lo que un yanqui se tome
> de una visita a la barra
> to un año cualquiera come...[15]

Guillén continues growing more intense each day, and reaches his culmination in his songs to Spain. We may remark, among his most noteworthy compositions, the profound *Mis dos abuelos* (My Two Grandfathers) and the following poem:

> No sé por qué piensas tú,
> soldado, que te odio yo,
> si somos la misma cosa,
> yo,
> tú.

Tú eres pobre, lo soy yo;
soy de abajo, lo eres tú:
¿de dónde has sacado tú,
soldado, que te odio yo?

Me duele que a veces tú
te olvides de quién soy yo;
¡caramba! si yo soy tú,
lo mismo que tú eres yo.

Pero no por eso yo
he de malquererte, tú:
si somos la misma cosa,
yo,
tú,
no sé por qué piensas tú,
soldado, que te odio yo.

¡Ya nos veremos yo y tú,
juntos en la misma calle,
hombro con hombro, tú y yo!
Sin odios, ni yo ni tú,
pero sabiendo tú y yo
adónde vamos yo y tú...

¡No sé por qué piensas tú,
soldado, que te odio yo![16]

Another Cuban poet of merit is Emilio Ballagas, one of the purest poets in the language. He too cultivates the Negro theme, although I believe that he has not the least Negro element in his ancestry. Nevertheless, the transparent clarity of his poems in the true Spanish tradition reveals splendid maturity of approach.

In his effort to portray fully the Negroid element, Ballagas often sacrifices social significance in favor of the picturesque, and produces *comparsas, rumbas,* and *sones* now famous throughout all Spanish America. Among these are the especially noted *Elegía de María Belén Chacón* and his *Comparsa habanera* (Havana Comparsa). But Ballagas approaches the social aspect from a strongly racial viewpoint, more suitable to a North American poet such as Langston Hughes than to a Cuban bard. His poem *Actitud* (Attitude) contains a collective social protest of exceptional vigor.

The Negro theme has numerous devotees, including the Brazilians, Raul Bopp and Jorge de Lima; the Cubans, Tallet and Carpentier; and the Puerto Rican, Palés Matos—all serious and capable poets. In my opinion, should they abandon the desire to paint merely the picturesque and folkloric aspects and penetrate rather into the soul of the Negro, they could produce a cycle of Afro-Cuban poetry worthy the attention of the entire continent.

The indigenous theme is less picturesque than the Afro-Cuban or Afro-Brazilian. The latter includes predominant decorative elements: color, accelerated or syncopated rythm, warmth of vocabulary, richness of garb, gaiety. It approaches somewhat the medieval drama, the guild processions on Good Friday, the theater of the masses. The Indian, on the other hand, is liturgical. Striking splashes of color ill become him; in fact, they are almost in direct opposition to his nature. Rather than decorative, the indigenous mood is symbolic in its simplicity. In religious processions the Indian seems to be submerged in his own rhythm, seeking contact with the earth. His voice is plaintive and bears the cutting cold of his mountain abode. His rhythm is slow, monotonous, enveloping—almost tragic.

The Indianist theme has been, and still continues to be, abundantly exploited in the Spanish American novel. In fact, there exists today an entire indigenist school of poetry, the most genuine representative of which, in my opinion, is the Peruvian, César Vallejo.

Despite many vain attempts made in Peru to resurrect the Indianist vogue, the genuine shadow of Garcilaso de la Vega long held sway. But in 1918 the volume *Heraldos negros* (Black Heralds) of César Vallejo echoed for the first time the suffering and anguish of the native. It revealed the Indian's life of torment, which arises from the incongruity of his ageless soul with the world of modern technology. The Indian serves as subject today to many Peruvian poets: José Carlos Mariátegui defines the indigenous theme as "a state of conscience," not as a simple literary exercise; the radical *aprista*[17] movement has incorporated it and makes it the essence of its program; Ciro Alegría is disseminating the vogue throughout the entire Western world; Alejandro Peralta and César Vallejo endow it with the profundity befitting true poetry.

Ever since his youth Vallejo has undergone a strong social orientation. He observes the man of his own race and describes him in the context of his mountain country. He can remain but a short time passively objective before the overwhelming sadness of his exploited race awakens a note of protest.

> Arriero, vas fabulosamente vidriado de sudor.
> La hacienda Menocucho
> cobra mil sinsabores diarios por tu vida.
> Las doce. Vamos a la cintura del día.
> El sol que duele mucho.
> Arrìero, con tu poncho colorado te alejas
> saboreando el romance peruano de tu coca.[18]

And because of the protest, because he recognized the voice of his blood, he spent long months in prison. He succeeded in reaching Europe; he spent several years in France, traveled through Russia, and finally arrived in turbulent Spain aflame with civil war. There he felt the approach of death amidst that immense tragedy. And shortly before his demise he wrote his most intense work, *España, aparta de mí este cáliz* (Spain, Remove This Cup from Me).

The indigenous theme carried him to a revolutionary attitude of universal scope, to supreme confidence in the ultimate salvation of man. His social viewpoint is clearly defined in his poem *Masa* (Masses):

> Al fin de la batalla,
> y muerto el combatiente, vino hacia él un hombre
> y le dijo: «¡No mueras; te amo tanto!»
> Pero el cadáver ¡ay! siguió muriendo.

Se le acercaron dos y repitiéronle:
«¡No nos dejes! ¡Valor! ¡Vuelve a la vida!»
Pero el cadáver ¡ay! siguió muriendo.

Acudieron a él veinte, cien, mil, quinientos mil,
clamando: «¡Tanto amor, y no poder nada contra la muerte!»
Pero el cadáver ¡ay! siguió muriendo.

Le rodearon millones de individuos,
con un ruego común: «¡Quédate hermano!»
Pero el cadáver ¡ay! siguió muriendo.

Entonces, todos los hombres de la tierra
le rodearon; les vió el cadáver triste, emocionado;
incorporóse lentamente,
abrazó al primer hombre; echóse a andar...[19]

Once again we discover the Spanish theme, incandescent, alive with fiery emotion. The two chief social poets approached it enthusiastically. Guillén returned to his island of Cuba; Vallejo died on European soil. Some could return; others died—such men as Miguel Hernández, Antonio Machado, and García Lorca. There, both man and poet became greater, because the Spanish civil war was the noble and pure defense of a liberty-loving people. The lyric poet, in the presence of suffering, heroism, and death, turned infallibly to the epic. Death, pain, and heroism determine the poetic formula of León Felipe in his long works, *El Payaso de las bofetadas y el Pescador de caña* (The Clown Who Is Slapped and the Fisherman with the Rod) and *El Hacha* (The Ax). His is the formula of fire. He defines it thus: "Every good fuel is excellent poetic material. Everything, even prose—the prose here in this very passage,—is neither an excipient nor an exegesis in itself. It is a poetic element which gains in quality, not with rhythm, but with temperature. The line of the flame is today the organizing and architectural line of the poem. Fire now has a logic and dialectics of its own, just as does reason. The image, indeed, the burning image equals the law in worth. And in order to win a place among the advance outposts of the intellect, the poetry of today must not be music or measure, but fire."[20]

Imbued with this aesthetic and human fervor, León Felipe sang of his country, a land treacherously murdered by its own sons and betrayed by all the democracies of the world, by those whom he calls "merchants and their servants." We find here the poet and perennial Quijote, who offers the business tycoons "all the blood of Spain for a drop of light." Spain has died, betrayed by all Spaniards, and the poet's lament recalls the role of the ancient Greek chorus.

León Felipe approaches the social theme from a profoundly ethical viewpoint. In doing so, he merely continues the moral attitude of his Spanish predecessors, Quevedo, author of the celebrated *Epístola moral* (Moral Epistle), Jovellanos, and Unamuno. To León Felipe, and in the eyes of the other poets, the world belongs not to the merchant, the gambler, the soldier, nor the archbishop, but to "him who will redeem it," to the Promethean poet, to the apostle of justice. That is why the poet—in effect, the hero—offers "all the blood of Spain for a drop of light."

Another poet worthy of mention here is Pablo Neruda, for his inner torment and profound despair over the tragic history of Spain have left engraved in fire the drama of that turbulent nation. In several respects Neruda is a poet of continental scope, as were Walt Whitman in the United States and Rubén Darío in Spanish America. I call him "continental" because he is the synchronizer of experiences and the assimilator of poetic forms. His background is the entire Hispanic American world—confused, bitter, pessimistic, audacious. He is the interpreter of his times and will always have to be defined in accordance with his epoch rather than with rules of style and rhetoric.

Neruda was born in Chile, and has Indian blood in his veins. I would say that he is the most faithful representative of the indigenous soul of America. Let us begin with the Araucanian, whose life is inextricably entwined with wheat and the mountain range, with cold and tempests. He is a timid yet heroic being; he seems to be carved of stone and engendered in the hostile obscurity of the forest. He is a solitary, isolated man, filled with mild desires, affections, and unconscious hatreds. He lives with his sorrow and sensuality in the eternal humidity of the lands of Arauco.

But this Indian suddenly comes out into the world. He discovers Western culture and finds his poetic language; the Castilian tongue, flexible, rich, sensuous, and slow of movement, is his vehicle. He begins to collect primary experiences and to express them, instinctively, with precipitate, unmeasured movement. He discovers love, but love on the brink of death:

Besadora, dulce y rubia,
me iré,
te irás, besadora...[21]

An inexplicable sadness gnaws at his heart. He feels the influx of primary emotions, for which he cannot find outward expression. Can it be the sorrow of parting? Or the painful fear of the infinite? The poet does not know: he is lost, and alone in the world, like the American Indian.

Yo me voy. Estoy triste; pero siempre estoy triste;
Vengo desde tus brazos. No sé hacia dónde voy.
Desde tu corazón me dice adiós un niño
Y yo le digo adiós.[22]

The poet lives yonder in southern Chile, in a drab, bleak town of long streets, permeated with the odor of the general store and the stench of turbid wells, alive with the ugly souls of embittered men. There is no poetry amid such environs, except for that of his heart, except for that of a lost love, "which is a white rose that opens in the silence." Now begins the true role of the poet. He creates out of pain; he writes with blood; but he seeks a more polished expression, and beseeches aid from traditional literary culture.

¡Yo lo comprendo, amigos, yo lo comprendo todo.
Se mezclaron voces ajenas a las mías,
yo lo comprendo, amigos!

Como si yo quisiera volar y a mí llegaran
en ayuda las alas de las aves,
todas las alas,
así vinieron estas palabras extranjeras
a desatar la oscura ebriedad de mi alma.[23]

From the very start the poet exhibits a conflicting attitude of generosity and selfishness; moreover, a commingling of earthly mud and celestial skies; light and obscurity; animal instincts and lofty spirituality; joy and grief. Thus he says: "May my dark sorrow not die on your wings . . ."

«Y así una tarde—amor de manos crueles—
arrodillado, te daré las gracias.»...

Amigo, con la tarde haz que se vaya
este deseo mío de que todo rosal
me pertenezca.
Amigo,
si tienes hambre come de mi pan.[24]

He would sing about the lofty, magnificent life if he were not weighted with those black sediments of disillusion. But he has seen the eternal contradiction of life. He has observed how the wind and the rose do not complement each other to form a whole harmonious in beauty, but rather that "the wind bears a bit of clay to each rose."

Ever since he was a child, his poetic soul contemplated life with the unwavering, critical eyes of a man, with the eyes of a Chilean man, whose exacting scrutiny interprets all with perfect clarity. From his early years he was prepared for the role of the antipoet, which he later became. How can we expect any other formula from a man who has seen:

Las ciudades—hollines y venganzas—
la cochinada gris de los suburbios,
la oficina que encorva las espaldas,
el jefe de ojos turbios?[25]

How can we criticize him if he knows that in the factories the souls of dead workers pierce the black of night with their sobs and fleeting steps? That is why he is drawn by the blood red of the sunset, the dark agony of night; he sees barren countrysides and the motionless anguish of steel.

In the process of his poetic formation the wild, uncontrolled, creative exaltation was to remain predominant. From that time, therefore, he is a romantic, dramatic poet, giving voice to the exultant strength of his sensuous, vigorous temperament. It is useless to explain in detail his images, rhythm, and selection of vocabulary; for everything is merged in his poetry, irregularly—in appearance haphazardly,—into a thick, black mass, a cold, thick, black mass from which flames seem to spring forth. There would be little purpose in making a study of his symbols, for they never have the same significance. It is futile to attempt a definition of his use of the adjective, for it is ever varied in concept. This bleak, cold, viscous, and yet ardent poet defies classification and must be accepted merely as an organic force in the act of creative endeavor.

His own definition of his soul is an inexact, capricious, contradictory statement, yet it gives us the uncertain key to its comprehension; in his own words his soul is:

> A shadowy zone, a narrow, pensive line. A vine crucified on a wall. A song, a dream, destiny. My flower, flower of my soul. The winged movement of sleep, of a butterfly, of twilight...
>
> My flower. Flower of my soul. Terrain of my kisses. Bell-stroke of tears. Whirlpool of murmurs.

Before turning to his *Residencia en la tierra* (Residence on Earth) we should acquaint ourselves with the poet's own concept of his work. He speaks to us of an impure poetry, one of material things in repose: wheels, coal sacks, barrels, baskets, handles, hafts of implements. It is interesting to note the interdependence among these objects, man, and earth. The objects symbolize the confused impurity of mankind. In other words, they depict an atmosphere of sweat, smoke, or flowers, according to the various professions.

Poetry should be impure, should contain everything, should be like a body, nourished with food and fantasy. Nothing should be omitted, not the ugly nor the bestial. The poet, moved by an impulse of love, should penetrate to the depths of all worldly things; he must acquire the suavity of the instrument played without ceasing, the polish of skillfully wrought wood, the smooth perfection of steel. Flowers, wheat, water have that very consistency, that quality of magnificence to the touch. Along with this, however, the poet must not forget his melancholy, his sentimentalism, the impure fruits.

Consequently, in *Residencia en la tierra* the poet lives in a realm of dreams integrated by concrete realities. He scorns nothing, neither the sublime nor the commonplace, in his absolute freedom of creation. He places ordinary, everyday objects in abstract zones of ideal beauty, with a highly unusual gamut of values:

> Hay un país extenso en el cielo
> con las supersticiosas alfombras del arco-iris
> y con vegetaciones vesperales:
> hacia allí me dirijo, no sin cierta fatiga,
> pisando una tierra removida de sepulcros, un tanto frescos,
> yo sueño entre esas plantas de legumbres confusas.[26]

The entire material world surrounds his soul, in perfect harmony with it and with the spiritual domain. Just as the classical poet speaks of the music of the heavens, so does Neruda, who is more of our times, feel the music of the earth, "as I stand surrounded by silent geography."

> Me rodea una misma cosa, un solo movimiento,
> el peso del mineral, la luz de la piel,
> se pegan al sonido de la palabra noche:
> la tinta del trigo, del marfil, del llanto,
> las cosas de cuero, de madera, de lana,
> envejecidas, desteñidas, uniformes,
> se unen en torno a mí como paredes—[27]

This sensation provides the impulse for *Tres cantos materiales* (Three Material Songs), *Entrada a la madera* (Entrance into

Wood), *Apogeo del apio* (Apogee of the Celery Stalk), and *Estatuto del vino* (The Statute of Wine). His approach to wood, the movement of the spirit toward the world of wood, is in itself poetry,—poetry aroused by the life and death of the plant world. He enters that sphere as a suffering man. The following lines convey powerfully the emotion of the poet in the presence of the phenomena of nature:

> Soy yo ante tu ola de olores muriendo,
> envueltos en otoño y resistencia:
> soy yo emprendiendo un viaje funerario
> entre tus cicatrices amarillas:
> soy yo con mis lamentos sin origen,
> sin alimentos, desvelado, solo,
> entrando obscurecidos corredores,
> llegando a tu materia misteriosa.[28]

In his *Apogeo del apio* Neruda continues his trip through the world of plant life. At night the poet's alert ear perceives the secrets of the earth; and amid the deep obscurity the stalk of celery merges with his being and grows there, instilling into his soul the subterranean light, the profound beauty of the subsoil. The celery stalk is everywhere apparent, with its cloven feet, its green eyes, its moist hands. It acquires life, and later enters into death with the celestial beauty of a blond child who lies dead among the lilies.

APOGEO DEL APIO

> Del centro puro que los ruidos nunca
> atravesaron, de la intacta cera,
> salen claros relámpagos lineales,
> palomas con destino de volutas,
> hacia tardías calles con olor
> a sombra y a pescado.
>
> ¡Son las venas del apio! ¡Son la espuma, la risa,
> los sombreros del apio!
> Son los signos del apio, su sabor

de luciérnaga, sus mapas
de color inundado,
y cae su cabeza de angel verde,
y sus delgados rizos se acongojan,
y entran los pies del apio en los mercados
de la mañana herida, entre sollozos,
y se cierran las puertas a su paso,
y los dulces caballos se arrodillan.

Sus pies cortados van, sus ojos verdes
van derramados, para siempre hundidos
en ellos los secretos y las gotas:
los túneles del mar de donde emergen,
las escaleras que el apio aconseja,
las desdichadas sombras sumergidas,
las determinaciones en el centro del aire,
los besos en el fondo de las piedras.

A medianoche, con manos mojadas,
alguien golpea mi puerta en la niebla,
y oigo la voz del apio, voz profunda,
áspera voz de viento encarcelado,
se queja herido de aguas y raíces,
hunde en mi cama sus amargos rayos,
y sus desordenadas tijeras me pegan en el pecho
buscándome la boca del corazón ahogado.

¿Qué quieres, huésped de corsé quebradizo,
en mis habitaciones funerales?
¿Qué ámbito destrozado te rodea?

Fibras de obscuridad y luz llorando,
ribetes ciegos, energías crespas,
río de vida y hebras esenciales,
verdes ramas de sol acariciado,
aquí estoy, en la noche, escuchando secretos,
desvelos, soledades,
y entráis, en medio de la niebla hundida,
hasta crecer en mí, hasta comunicarme
la luz obscura y la rosa de la tierra.[29]

The elements of Neruda's *Estatuto del vino* are not quite so well fused; rather, they seem superimposed. First, we contemplate the natural existence of wine, "flying with its body of saturated red wings"; then we see man as a poet, and man as a tormented, anguished drinker; at the end, wine once again recovers its material existence.

In these three poems Neruda reveals unknown worlds, intimate relationships between the tangible things of familiar ken and the world of emotion and dreams. In fact, if he had always maintained a lofty sense of aesthetic purity, I would say that he had created the mystic soul of matter. But had he done so he would have attained the summit of creative art; and the fact is, we cannot expect so much of this poet, who is limited by factors of temperament and culture.

The outbreak of the Spanish civil war surprised Neruda in Madrid. In the presence of its tragic spectacle there arose in him the social poet, the revolutionist, the civic bard. Ever since his youth Neruda had manifested great admiration for the sweeping lyricism of Walt Whitman, for the American's slow development of images and his exhaustive enumerations, and so, bearing fresh in mind the vivid impression of the conflagration that was leveling the Spanish peninsula, Neruda returned to that formula of civic poetry, but with a zeal of greater intensity and virility than ever before. *España en el corazón* (Spain in the Heart) is a work of flaming tenor. Though it contains less true poetry than *Residencia en la tierra,* it is a poem of greater humanity. In it the Chilean Indian from Parral approximates a universal concept of poetry, one in which frontiers are nonexistent, one which is free from vulgar "patriotism."

He wishes to create an immense song, a song of war and blood, yet also a song of tenderness for that Spain which has just died because of our indifference. And he sings of the young poet so cruelly murdered by the Fascists, García Lorca, the pure singer, and the friends of the unfortunate youth. He curses the Nazis, the

Fascists, and their Moorish troops; and he sings of the Madrid of July, 1936, the illustrious city, surprised by

> un hipo negro de generales
> y una ola de sotanas rabiosas...[30]

There the poet lived, surrounded by friends, close to the eternal smile of Federico García Lorca:

EXPLICO ALGUNAS COSAS

> Preguntaréis: ¿Y dónde están las lilas?
> ¿Y la metafísica cubierta de amapolas?
> ¿Y la lluvia que a menudo golpeaba
> sus palabras llenándolas
> de agujeros y pájaros?
> Os voy a contar todo lo que me pasa.
>
> Yo vivía en un barrio
> de Madrid, con campanas,
> con relojes, con árboles.
>
> Desde allí se veía
> el rostro seco de Castilla
> como un océano de cuero.
>
> Mi casa era llamada
> la casa de las flores, porque por todas partes
> estallaban geranios: era
> una bella casa
> con perros y chiquillos.
>
> ¿Raúl, te acuerdas?
> ¿Te acuerdas, Rafael?
> ¿Federico, te acuerdas
> debajo de la tierra,
> te acuerdas de mi casa con balcones en donde
> la luz de junio ahogaba flores en tu boca?[31]

And then came the generals, airplanes, Moors, Germans and Italians—assassins all of the lily, the dove, and of fair infants; joy and beauty came to an abrupt end in that once glorious capital, and there resounded only the roar of rifles and bombs; and grief, like a great black tempest, fell upon the city. And then, when faith and the flower had been destroyed forever, the dismayed populace witnessed the arrival of the International Brigade, the inspiration for epic enthusiasm. Heroic battles followed, victories and defeats, frenzied struggle, exultant joys, and tears. All this is reflected in the work of the poet as he stands amid the ruins of a civilization, as he glories in the occasional triumphs of the unaided forces of liberty.

Weary of the blood and burning powder of war, he hurls virulent imprecations upon the figure of the Fascist General Franco. Spain has succumbed, but the poet may still turn to the great, free world of America, and to the torrential floods of light emanating from the vast steppes of Russia. His song will continue, but his lowered voice will echo the grief that has afflicted the soul of all poets upon the death of Spain, and throughout the world their voices, now profound and grave, will rise forth as from a cemetery or from a petrified sea. Their words shall be heard till the end of the world; and with each new song they shall have renewed life; they shall be perpetuated through the generations, as is the heroism incarnate in history-making men, and so on till the end of time.

Neruda's voice rises again in a civic poem, robust and new, dedicated to the great liberator, Simón Bolívar:

Un Canto para Bolívar

Padre nuestro que estás en la tierra, en el agua, en el aire
de toda nuestra extensa latitud silenciosa,
todo lleva tu nombre, padre, en nuestra morada:
tu apellido la caña levanta a la dulzura,
el estaño bolívar tiene un fulgor bolívar,
el pájaro bolívar sobre el volcán bolívar,
la patata, el salitre, las sombras especiales,
las corrientes, las vetas de fosfórica piedra,
todo lo nuestro viene de tu vida apagada:
tu herencia fueron ríos, llanuras, campanarios:
tu herencia es el pan nuestro de cada día, padre.

Tu pequeño cadáver de capitán valiente
ha extendido en lo inmenso su metálica forma:
de pronto salen dedos tuyos entre la nieve
y el austral pescador saca a la luz de pronto
tu sonrisa, tu voz palpitando en las redes.

¿De qué color la rosa que junto a su alma alcemos?
Roja sera la rosa que recuerde tu paso.
¿Cómo serán las manos que toquen tu ceniza?
Rojas serán las manos que en tu ceniza nacen.
¿Y cómo es la semilla de tu corazón muerto?
Es roja la semilla de tu corazón vivo.
Por eso es hoy la ronda de manos junto a tí.
Junto a mi mano hay otra, y hay otra junto a ella,
y otra más, hasta el fondo del continente oscuro.
Y otra mano que tú no conociste entonces
viene tambien, Bolívar, a estrechar a la tuya.
De Teruel, de Madrid, del Jarama, del Ebro,
de la cárcel, del aire, de los muertos de España
llega esta mano roja que es hija de la tuya.

Capitán, combatiente, donde una boca
grita Libertad, donde un oído escucha,
donde un soldado rojo rompe una frente parda,
donde un laurel de libres brota, donde una nueva
bandera se adorna con la sangre de nuestra insigne aurora,
Bolívar, capitán, se divisa tu rostro.
Otra vez entre pólvora y humo tu espada está naciendo.
Otra vez tu bandera con sangre se ha bordado.
Los malvados atacan tu semilla de nuevo:
clavado en otra cruz está el hijo del hombre.

Pero hacia la esperanza nos conduce tu sombra:
el laurel y la luz de tu ejército rojo
através de la noche de América con tu mirada mira.
Tus ojos que vigilan más allá de los mares,
más allá de los pueblos oprimidos y heridos,
más allá de las negras ciudades incendiadas,
tu voz nace de nuevo, tu mano otra vez nace:
tu ejército defiende las banderas sagradas:
y un sonido terrible de dolores precede
la aurora enrojecida por la sangre del hombre.

Libertador, un mundo de paz nació en tus brazos.
La paz, el pan, el trigo de tu sangre nacieron:
de nuestra joven sangre venida de tu sangre
saldrá paz, pan y trigo para el mundo que haremos.

Yo conocí a Bolívar una mañana larga
en Madrid, en la boca del Quinto Regimiento.
«Padre,» le dije; «¿eres, o no eres o quién eres?»
Y mirando el Cuartel de la Montaña, dijo:
«Despierto cada cien años cuando despierta el pueblo.»[32]

Continuing along ever more distant horizons, and in constant growth, the poet finally discovers the theme for which he seemed predestined: the heroism of the Russian people in the defense of Stalingrad. Here the social poet assumes epic proportions, although, of course, in an ever new form, an extremely modern concept of the epic. We all recognize that the subject matter has little actual relation to the greatness of the poem, and that the essence of its artistic value lies in the poet's penetration into his theme. Here, however, there is a close correlation between form and content, and in my opinion *El Canto a Stalingrado* marks the lyrical height of Pablo Neruda.

At present the poet is engaged in the composition of a work of epic conception, entitled *Canto general de Chile*. It is a poem of cosmic inspiration in which the mineral, plant, animal, and human worlds explain themselves and clash in an anguished desire for comprehension and revelation. The bard sings of the discoverers and the conquerors, of climates, deserts, and seas; of high mountains and rivers. He ascends rather vertiginously, but pauses, his refined, tender glance at rest on a rose, to say:

Veo una rosa junto al agua, una pequeña copa
de párpados bermejos,
sostenida en la altura por un sonido aéreo...[33]

Be his subject grandiose or minute, the poet is ever apparent, interpreting his people and his epoch; his soul overflows with emotional experiences seeking outlet; he is tempered with light and shade, exultant with numerous metaphors, overwhelmed with images judiciously and injudiciously employed; his work is a combination of the fantastic and the real.

He approaches the realm of the baroque, plunges headlong into the marshes, speaks the jargon of the ruffian, and emerges transfigured, soaring toward the stars. Finally, he returns to the pristine clarity of his childhood and purifies himself in the arms of his country.

Himno y regreso

Patria, mi patria, vuelvo hacia ti la sangre.
Pero te pido, como a la madre el niño
lleno de llanto.
Acoge esta guitarra ciega
y esta frente perdida.

Salí a encontrarte hijos por la tierra,
salí a cuidar caídos con tu nombre de nieve,
salí a hacer una casa con tu madera pura,
salí a llevar tu estrella a los héroes heridos.

Ahora quiero dormir en tu substancia.
Dame tu clara noche de penetrantes cuerdas,
tu noche de navío, tu estatura estrellada.

Patria mía: quiero mudar de sombra.
Patria mía: quiero cambiar de rosa.
Quiero poner mi brazo en tu cintura exigua
y sentarme en tus piedras por el mar calcinadas,
a detener el trigo y mirarlo por dentro.
Voy a escoger la flora delgada del nitrato,
voy a hilar el estambre glacial de la campaña,
y mirando tu ilustre y solitaria espuma
un ramo litoral tejeré a tu belleza.

Patria, mi patria
toda rodeada de agua combatiente
y nieve combatida,
en ti se junta el águila al azufre,

y en tu antártica mano de armiño y de zafiro
una gota de pura luz humana
brilla encendiendo el enemigo cielo.

Guarda tu luz, ¡oh patria!, mantén
tu dura espiga de esperanza en medio
del ciego aire temible.
En tu remota tierra ha caído toda esta luz difícil,
este destino de los hombres,
que te hace defender una flor misteriosa
sola, en la inmensidad de América dormida.[34]

I have presented here an incomplete picture of our social poetry. I have only spoken of five poets of socializing attitude. In conclusion I should like to reaffirm my belief in pure poetry as a goal. But I am convinced also that poetry must bear the mark of its epoch. The poets of today have a duty to fulfill, a mission which would amplify the merely artistic aspects of the muse. Once, several centuries ago, the sword of Francisco Pizarro became a pen, and traced an eternal inscription in the sands of America. Now it is time for us to turn the pen into a sword and plunge it into the core of human suffering—into the flames and the blood.

Chapter X ◇ The Poetry of the Future

It is always a pleasant occupation to extend the antennae of intuition into an unknown world of vague shadows and light and to inhale with a mixed emotion of fear and joy the air of the most lofty zones. So it is to glance toward the future of our poetry, toward the expression so eagerly desired by our new world. Clearly it is an adventure in fantasy, a dream impossible of complete fulfillment, the wing of an idea which appears suddenly in a new atmosphere, and which stirs with spiral movement, scorning the impulse of experience and deduction. A theme wholly suitable to the poet, who rejoices in its mystery and indefiniteness, it is despised by the scholar, who requires certainty, horizontal or vertical movement, exact dimensions.

Nevertheless, it is a provocative, suggestive subject, one in which the imagination finds limitless horizons, in which reality may struggle with fantasy, and reasoning with dream. This is its great attraction for us, but at the same time we are restrained by fear of wandering astray or of approaching the paradox through the blue mist of speculation.

In order to ponder the poetry of the future, we must always bear in mind two fundamental factors: the poetry of the past and present, and the cultural transformation that the American peoples may undergo. Our efforts today contain the germ of the work of tomorrow; and if our cultural growth is effected naturally, without great changes due to foreign influences, we are justified in contemplating a poetic development which will obey certain norms and tend in determinable directions.

Any discussion, then, of the poetry of the future will imply merely a résumé of our poetic production during the past century and an analysis of our cultural conceptions in a new world desirous of creating its own values in opposition to the old, already finished, and apparently senile sphere. If we could believe with certainty that Europe and Asia were culturally extinct, our proposed task of augury would be simple and logical. But fortunately we are moving in an orbit of sheer hypothesis.

Our romantic movement, which, aside from blind imitation, was a protest against the cold, sterile poetry of the eighteenth century, sought in American themes the diversity that could lend it distinctive character. Hence it was that Andrés Bello conceived his *Silvas americanas,* in which tropical nature offers a great variety of shades to the contemporary landscape. José María Heredia strove to portray the emotion of his continent in the lyrical verse of his *Canto al Niágara,* and of *Al Teocalli de Cholula,* the first manifestation of authentic romanticism in America. Olmedo found inspiration for his vigorous poem *A la victoria de Junín* in the deeds of our greatest hero. Echeverría felt the first vibrations of the pampas in his lengthy poetic work, *La Cautiva* (The Captive Woman); Mármol exalted his country in *Los Cantos del peregrino* (The Pilgrim's Songs); and the prose poet Domingo Faustino Sarmiento affords us in his *Facundo* the most virile example of literary Americanism.

Poetic technique continued to be imitative, as were the references to the countryside, the images and symbols, the appeals to the muse, the apostrophes to the sun, the sea, and the moon. Neither Tabaré nor Cumandá succeed in convincing us; but we are charmed at the idea that these creatures inhabit our land, though they speak a foreign tongue, and though their sentiments be far from those of our real, indigenous peoples. At least, there existed in romanticism an internal conflict between American sources of inspiration and European form. If the former did not triumph, it was because the whole civilization of our continent aspired to a European conception of culture and because our poetry was the production of an infinitesimal group of devotees.

This victory of form defines the modernist movement: evasion of reality, escape from a world which our poets thought devoid of beauty and heroic stature, flight from an existence lacking in poetic materials, withdrawal in time and space toward an excessively literary form. The early critics of modernism found it difficult to accept the formula of Darío's *Azul,* and even today we are slightly confused by the verbal capers and technical acrobatics of Julio Herrera y Reissig.

When the modernist poet adopts themes from the immediate world of reality, one feels a discrepancy between subject and expression. For example, Chocano sings of the Indians and the *conquistadores;* he describes the Andes, the Amazon, the tropics; he speaks of the fauna and flora of the American continent. But his grandiloquent, mannered rhetoric rarely jibes with his theme. All his work gives us the sensation of a lack of internal vigor, for which the poet wishes to compensate with a superabundance of the merely decorative. This phenomenon is also visible in Darío, even in poems, such as the *Salutación del optimista,* which have been considered typically American.

Modernism is, in part, a kind of inverted realism. We note its constant escape from immediate reality to the ideal aspiration of life—in effect, an aspiration that exists in all our cultural activities. The same impulse which led Darío to sing of Verlaine and of Versailles made the Argentinian millionaire go to Paris to squander his fortune; drew the interest of the archaeologist to Greece, despite the proximity of the ruins of the great indigenous empires; and enticed the student to the investigation of Roman history, to the neglect of that of his own country. Thus we can understand the presence of the swan, the acanthus, the lotus, the nightingale, the nymph and the satyr, and the absence of the wild pigeon, the linnet, the parakeet, the llama, the iguana, and the mango. And even when, like González Martínez in his famous sonnet, we wring the swan's neck and replace that bird with the owl, it still will not be the American owl that hides in dilapidated houses and among the trees, but the mythological owl that leaves the lap of Pallas and spreads its wings from Mount Olympus.

What immediately strikes the eye in the development of our poetry is its apparent lack of roots; it seems that our poets produced their works by sheer miracle, from an infused art. For example, there is a manifest discrepancy between the daily life and the sonnets of Julio Herrera y Reissig; there is an abyss between Darío's *Prosas profanas* and the mediocrity of almost all the Hispanic American nations. Our entire culture is formed of superimposed planes, without respect for the law of cause and effect, and without true fusion of elements. Just as the Paraguayan Indian uses the rifle or machine gun without having played the least part in its invention and manufacture; just as the college student employs the microscope in a haphazard manner; just as the pedantic instructor explains Einstein after his own fashion, so does the Spanish American poet speak a language which the man of average culture does not understand, a language that is not the result of a proper linguistic preparation. Hispanic America cannot boast a literary tradition parallel to that of Spain, and now that we have withdrawn so far from the Spanish approach we grow increasingly confused each day. The poetic sensibility of Hispanic America does not result from the events of our own world, but rather from those of a literary sphere completely alien to our reality. Hence, the aesthetic themes which produce emotional states are products of the study of foreign authors. In modernism, for example, there is far greater correlation between the literary themes of Hugo, Gautier, Leconte de Lisle, Verlaine, Baudelaire, and Mallarmé, and those of Darío, Lugones, Herrera, Nervo, and Valencia, than there is between these same subjects and the life of the American continent.

In other words, then, we may say that modernist poetry, because its essence is not the intimate interpretation of the historical development of Spanish America, did not attain to a definitive expression. We have seen that in technique as well as in poetic material the modernists drew inspiration from an alien tradition, thus showing the absence of an inspiration of their own.

The romanticists had a rather fixed concept of the poetic attitude. Bello, Echeverría, and Zorrilla de San Martín limit themselves to the role of descriptive writers; Olmedo, Heredia, Almafuerte, and Andrade assume the aspect of seers, augurs. At times the subject matter is American, but the poetry is not. In the modernists, emotion is subordinate to the intellect, and worldly happenings rarely touch upon their sensibility. When Darío sings of the glories of Chile, he adopts a Homeric or Hugoesque air, but when he points out the dangers that loom in the future of America, his voice sounds strange to our ears. Chocano, on the other hand, in order to sing of his people, adorns himself with Inca jewels and with the plumes of the *conquistador,* and declaims in pompous tones. It is well to note in this respect the enormous difference between Chocano and Walt Whitman, that truly faithful representative of the sensibility of his nation.

The postmodernist poets approach more closely the interpretation of the sensibility of our continent, although their fanciful innovations in form seem to alienate them from it. Pablo Neruda can serve us here as an example; for, despite his anomalous constructions, his mutilations, his carefully gleaned symbols, his repetitiousness, and his violent images, the Chilean poet expresses, first, the melancholy soul of his country, and subsequently, the anguish of his times. Neruda's work is tortuous, fragmentary, and obscure, filled with sadness and sensuality, as becomes the man of Chile, the mestizo harassed by his confused racial heritage; impassioned, torn by formless desires and vague dreams. Although Neruda aspires to be the antipoet, his entire style is the result of an assimilated literary culture, of careful poetic training, of a constantly tormenting desire for aesthetic expression. But the essence of his soul, his fear of death and destruction, his continual dissolution into time and matter, and his unsocial, lachrymose attitude are elements generally alien to the Chilean soul.

Luis Carlos López, on the other hand, reveals the graciously waggish spirit of the coastal Colombian. He delights in employing archaic vocabulary, interpreting thus the highly Spanish sensibility of his nation. But his lyrical rebelliousness obliges him to adopt an attitude of defiance and effrontery. In his consistently antipoetic position he merely interprets the sensibility of the small town, the tedium of unheroic existence, the monotony of provincial life. Here, style and subject matter blend in close harmony to form a faithful mirror of life.

No Spanish American poet has surpassed Ramón López Velarde in the intimate fusion of local or everyday themes with the current forms of the spoken language. We discover in his poetry the simplicity and mellowness of Mexican speech, its typical flavor, the inflection of its voice, and the authentic revelation of its environment: its provincial atmosphere, with its naïve customs and its romanticism; the humble devotion of its women, the odor of candle wax and incense, the dress of percale, the flowerpot on the window sill; the virile aspect of the rustic, the childlike *fiesta* in the village square. López Velarde's Mexicanism, both within and without, is thoroughly convincing; and, therefore, Mexico's young poets have seen in him, and not in Gutiérrez Nájera, Amado Nervo, or González Martínez, the most genuine representative of their poetic nationalism.

America finds its voice also in the mulatto poet Nicolás Guillén; for he expresses its ideals of justice, social reform, and democracy. He feels with deep humanity the tragedy of his country, of the exploited Cuban peasant and the long-suffering Negro, and he amplifies these materials with simple, vital verses, aflame with passion and fury. In the presence of social and human problems the poet's voice seems as if risen from the very soul of our continent. And his example has created a school, because the new writers have recognized in him the lyric strength accruent from his impartiality of vision and sincere interpretation. There exists an intimate harmony between the popular style of Guillén and the speech of the Negroes and mulattoes; in effect, his poetry is a continuation of natural modes and precise rhythms.

The women who have cultivated the poetic muse in Spanish America reveal a new element, a passion nonexistent in the great modernists. It is true that the expression of Delmira Agustini, Alfonsina Storni, Juana de Ibarbourou, and Gabriela Mistral approximates the idiomatic forms of modernism, but the intensity of their experiences lends to their poetry a distinctly new tone and a clearly American aspect. We may affirm that the sensibility of the Spanish American woman has found its most faithful interpreters in these writers. An integral part of their times, they cry out in constant protest against social hypocrisy and convention: against "square ideas," to use the phrase of Alfonsina Storni; against the narrowness of men and of the laws which keep women ever repressed. Just as the modernists maintained their pure, idealistic attitude toward art, so do these women toward life. And in their enjoyment of it they realize the need of insisting upon the recognition of feminine rights. Here again, as is evident, they are the product of their society.

We may note in Delmira Agustini the all-pervading obsession of physical, sexual love, expressed in a form of delirious rapture, since the restrictions that had made of feminine poetry in America a perfect veil for the concealment of emotions and violent desire were now broken. Her ever-turbulent spirit cries for fulfillment in the lines of the celebrated sonnet, *Lo Inefable* (The Ineffable).

> Yo muero extrañamente... No me mata la vida,
> no me mata la Muerte, no me mata el Amor;
> muero de un pensamiento mudo como una herida...
> ¿No habéis sentido nunca el extraño dolor
>
> de un pensamiento inmenso que se arraiga en la vida,
> devorando alma y carne, y no alcanza a dar flor?
> ¿Nunca llevasteis dentro una estrella dormida
> que os abrasaba enteros y no daba un fulgor?...
>
> ¡Cumbre de los Martirios!... ¡Llevar eternamente,
> desgarradora y árida, la trágica simiente
> clavada en las entrañas como un diente feroz!...

¡Pero arrancarla un día en una flor que abriera
milagrosa, inviolable!... ¡Ah, más grande no fuera
tener entre las manos la cabeza de Dios![1]

Discontented with the actuality that surrounds her, she seeks escape in a world of dream:

La Barca milagrosa

Preparadme una barca como un gran pensamiento.
La llamarán «La Sombra» unos; otros «La Estrella.»
¡No ha de estar al capricho de una mano o de un viento,
yo la quiero consciente, indominable y bella!
¡La moverá el gran ritmo de un corazón sangriento
de vida sobrehumana; he de sentirme en ella
fuerte como en los brazos de Dios! ¡En todo viento,
en todo mar, templadme su prora de centella!
La cargaré de toda mi tristeza, y, sin rumbo,
iré como la rota corola de un nelumbo,
por sobre el horizonte líquido de la mar...
Barca, alma hermana: ¿hacia qué tierras nunca vistas,
de hondas revelaciones, de cosas imprevistas
iremos?... Yo ya muero de vivir y soñar...[2]

Aflame with an insatiable thirst, she is soothed with the pure waters of the infinite:

La Sed

¡Tengo sed, sed ardiente!.—dije a la maga, y ella
me ofreció de sus néctares.—¡Eso no, me empalaga!—
Luego, una rara fruta, con sus dedos de maga
exprimió en una copa clara como una estrella;
y un brillo de rubíes hubo en la copa bella.
Yo probé.—¡Es dulce, dulce. Hay días que me halaga
tanta miel, pero hoy me repugna, me estraga!—
Vi pasar por los ojos del hada una centella.
Y por un verde valle perfumado y brillante,
llevóme hasta una clara corriente de diamante.
—¡Bebe!— dijo. —Yo ardía, mi pecho era una fragua.
Bebí, bebí, bebí, la linfa cristalina...
¡Oh frescura! ¡Oh pureza! ¡Oh sensación divina!
—Gracias, maga, y bendita la limpidez del agua![3]

---

[1] For notes to chapter x see pages 240–241.

Alfonsina Storni was a desolate, lost soul; a tender, refined woman misplaced amid the brutality of the modern metropolis. Ever doubting, unsatisfied, generous without heroic manifestation, she protested bitterly against the vulgarity of the atmosphere in which she lived, and at last, a true daughter of her city and time, she committed suicide at the age of forty-six. A woman rather than a poetess, she expressed herself poignantly, leaving to us the inspiring example of unfailing sincerity in art and in life.

Juana de Ibarbourou sings simply and clearly of the normal love of a woman's heart. An exaltation of joy endows her entire work with the sensuous charm of ripe fruit, the freshness of running waters. Her amorous poetry interprets naturally, optimistically, the sensibility of the Spanish American woman.

The last figure whom we approach is the recent Nobel Prize winner, the Chilean Gabriela Mistral, who is unsurpassed in the representation of the basic emotions of her continent. She carries the social disquietude of America into her poems; she apostrophizes, shouts, hates, and eulogizes with the primitive strength of her race. In effect, here is the most intense voice of contemporary Spanish American poetry.

We find in the work of these four women a notably American feeling, a poetic idiom more closely correlated with normal speech, and the constant palpitation of real life. There still remains in them an element of the modernist approach, but it is evident that social events wield great influence in determining the orientation of their lyricism.

Turning to other aspects of the present scene, we note the persistence of the desire to interpret in poetry the soul of our Indians, Negroes, mulattoes, social and economic types, and regional characters. Prominent in this field are Miguel Otero Silva, Fombona Pachano, Guillén, Palés Matos, Ballagas, and Franco. However, a clear conception has not yet been reached of exactly what this poetry should be as a representation of states of mind and modes of expression. In truth, this theme has enjoyed greater development in the field of the novel through the efforts of such vigorously American writers as Rivera, Gallegos, Lins do Rêgo, and Jorge Amado. But little by little we are discovering our world and our voice. The day will come when our poetry will be to us the essence of an inspiration based upon the succession of Spanish American cultural phases and intellectual experiences. Chaucer, Shakespeare, and Shelley mark the trajectory of the development of the English sensibility. We, lacking a tradition of our own, cannot reduce this phenomenon to a series of names. At one moment of our history we adhere to the Spanish heritage; at another, to the French; at still another, we veer toward an anarchical cosmopolitanism.

The Spanish language is being enriched in America, not only in vocabulary and syntax, but also in its racial significance. Consequently, our poets of the future will wield a more highly evolved instrument of expression, one more in harmony with their emotional and ideological life. Poets will then use this language, and in their turn will perfect it according to their creative genius. And as the Spanish spoken in America differs from that of Spain, so is it only logical to expect a deviation in our literary style. Increasingly we shall avoid the conventional forms of European poetry in proportion as we plunge more deeply into the life of our own continent. When sociological, racial, and economic struggles shake the very foundations of our American world, the poet of the future will echo the resounding cry of this impulse. When learned men, tired of the commerce and the vulgarity of the great urban centers, seek the quietude of nature, in the shade of its forests and in the freshness of its lakes and fields, the poet of the future will interpret that bucolic mood. And when our culture manifests clearly its individual personality, when it synchronizes and defines its essence, offering its mature fruits to the world, then will the voice of America's poets ring with a timbre of its own; then shall we learn again that, despite the temporary victories of materialism and violence, poetry is eternal.

It is probable that technique will undergo increasing simplification with the course of time. There are already indications that our poets are aware of the basic bond of unity afforded by a more integrated form. They are beginning to realize that the dispersion and mental anarchy so characteristic of many contemporary poets are often a result of the excessively free forms now prevalent. The old Spanish ballad still provides noble inspiration to the poets of popular and narrative tendency, and the sonnet valiantly appears once more in the foreground of vanguard production.

America will be the most active cultural center that the world has ever known. And since America's life is the eternal creation of spiritual worlds with unshakable idealism, our poetry will assimilate and amplify the beauty of the past, and will be the most lofty aesthetic revelation of the future.

Chapter XI ◇ The Parallel between Brazilian and Spanish American Literature

THE GREAT Brazilian poet, Mário de Andrade, once wrote me: "I maintain my opinion that *calle* is not translatable by *rua,* nor by *rue,* nor by *street,* nor *Strasse.*" This could well give rise to an essay on the art of translating; but I do not wish to tackle that subject here. Our purpose in this discussion is not to determine the meaning of words, for that is the task of the lexicographer. Rather, our interest centers about the poet's use of the word, in its phonetic force, as an instrument of aesthetic production, and in its sensibility. The root of our study is always the word, in its multiple aspects of a living organism in continuous evolution, of the representative of concepts, of pure beauty of sound, of mysterious, evocative connotation, of a syntactical foundation, and of yet other qualities. Every translator of poetry should always bear in mind the theory of Mário de Andrade. If *calle* is not *rua* in a general lexicographical sense, how can it be so in the individual usage of a poet, in his personal interpretation of its context? Further, a poem in Portuguese in which *rua* appears would become an entirely different thing were the word replaced by *Strasse* in translation; in effect, it would be the direct antithesis of the Portuguese work.

Therefore, it is preferable not to make exact translations between dissimilar languages, but to create something new through the translation. The original then serves as an internal stimulus, exactly as would a beautiful landscape, an intense emotion, or an aesthetic discovery. The problem of translation exists also between Spanish and Portuguese, although, since these are languages of common root and similar development, it concerns essentially small details more evident to the eye of the artist than to that of the ordinary reader. For example, let us consider the word for butterfly: in Spanish, *mariposa;* in Portuguese, *borboleta.* We notice that in any Spanish poem of elegiac tone the word *mariposa,* soft and melancholy, creates the atmosphere of the work, whereas *borboleta* introduces an element of sonority and gaiety that is almost the contrary of the elegy. Of course, there still remains the alternative of maintaining the word *mariposa* in Portuguese, in its sense of "moth"; but that also is a confession of inadequacy. We come, then, to yet another conclusion: that between two languages as similar as Portuguese and Spanish it is preferable not to translate, but to make an effort to read the work in its original form.

The great similarity in history, language, literary themes, and ethnological formation of the two Latin races of America leads often to a gross misconception; for the uninstructed person fails to take into account the differentiating shades that set off the one from the other, differences not only in poetry but in the general usage of the language as well. One should be wary of the common belief that the Portuguese of Brazil is becoming increasingly similar to the Spanish of the other American countries. Rather, the Spaniard—or the Spanish American—who arrives in Brazil for the first time complains that he cannot understand the language. But the selfsame man, when visiting France or the United States, is content in his linguistic ignorance. The reason is apparent: In Brazil, he had fully expected to understand the language; he had considered Portuguese as merely a dialect of Spanish, one somewhat different from his own. Then, as he goes along studying Portuguese, he firmly declares that it is "a very difficult language," one of "terribly complicated phonetics and absurdly irregular verbs." In brief, he continues to consider it as a Spanish tongue with variants that strike him as rather arbitrary. It is obvious, of course, that Portuguese, when approached as a foreign language and not as a mode of the Castilian, is the easiest in the world for Spanish-speaking peoples.

In this very failure to view the language of Brazil as different from our own there is a great amount of unavowed kinship, a subconscious, familiar confidence. As is only logical, there are many essential differences in the language, literature, history, and psychology of the two peoples; but our interest will be focused as present on other aspects: on the series of historical processes common to both, on the common spiritual root, on the similar contemporary social factors. I shall comment on these correlations briefly and superficially, for an exhaustive study of the subject would require many volumes and an enormous quantity of details and literary documents which I do not have at my disposal at the moment.

The similarities in the systems of colonization of the Americas stem undoubtedly from those elements which Spain and Portugal share alike, and the differences, from the geography and topography of the colonies. The excited imagination of the early discoverers created a fabulous, legendary continent which at times approached reality and at others distorted it.

The Portuguese soldier, drunk with his desire for adventure and heroic grandeur, corresponded in his most complete definition with the type of the Spanish soldier. And the product of Renaissance culture—be his name Colón, Cortés, Anchieta, or Alvarez Cabral—expressed himself in the same way before the miracle of the discovery. In fact, José de Anchieta is a perfect symbol of the racial harmony that reigned on the virgin continent. Of Spanish-Portuguese origin, Anchieta brought to the New World the disquietude of his dual heritage and the severe cultural discipline of the University of Coimbra. He devoted himself ardently to the study of the *tupí* idiom, and wrote an *Arte da Gramática da Língua mais usada na Costa do Brasil* (A Grammar of the Language Most Used on the Coast of Brazil). He was an exemplary missionary, a founder of schools, initiator of the first dramatic enterprises among the Indians, and author of plays in the native tongues. His work is identical with that of the early friars, who helped mold the nascent Mexican culture, and whom we have already discussed in this series of essays.

But Anchieta cultivated his own soul as well, and like the Spaniards he wrote poetry in Latin, Spanish, Portuguese, and *tupí.* All Brazil was a constant source of wonder to him; and thus he says: "All Brazil is a cool forest garden and all year long one never sees a dried-up tree or plant. The groves of trees climb cloudward, wonderfully tall, thick and of varied species. Many produce good fruit. Their charm is enhanced by numerous beautiful birds whose songs are not excelled by the nightingales, goldfinches, linnets, and canaries of Portugal. When a man walks on the forest path, the birds sing so harmoniously that it makes him praise God, and the woods are so pleasant that the beautiful, man-made ones of Portugal rate much lower."[1]

Christopher Colombus, too, had discovered this luxuriant garden, this earthly paradise, when he viewed his first island, a land resplendent with giant trees, exquisite tropical flowers and birds, among which (imagination worthy of an Italian poet!) the nightingale (a purely European bird) gave forth its song. This marvelous new world, peopled with strange beings; with enormous sea cows, pearl-bearing oysters, fireflies by whose light one could read a book, men whose bodies were covered with gold dust; with mysterious *quetzal* birds which died upon being profaned by the eye of man; with fountains of eternal youth—all this was described in the same fashion by Pero Vaz de Caminha, Anchieta, Cortés, Díaz del Castillo, Acosta, Las Casas, and in general by all the missionaries and *conquistadores,* both Portuguese and Spanish, who possessed the divine gift of poetry.

Ever since the early days of the occupation of Mexico, the Spaniards used the theater as an effective means of catechization. The Indians, as we have seen already, contributed to these religious

[1] For notes to chapter xi see page 242.

festivals and even modified them with their dances, rhythms, musical instruments, masks, and plumage. The missionaries themselves composed these pious works, which the Indians enjoyed tremendously. *Misterios de Jesús, Autos de Adán y Eva,* and *Autos del Juicio Final* (*Autos* of the Day of Judgment), were presented on the Mexican plateau, on the highlands of Cuzco, on the *sertão* and in the jungles of Brazil, with Indians playing the role of Adam, Eve, or of the Holy Virgin, and with the entire performance directed by an Anchieta or a González de Eslava. The *auto sacramental* in Brazil and in the other American colonies marks a stage of more advanced evolution than the European; for the latter remained purely doctrinal, whereas the former was amplified with the profane moral theme and with commentaries on current incidents, which served to reveal to the Indians through concrete facts certain abstractions of dogma that otherwise were incomprehensible to them. And in these religious works, verses in *tupí* were mingled with the Portuguese, and commentaries in Aztec or Quechua with the florid Spanish.

The sixteenth century abounds in descriptions of the land: geographical treatises, narratives about the Indians, and innumerable letters to kings and governors. The names of Cardim, Gabriel Soares, and Pero de Magalhães Gandavo, in Brazil, and Sahagún, Xerez, and Acosta, in the Spanish colonies, are especially prominent in this regard. Shortly afterward a curious new genre came into vogue in America. This descriptive, novelesque type—as exemplified by *El Cautiverio feliz* (Happy Captivity) in Chile—recounts the adventures and suffering of white men who had fallen into the hands of the Indians. One of the first essays of this kind is the *Viagens e cativeiro entre os selvagens do Brasil* (Travels and Captivity among the Indians of Brazil), which was published in 1557 by the German, Hans Staden. The voyager, who was shipwrecked off the shores of America and taken prisoner by the Indians, offers numerous elements of reality as well as fiction in this work. Stories of captivity were exceedingly common in America, from the United States and Mexico to Chile, throughout the entire seventeenth century.

However, before continuing this brief account of the similarities and correlations in the cultural development of Brazil and the other American countries, we must pause to take full cognizance of a fact of extreme importance in an atmosphere of historic-literary creation: the early Hispanic American writers were heroic warriors of the conquering forces, men such as Bernal Díaz del Castillo and Ercilla y Zúñiga. The former, a humble soldier in the army of Cortés, never described a single deed that he had not seen with his own eyes. The latter, a fiery Spanish captain, mingled fantasy and imagination with the record of his experiences, in his noted epic *Araucana*. On the contrary, the first Portuguese writers of the colonial period, men such as Teixeira Pinto and Gabriel Soares, were farmers, and consequently wrote their interesting treatises on the land, describing the customs of the people, the flora of the region, and the strange aspects of life in the New World.

The first Brazilian poet, Teixeira Pinto, wrote his celebrated poem, *Prosopopéia,* toward the end of the sixteenth century, and a more patriotic than literary criticism has seen in its geographical descriptions, especially in those of Recife, the first true example of nativism. The work is written in a grandiloquent, hyperbolical style, encumbered with erudite quotations and mythological allusions. Highly involved and labyrinthine, it is one of the first indications of Gongorism in America. As in the case of Bernardo de Valbuena, it is not known whether the poet was born in Europe or in the New World. His poem, like Valbuena's *Grandeza mexicana* (The Greatness of Mexico), presents a superficial Americanism, based on the admiration that the author feels for the beauties of the land. We note in Teixeira's defense and encomium of Governor Jorge Dalbuquerque Coelho the emphasis upon the individual which is characteristic of the Hispanic American epic. This is further exemplified by the *Araucana* of Ercilla, and even more by the *Arauco domado* (Arauco Tamed) of the Chilean, Pedro de

Oña. In all these epics the poets are more concerned with the deeds of a specific hero than with the nobility of a people or a race.

The eighteenth century is characterized by the enormous influence of Gongoristic euphuism on American poetry. No country was exempt from the formula of affected style, nor was any poet free from the influence of Góngora and his *Soledades*. Preachers, orators, poets, and ordinary folk, from Mexico to Lima, sought to imitate in speech and writing the baroque elegance of *culteranismo,* adorning their style with Latin phrases, rare metaphors, and violent contrasts. Pedro de Oña, Peralta y Barnuevo, Espinosa y Medrano, Sigüenza, and even Sor Juana Inés de la Cruz, all fell into the excesses of Gongorism. Brazil underwent the same epidemic. According to Ronald de Carvalho: "Literature enjoyed great esteem, especially in Bahia. Poets of the Italian, Spanish and Portuguese Renaissance, such as Tasso, Góngora, Lope de Vega, Gabriel de Castro and others, were read and imitated. As among those of the Portugal of Don Francisco Manoel de Melo, the influence of Góngora and his followers prevailed among our literary men, almost all of whom had been educated abroad in Coimbra."[2] Thus, Bento Teixeira, Eusébio de Matos, Botelho de Oliveira,[3] and the most important poet of seventeenth-century Brazil, Gregório de Matos, adhered to the Gongorist school.

Gregório de Matos, we remark, is extremely simple in his satires, but affected and decorative in his more serious lyric compositions. In effect, he manifests amazing similarity to his contemporary, the Peruvian Juan del Valle y Caviedes. Both were men of high social position, reduced to a pitiful condition by their dissolute character and a life of vice. Both received an excellent education, but lost everything because of their licentious existence and caustic tongue. Both could have been exceptional lyric poets, but they prefered to sacrifice their talent in order to lash out at their enemies with cruel satires, coarse tirades in the worst taste, and affronts blazing with hatred. The vulgar language employed by both poets was also a concession to the taste for obscene poetry which then raged in Europe. The only difference between the two resides in the fact that Gregório de Matos utilized his cutting style in attacks upon all society—great and small, potentates and humble, black and white,—whereas the impoverished Peruvian, the roving vendor at Lima's doorways, the incurable syphilitic, concentrated all his hatred on the doctors of his time.

Juan Del Valle y Caviedes and Gregório de Matos have a personal, picturesque style, abounding in piquant, savory, popular expression. The academic, pseudo-classical, euphuistic style of the other poets sounds hollow alongside these poems which are alive even today. What a strange fate for these two strong personalities! It seems that their own sensibility was the cause of their destruction. First, they sacrificed the comforts of life in order to indulge an acrimonious tongue; later, they immolated their art, preferring incisive satire to the higher forms of lyricism. In spite of all this, I wish to do them the justice that mild critics have long denied them. In my opinion, they are the most genuine representatives of seventeenth-century poetic production. And although they may not be classified as great poets, it is indisputable that Juan del Valle y Caviedes is the most essentially Peruvian poet of his time, and Gregório de Matos the most profoundly Brazilian. Oliveira Lima says of his compatriot, in this respect: "A page from any of his contemporaries of Bahia could be considered the product of a Portuguese writer. But a satire of Gregório de Matos, on the contrary, is unmistakable: it bears the impress of Brazil, stamped with a die hitherto unknown."[4]

By changing only one word, the Peruvian could echo these words of Matos:

> Eu sou aquêle que os passados anos
> cantei na minha lira maldizente
> torpezas do Brasil, vícios e enganos.[5]

The influence of Gongorism continued dominant throughout Hispanic America during the eighteenth century, although neoclassicism offered serious opposition. One of the Brazilian disciples of euphuism was Antônio José da Silva, called *o Judeu* (the Jew), whose style is a mixture of popular and affectedly erudite elements. It is he who speaks of "the funeral urns of my sighs," of "the liquid monument of my tears," of "the conceits which spring from my lips like whirlpools." In effect, the style of this author reflects, like that of most Hispanic American pedantic writers of the epoch, the clash between dying Gongorism and neoclassicism of French origin, which was destined for a brilliant triumph.

It may be said that the rise of the school of Minas Gerais at the end of the eighteenth century marked the end of Gongorism, at least in its most salient characteristics.

The epic poets of this school, José Basílio da Gama and Santa Rita Durão, delayed in cultivating the genre, following the Spanish American writers by almost two centuries. Both *Uraguay* and *Caramurú* give evidence of the latent desire of their authors to introduce the literary myth of the Indian, to create nativist poetry. Despite these writers' use of classical mythology and allegory, Americanism is a fixed idea in their minds. It is a fictitious Indianism, of course, that paints the native girl, Paraguassú, "as white as the white snow," and another, Lyndoia, fading away by reason of frustrated love, in a melancholy yet delightful place of reverie:

> Onde ao pé de uma lapa cavernosa
> cobre uma rouca fonte que murmura,
> curva latada de jasmins e rosas.[6]

Nevertheless, this Indianism is no more false than that of Ercilla, who presents an Araucanian chieftain delivering a speech worthy of the oratory of Castelar, and the heroine Fresia flinging the son born of their love at the feet of her captured husband, in a heroic gesture typical of Calderón. Nor is it more artificial than the nativism of Pedro de Oña in his description of the beauty of this very heroine, "snow among the roses," as she leaves her bath; or in his picture of the swoon of the Indian girl, Gualeva:

> ¿Qué lilio, qué azucena o blanca rosa,
> a quien rompiendo el campo de pasada,

la reja descortés dejó cortada,
cayó sobre la yerba tan hermosa?
¿Ni cuál adormidera granujosa
inclina su cabeza coronada,
cual reclinó Gualeva el rostro bello
sobre el marmóreo laso y débil cuello?[7]

Nor is it more apocryphal than the Indianism of the Spanish American romantic poets and novelists, some of whom were strongly affected by the Brazilians. I may cite the poetry of the Uruguayan Magariños Cervantes, through whose veins coursed Portuguese blood. This poet also wrote his *Caramurú*, an Indianist novel, in which the traces of Basílio da Gama and Santa Rita Durão are clearly visible, and which manifests the direct influence of the *Confederação dos Tamoios* of Gonçalves de Magalhães.

This nativism, or rather indigenism, which appeared in Hispanic America toward the end of the eighteenth century, marks an easy transition to romanticism.

The founding of academies encouraged naturally a desire to shine in society, to vie in intellectual endeavors with the élite of the mother country, to exhibit a vast quantity of pseudo-literary and pseudo-scientific information. Consequently, there spread an epidemic of ultralearned literary efforts, exemplified by the beautiful poem *Rusticatio Mexicana,* written in Latin by the Guatemalan, Rafael Landívar, and *Tripoli,* also in Latin, by the Brazilian poetaster, José Francisco Cardoso. These works are indicative of the times: they represent identical ways of understanding the mission of poetry. They mark, in a sense, periods of artistic fatigue, which denote the death of one epoch and the birth of another, drawn from new sources, so that poetry may not die completely. The era announced by these manifestations is that of romanticism, a movement which assumed the same forms in Brazil as in the rest of Spanish America, where the literary vogue was intimately linked with the political philosophy of the times. The ideal of political independence, nurtured in the principles of the French

Revolution, found expression in the credo of the romanticists, thus removing them somewhat from the natural founts of inspiration of their race—from the Galician-Portuguese *cancioneros*[8] and the Castilian *romanceros*.[9] What we observed in Heredia, Echeverría, and the romanticists of the Indianist school is repeated in Gonçalves de Magalhães, Gonçalves Dias, Castro Alves, and the other Brazilian indigenists, who, paradoxically enough, acquired the cult of the "noble savage" from the Frenchman, Chateaubriand. This literary nationalism which rests on nature and primitive man induced Gonçalves de Magalhães to proclaim firmly that all Brazilians are the descendants of the Indians of the conquest. To this poet, as Sergio Buarque de Holanda observes, independence was merely the revolt of the rightful owners of the land against the Portuguese usurpers. The Spanish American romanticists, from Olmedo to Zorrilla de San Martín, defended this view. In fact, even present-day heirs of the romantic school in Mexico and Peru continue this very struggle.

Brazilian romanticism, which, like the Argentinian, was born in Paris about 1833, has its perfectly delineated elements: frustrated love, solitude, the sepulchral themes, the glorification of historic ruins, the sentimental interpretation of nature, and the struggle against slavery and tyranny. It is futile to seek its origin in the *mineira* school of Brazil or in the Latinist eclogue writers of Mexico and Guatemala; the great themes will always be, throughout the entire continent, those of the French poets and Lord Byron.

A comparative study of the works of Esteban Echeverría and Gonçalves de Magalhães would be of great value to an appreciation of the profound similarity that existed in the genesis of romanticism as between the two peoples. Both writers reflect the marked influence of Byron and Hugo; both were poets essentially classical in temperament who were converted to romanticism because of the exigencies of the time; both maintain that American nature should be the source of inspiration of the poets of the New World; both are the true initiators of romantic poetry in their respective countries; both are minor poets whose unique historical and anecdotal importance lies in their having inaugurated a movement; both are deeply concerned with the Indian, about whom they know nothing. Here—as later with respect to the gaucho—the Indian is a personage well suited to an operetta or melodrama, a figure who bears no resemblance to the actual being he is supposed to represent; an Indian who in many ways is the direct antithesis of the real Indian, but who, through Gonçalves Dias and Echeverría, is transformed into a national myth.

After the achievement of independence, Brazil and the Spanish-speaking nations of America continued their development in a like manner. All Brazilian efforts toward the establishment of their own national genius found their echo in Spanish American literature. At the outset, there predominated a desire to create the national literature of each people, a literature inspired by a picturesque language, native legends, or the historic roots of our early society. The names of Magariños Cervantes, Echeverría, Juan León Mera, José de Alencar, and José Hernández may be cited as examples of this tendency. Then there appeared several new types: the Indian in his primitive state, the mestizo, the inhabitant of the *sertão,* the pampa Indian of Argentina; the gaucho; the great landholder and his slave; or the Indian in relation to his Portuguese or Spanish master—all fictional types who are still considerably removed from the absolute reality of life on the continent.

A book that penetrates deeply into Brazilian actuality, especially into the daily life of Rio de Janeiro, is *Memórias de um sargento de milícias* (Memoirs of an Army Sergeant), by Manuel Antônio de Almeida. Although it is actually rather a picaresque novel, its depiction of regional customs, its creation of popular types, its accurate portrayal of the life of the lower and middle classes, its violent evolution toward naturalism, and its avoidance of literary style, its adoption, instead, of the speech of ordinary folk—all tend to draw it toward the work of the first Hispanic American realists.

It is easy to establish correlations, kindred forces, and similarities in a parallel study of the two literatures under discussion. However, when we approach a figure of exceptional value and unique genius our task becomes complicated. For example, how can we describe the particular genius of Machado de Assis? With which Spanish American writer can we compare him? As a novelist and writer of short stories, he admits of no peers either in Spanish or in his own language. In short, his work is the culmination of a classical literary culture; he is the most disciplined writer of his time, the one of most refined taste—in effect, a marvel of aesthetic culture. Yet despite all this, at least in my opinion, he is the most essentially Brazilian writer of his nation; he is the absolute antithesis of that other great stylist, the Gallicist Joaquim Nabuco, whose ideas resemble strongly those of the Uruguayan master, José Enrique Rodó.

We may pause no longer on a comparison of individuals. Suffice it to observe in summary that the European literary movements were reflected almost simultaneously throughout all of Hispanic America.

The Parnassian school took firm root in our lands because of its voluptuous sensitivity and its cult of form. The great Parnassian, Olavo Bilac, a poet of metallic verse and vibrant color, produced superb sonnets, amazingly similar to those of José Santos Chocano. The former, an emerald-seeker, was also the bard of the *bandeirantes* (those dauntless pioneers into the hinterlands of Brazil), the creator of heroic types. The Peruvian was the poet of the *conquistadores,* of the colonies, of the interior. Both chiseled their verse with the zealous care of the sculptor. In brilliance of form, resonance, and lyrical grandiloquence the poetry of Bilac and Chocano satisfies our conception of tropical inspiration.

The symbolist movement, with its soft, melancholy note and its primordial subjectivism, reached us through the poetry of Verlaine and found expression in America in the form of Catholicism, in such poets as Alphonsus de Guimaraens and Amado Nervo, and in a mystic sensuality in Rubén Darío and Cruz e Sousa. And here I must note the work of that exquisite poet, Alphonsus de Guimaraens, author of *Kiriale* (Kyrie), *Dona Mística, Câmara ardente* (The Burning Chamber), *Septenário das Dôres de Nossa Senhora* (The Seven Sorrows of Our Lady), and of numerous sonnets of admirable perfection in the Portuguese language. This fine symbolist poet at times approaches pure poetry, and reproduces in Portuguese a crepuscular type of verse such as Verlaine cultivated in French and Leopoldo Lugones in Spanish. In certain innovations of form Guimaraens may be compared with Julio Herrera y Reissig, but in his profound mysticism he bears closer resemblance to the Mexican mystic, Amado Nervo.

The superficial influence of symbolism fell into a precipitous decline, and poetry, strengthened internally by the succession of varied ideological schools, attained its pure essence in the writers who mark the culmination of its development, the Peruvian José María Eguren, and the Brazilians Cecília Meireles and Manuel Bandeira.

Returning to prose, we observe that the romantic novel had come to an end everywhere by 1880. The succeeding movement was naturalism, which was intensely concerned with social themes, the careful scrutiny of details, local color, and the somewhat capricious application to the novel of scientific principles of evolution and determinism. The end of this period witnessed the publication of the great work of Euclides da Cunha, *Os Sertões* (The Backlands of Brazil), which has been compared repeatedly with the *Facundo* of Sarmiento. It is true, of course, that both writers were especially interested in sociological themes, that many of their works treat of topographical, geographical, and ethnological subjects, and that their characters are the natural product of the barbarous land in which they live, and of the conflict between the civilizing force of the capital and the rude strength of the primitive interior, capable of producing an Antônio Conselheiro and a Facundo Quiroga. These works are the dramatic exaltation of the

American man and his atmosphere, the symbol of our future societies; in other words, they are the most finished examples of our regional literature. Euclides and Sarmiento are the first creators of a personal, vigorous style on the Hispanic American continent.

Sociological, racial, psychological, and political problems rise to the fore also in Graça Aranha's celebrated work, *Canaan,* a novel that was accepted enthusiastically by the Spanish American modernists. It is interesting to note that there exists among the Spanish American writers devoted to this genre—a genre especially cultivated by Carlos Reyles and Díaz Rodríguez—a strong preoccupation with nationalism, and simultaneously a rather euphuistic style which for manifold reasons does not harmonize with the theme.

Regionalism lends a fertile element of variety to our novel. In Brazil, the novel of the *sertão,* of the droughts, the mining zones, the south, and of the Amazon territory has long been prominent, with the more recent addition of the type dedicated to the region of Rio de Janeiro and São Paulo. In the other American nations the same criterion, more geographical than psychological, plays an important role in the following types of the novel: the Uruguayan and Argentinian gauchesque genre; the novel of the Andes, of the Amazon, of the tropics and of the great cities, with their respective atmospheres; and the novel of the saltpeter-mining area, of the highlands of Quito, of the northern ports on the West Coast, and of the Mexican plateau.

Spanish American modernism of 1888 was essentially a cultured movement, with little American vigor, except on occasion, in theme. But of what avail are such poems as Chocano's songs to the native fauna and flora if the form of expression is highly conventional? Darío himself in his *Canto a Roosevelt* and *Salutación del optimista* offers an Americanism of ideological approach, but his poetry remains intimately European.

I have few illusions about the possibility of a purely American art. I believe that, since culturally we are Europeans, any attempt to seek expression in primitive forms would seem like attempting a return to the era of the bow and arrow. Rather, our task is to equal and even to surpass the artistic production of Europe; our duty is to be super-Europeans, with the natural modifications imposed on us by the American atmosphere and racial growth.

Since 1920, poets have striven to free themselves from the yoke of French poetic intellectualism, from the sensibility that had given birth to French symbolism and to Spanish American and Brazilian modernism. In their search for freedom of expression these poets renounced the immediately preceding school; and we find many a writer truly representative of the current vogue who yet harbors within himself the germ of revolt. This phenomenon is evident today in the Brazilian Manuel Bandeira and in the Mexican González Martínez. In short, then, poets are struggling to substitute a new sensibility, new themes, new poetic forms, and a new language for the old. They have not accomplished, as some would desire, the decisive nationalization of literature, but they are doing something constructive and meaningful.

Leopoldo Lugones initiated the cultivation of themes pertinent to ranching and husbandry, with his volume *Los Ganados y las mieses* (Cattle and Grainfields). About 1920 the Mexican López Velarde created a new mode of expression with his provincial poems. The Colombian Luis Carlos López is the poet of the commonplace things of daily life, and Borges, Huidobro, Salvador Novo, Oribe, Vallejo, Hidalgo, and Carrera Andrade represent a new aesthetic consciousness similar to that represented in Brazil by Mário de Andrade, Jorge de Lima, Oswald de Andrade, Murilo Mendes, Raul Bopp, Schmidt, and Carlos Drummond de Andrade.

Mário de Andrade, in speaking of the modernist movement of destructive tendency, sees in it a profound convulsion of Brazilian reality, a sweeping change characterized by the fusion of three fundamental principles: the inviolable right of aesthetic investigation; the actualization of the Brazilian artistic intelligence, and the stabilization of a national creative conscience. These three norms are merged into an organic whole, a collective conscience. That was the innovation presented by the Brazilian modernism of 1922.

The modernist attempts to harmonize the national reality with "the instrument of work," in order to attain authenticity of expression. Consequently, efforts were made to introduce a national language into several of the Hispanic American nations. This theory reached its height in the admirable *Macunaíma* of Mário de Andrade and in *Cobra norato* of Bopp. The same process is manifest in the *Altazor* of Huidobro, in the poetry of Nicolás Guillén and, later, in the work of the young Ecuadorian novelists.

We have noted previously in these studies the influence that folklore and popular poetry exerted on the romantic movement. Now, with Brazilian modernism and the vanguard schools, we are once again witnesses to the same spectacle of popular pressure in themes, forms, and rhythms.

The poet of today aspires to the expression of his environment and times. He seeks the vibrant topic, the reflection of the masses, the theme of social struggle. Unfortunately, however, there still exists, at least among us Spanish Americans, a lack of harmony between the subject matter and the form of poetic expression.

This correlation is effected more successfully in the field of the novel. The Brazilians consider as a duty the accurate depiction of their national reality. We cannot fail to mention José Américo de Almeida, José Lins do Rêgo, Jorge Amado, Raquel de Queirós, and Graciliano Ramos, whose powerful novels give virile expression to the land, in a language that contains much of the earth's true savor. Theirs are works which interpret faithfully the atmosphere, the historical moment, and the typically Brazilian personage. The Spanish-speaking counterparts of these authors are José Eustasio Rivera, Rómulo Gallegos, Jorge Icaza, Aguilera Malta, Ciro Alegría, Nicomedes Guzmán, and José Rubén Romero, all of whom, deeply ensconced in the social theme and consistent in their regionalism, live in close contact with the man of their time. The novelist of today, throughout all Hispanic America, feels a profound disdain for "academic style" and for highly involved, scrupulously studied writing. He prefers to express himself in a vigorous American idiom, one which undergoes daily renovation. He scorns the historical novel and, in effect, all escape mechanism toward unknown worlds of fantasy. He is factual, without falling into the vulgarity of the newspaper columnist or the radio commentator. If at times we find him excessively crude in style, as happens in the work of Icaza, Gil Gilbert, Jorge Amado, and others, we must bear in mind that we are in a transition period, one of experimentation and artistic investigation. These Americanist writers were confronted with a task infinitely more difficult than that of their predecessors, who merely utilized the European models at hand. And, in truth, they have fulfilled their mission admirably.

◇ ◇ ◇

In this essay on literary relationships I have not tried to arrive at any conclusion, nor to achieve anything beyond the mere presentation of facts. I repeat here what I have said frequently in the past: the greatest and most genuine possession of the Hispanic American continent is its aesthetic vocation and, in part, its artistic realization. It is time for us to take serious interest in the men who dedicate and sacrifice their lives to the cultivation of beauty, for they are forming a nation—the realm of true culture that we are constantly building, slowly but surely.

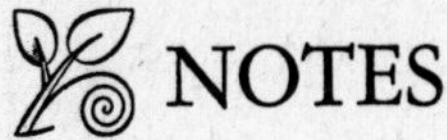

NOTES

NOTE TO CHAPTER I

Introduction

(Pages 1–19)

[1] M. Oliveira Lima. See *Aspectos da literatura colonial* (Leipzig, 1896), also *Aspectos da historia e da cultura do Brasil* (Lisboa, 1923).

NOTES TO CHAPTER II

Colonial Culture in America

(Pages 20–38)

[1] A high tribunal of varied jurisdiction.

[2] A native grinding stone for corn and maize.

[3] J. García Icazbalceta, *Obras,* Vol. 1, *Biblioteca de autores mexicanos* (México, 1896), pp. 166, 167.

[4] The *volador* is a ritual dance in the course of which the participants climb to the top of a hundred-foot pole, where they execute various turns and stops. Then, suspending themselves by the legs from a long rope tied to the top of the pole, they whirl about, head down, until the gradually unwinding rope allows them to reach the ground.

[5] M. Orozco y Berra, *Historia antigua y de la conquista de México* (México, 1880), Vol. 2, p. 540.

[6] Padre José de Acosta, *Historia natural y moral de las Indias* (México, 1940), p. 461.

[7] Great landlords to whom the Spanish king had granted large estates in the New World, and whose absolute jurisdiction extended over the Indians as well as over the natural resources of the region.

[8] H. I. Priestley, *The Mexican Nation* (New York, Macmillan, 1935), p. 98.

[9] The earliest novel of chivalry in Spain. Although its existence has been traced as far back as the fourteenth century, its first known edition appeared in 1508, to be followed by numerous sequels.

NOTES TO CHAPTER III

Sor Juana Inés de la Cruz

(Pages 39–67)

[1] Excessive subtlety of thought, characterized by highly involved, artificial, obscure metaphors—all in an effort to raise art above the level of the average intellectual. This school was given impetus by the Cordovan poet, Luis de Góngora (1561–1627).

[2] A one-act religious play, performed during the celebration of certain Church festivals, especially that of Corpus Christi. The renowned Spanish dramatist, Pedro Calderón de la Barca (1600–1681), excelled in this form.

[3] A *loa* is a short dramatic panegyric or prologue to a play.

[4] A *sainete* is a one-act farce or satirical piece. This form was later perfected by the Spaniard, Ramón de la Cruz y Cano (1731–1794).

[5] I know not why I feel this torment of love that in my heart arises, but indeed I know that I feel it.

[6] Pedro Salinas, *En busca de Juana de Asbaje* (*Memoria del Segundo Congreso Internacional de Catedráticos de Literatura Iberoamericana;* Berkeley, University of California Press, 1941), p. 189.

[7] *Ibid.*

[8] José María Vigil, "Sor Juana Inés de la Cruz," *Revista Europea* (October, 1876).

[9] Padre Calleja, *Aprobación, Fama y Obras posthumas* (Edition of 1701).

[10] That Fabio does not love me, when I adore him,
Is an unequaled grief, and hurts my will;
But that Sylvio loves me, though I abhor him,
Is no less penance, if a lesser ill.
Such suffering is hardly to be borne,
When toward my ears ever and ever move
Both the vain arrogance of a man I love
And the irksome sighing of a man I scorn.

If Sylvio's surrender wearies me,
I weary Fabio by surrendering;
By one I keenly seek to be approved,
The other courts my approval eagerly.
Active and passive is my suffering:
I grieve in loving, and in being loved.

(Translated by S. Griswold Morley)

[11] Love, at the first, is fashioned of agitation,
Ardors, anxiety, and wakeful hours;
By danger, risk, and fear it spreads its powers,
And feeds on weeping and on supplication.
It learns from coolness and indifference,
Preserves its life beneath faithless veneers,
Until, with jealousy or with offense,
It extinguishes its fire in its tears.

Love's beginning, middle, and its end are these:
Then why, Alcino, does it so displease
That Celia, who once loved you, now should leave you?
Is that a cause for sorrow and remorse?
Alcino mine, no, love did not deceive you:
It merely ran its customary course.

(Translated by S. Griswold Morley)

[12] This evening when I spoke with you, my love,
From your face and gesture well I knew
That with words I had not persuaded you
Of what you saw my heart desired to prove.

And love, who aided me in what I willed,
Achieved what seemed impossible to attain,

Since in the tears wherewith I clothed my pain
All my heart was melted and distilled.

Enough of rigors, belovèd: let them end!
No more shall tyrant jealousies intervene,
Nor vile suspicions your quietude offend

With hideous shadows and with vain demands;
Since in liquid essence you have touched and seen
All my heart melted here between your hands.
(Translated by Muna Lee)

[13] Tarry, shadow of my elusive treasure,
Image of witchery that I most desire,
Fair illusion for whom blissful I expire,
Fiction sweet I live for, anguished beyond measure.

Since to magnet of your graces turning
Obedient as steel is my devoted breast,
Why with beguilements make my heart your quest,
Then flit away in mockery of my yearning?

Yet can you never boast, as satisfied,
That crushed beneath your tyranny I fall;
Since mockingly though your fleet form evade
The close strait cincture that my arms had made,
Nor arms nor breast it avails you to deride:
Inescapable, my fancy builds your prison wall.
(Translated by Muna Lee)

[14] Silvio, I abhor you and still condemn
Your being in such wise present to my sense;
Iron to the wounded scorpion is offense,
And mud to whom its slime distains the hem.

You are like a poison wherein death throes wait
For whosoever pours it forth by chance;
You are, in brief, so false and foul of stance
That you are not even good to hate.

I give your sorry presence place again
In memory, though memory would say nay,
Forcing myself to bear deservèd pain;
For when I recall how once my heart approved you,
Not only you I come to loathe straightway,
But myself also, for what time I loved you.
(Translated by Muna Lee)

[15] You say I forget you, Celio, and you lie
In saying that I remember to forget you.
For within my thoughts there is no place let you
Wherein—even forgotten—to stand by.

Forgetfulness must take some memory's place
As the ash must be preceded by the ember.

But you have never won so great a grace:
There's nothing to forget nor to remember.

If you could be forgotten you might find
Joy to have been once remembered—even glory
Might fleetingly have known of being loved.
But so far are you from any such proud story,
Unremembering you not forgetfulness is proved
But merely a negation of the mind.

(Translated by Muna Lee)

[16] Dorothy Schons, "Some Obscure Points in the Life of Sor Juana Inés de la Cruz." *Modern Philology*, Vol. XXIV (November, 1926), p. 143.

[17] Padre Calleja, *Vida de Sor Juana* (México, 1936).

[18] You foolish men who unjustly accuse women, without realizing that you are the cause of what you censure.

[19] Pedro Salinas, *op. cit.*, p. 174.

[20] Rose divine, of gentle nurture,
With fragrant subtlety you are
Beauty's crimsoned avatar,
Snowy lore for grace's culture.

Image of our human doom,
Loveliness born to be blighted,
In whom nature has united
Happy cradle, mournful tomb.

How proud, how arrogant, in your disdain
You scorn the thought that you might chance to die;
Then when your petals shrunk and faded lie,
What withered symbols of your fate are plain!
Thus with wise death and foolish life you may
Living, mislead us, but dying, show the way.

(Translated by Muna Lee)

[21] Quatrains of eight-syllable lines, rhyming *abba*.

[22] See footnote 5.

[23] And when, so tenderly, I bewail my unhappy plight, I know that I am sad, but its cause eludes me.

[24] Offended for little reason, I am wont, despite my love, to deny the slightest favor to him to whom I would give my life.

[25] O sadness that pervades me, let us feign for a while that I am happy; perhaps you can persuade me, although I know the contrary.

[26] If a skillful hand does not prune the topheavy tree, the exuberance of the branches will starve the fruit.

What does it matter to the flowery field if autumn finds no fruit in a pleasant but not useful place which in May shows abundant flowers?

(Translated by Ruth J. Warner)

[27] There was a shepherdess of reflective mien, darling of the grove and envy of the heavens.

The Head Shepherd of Lofty Peak was wounded by her eye, snared in her hair.

Her beloved was precious myrrh to her, and she sheltered him on her snowy breast.

She has rich furnishings, well kept; her house is of cedar, her bed strewn with flowers.

She rejoiced that her dusky color was illumined by the rays of Phoebus.

For her, with lover-like anxiety, her Spouse passed through valleys, leaped over hills.

She inquired, in loving eagerness, where the lambs of her Spouse are grazing.

Her generous, tender beloved, with sweet endearments, calls to her from Lebanon.

To enjoy the embrace of her lover and lord, she exchanges the lowly valley for the lofty mount.

The holy shepherds on eternal Olympus sing praises to her in accents sweet.

But those of the valley, observing her flight, quickly say, in perplexed repetition:

(*Refrain*) To the mountain, to the mountain, to its summit, run, fly, you shepherds, for Mary is wafted away on the breeze; run, run, fly quickly, quickly, for she is carrying away souls and bodies, and, taking away for herself our riches, she leaves our village treasureless. (Translated by Ruth J. Warner)

[28] The flowers and the stars had a dispute. Oh, how clever they are! The stars speak through their sparkling and the flowers cry out with perfume. Listen to them wrangle, gentlemen, for they are now making their complaints.

First voice: Praise for the stars.

Second voice: Praise for the flowers.

Chorus: Praise for the stars and praise for the flowers.

The stars, it is plain to see, were honored by Mary so much that she adorned them with her eyes and her brow. Therefore, it is clear and evident that *they* were the most beautiful.

Chorus: Praise for the stars.

Was not any flower on Mary an affront to the stars, from the carnation of her lips to the lily of her feet? Therefore, it is more clearly seen that *they* were the best.

Chorus: Praise for the flowers.

The Virgin chose as the most worthy that with which she fashioned her crown, and her crown is made of flashings of light.

Chorus: Praise for the stars.

Most beauteous and shining is her flowery garment, and it is composed of many colors.

Chorus: Praise for the flowers.

On the stars the Virgin treads and among them she desires to reign, decorating with them the mark of her footsteps.

Chorus: Praise for the stars.

Among the flowers she acquired that state of glory which she attained; therefore, they are superior.

Chorus: Praise for the flowers.

First voice: Let the flashing stars fulminate.

Chorus: Praise for the stars.

Second voice: Let the glowing flowers radiate.

Chorus: Praise for the flowers.

First voice: Praise, praise for quarrelling.

Second voice: Praise, praise for crying out.

First voice: Battle against the flowers.

Second voice: War against the stars.

First chorus: Battle against the flowers.
Second chorus: War against the stars. (Transalted by Ruth J. Warner)

[20] Karl Vossler, *La décima Musa de México,* 1934.

NOTES TO CHAPTER IV

Independence and Romanticism

(Pages 68–87)

[1] Isaac Barrera, *Historia de la literatura hispanoamericana* (Quito, Ecuador, 1935), pp. 202–203.

[2] Depreciatory names applied to the Spaniards.

[3] My lyre! give me my lyre! My bosom feels the glow of inspiration.
(Translated by W. C. Bryant)

[4] Let God not permit that I die without my returning home, without my seeing the palms where the *sabiá* sings. (Translated by A. T.-R.)

[5] If there is a soft meadow covered with dew where one may find a sleeping flower, where you may find, my sweet love, violets and jasmine dying of love, I want to be that meadow full of flowers and light, where your feet, my love, sweetly tread; I want to be the soft breeze of that valley to kiss your lips and die.
(Translated by A. T.-R.)

[6] If you pass by my tomb some day and lover-like you call forth my soul, you will see a bird in the cypress tree; speak with it, for it is my soul.
(Translated by Ruth J. Warner)

[7] Sergio Buarque de Holanda, *Gonçalves de Magalhães* (Rio de Janeiro, 1939).

[8] Indeed I need to tell you that I love you, to tell you that I adore you, with all my heart; that I suffer a great deal, that I weep a lot, that I cannot stand so much strain, and with a loud cry I implore you, I implore you and I speak to you in the name of my final illusion. (Transalted by Ruth J. Warner)

[9] The title of this poem means "Pastoral Wedding." Its four parts read, in English, as follows:

I. The Village

Blue is the heaven, and the hillside gleams
with flowers and scents and woodland melodies;
murmuring doves seem floating on the breeze
and rushes are reflected in the streams.

Then comes Apollo with his dazzling beams
to bathe the beauteous vale on whose green flank
a sacred temple, as on a myrtle bank
a swan, stands white against the country scene.

Here Innocence, who with shepherds oft reposes,
spends in the peaceful village happy hours
among acacias, greenery, and roses,

and in the night she kisses, chaste Febea,
two cottages that shelter, mid the flowers,
Myrtilo one, the other Galatea.

II. The Meeting

With loosened locks the gentle shepherdess
comes to her door at the first morning choir;
she seems a lily clad in white attire
beflecked with gold, born with the dawn's caress.

And young Myrtilo in his rosiness
awaits her 'neath the verdant sycamores;
enamored swain, the virgin who adores
him knows his love for her is measureless.

She leads her flock of sheep with joyful crook,
and his uneasy goats he manages
toward a sheer rock above a shaded nook;

so the twain meet upon the slope: they see,
they speak, they kiss; and eagerly she says,
"My darling, when?" "Very soon," answers he.

III. The Wedding

The evening star has risen; and as Venus reigns
in heaven, so, within the hallowed church,
long waving streamers from the scented torch
scatter the darkness with their bluish flames.

The altar waits; soon there arrives the time
when the two lovers shall in wedlock meet:
she, like a pure and candid marguerite,
and he, a spikenard in its early prime.

The multitude uplifts a joyous cry:
"They come!" Alpheus the shepherd acolyte
directs the choir in simple pageantry.
There love attains the goal of its desire,
and, mid the perfume of the sacred rite,
"Hail bride! Hail bridegroom!" three times chants the choir.

IV. The Bridal Chamber

The bride draws near the marriage bed, disposed
with flowers by Joy and Love in rivalry;
clouded with mist is now the gentle eye
that once a loving mother's kisses closed.

Tears of virginity she sheds; the dress
that pridefully adorned the milk-white maid
slips from her tremulous shoulders, now displayed
in the same nudeness as her lovely breasts.

The goddess flees; toward the mysterious bed
the divine beauty goes, by Venus led,
and ill conceals the quivering of dismay.

Myrtilo, whispering, bends over her.
A cry is heard . . . But let no loiterer
draw from the nuptial couch the veil away.
(Translated By S. Griswold Morley)

[10] Sigh, O heart, so silent that no one hears the echo of your sigh. Without disturbing the dreams of the fortunate one, sigh, O silent heart. Feigning happiness and repose in the quiet shadiness of a secluded spot, sigh, O heart, so silent that no one hears the echo of your sigh. (Translated by Ruth J. Warner)

[11] The verses read, in English, as follows:

In every season of the year
A white rose I will gladly grow
For a true friend whom I know
To be frank and sincere.

And to the enemy whose blows
Destroy the peace in which I live
No thorn or thistle do I give:
I grow him a white rose. (Translated by S. Griswold Morley)

[12] Oh, how sweet a song! Limpid, it gushes forth, spreading its tender harmonies. And it seems to bear in each note much of my sadness and tenderness . . .

Whose is that voice? It seems to rise up near the blue lake, on a quiet night, mounting through space and scattering its notes when it touches the glass of the window which is half opened by the poet's sweetheart.

How many swans sport on the lake! How blue are the restless, leaping waves! How much moonlight in this quiet scene! But the souls, how sad and solitary they are! (Translated by Ruth J. Warner)

[13] One night, a night of murmurings, perfume, and the music of wings; a night when fantastic fireflies glowed in the humid, nuptial darkness, slowly at my side you walked, clinging to me, silent and pale, as though a presentiment of infinite sorrow shook you in the innermost fibers of your being. Forward on the flowery path that crosses the plain you walked; and in the boundless, fathomless blue sky the full moon spread its white light; and your slender, languid shadow and my shadow, projected by the moon's rays on the sorrowful sand of the path, joined together. And they were one, united, one single, long shadow.

Tonight, alone, my soul filled with the infinite sadness and agony of your death, separated from you by time, by the grave, by space, by the black infinity across which speech cannot reach, silent and alone I walked along the path; and dogs were howling at the moon, the pallid moon, and frogs were croaking. I felt cold. It was the cold of your beloved cheeks and temples and hands, there in your room between the snowy white sheets of your deathbed. It was the cold of the tomb, the ice of death, the cold of nothingness. And my shadow, by the moon's rays projected, went alone, alone across the lonesome plain; and your shadow approached, tall and nimble, slender and languid, as on that warm night of the now dead springtime, as on that night of murmurings, perfume, and the music of wings. Your shadow drew near and walked with mine. Oh, interlaced shadows! Oh, shadows of bodies which unite with shadows of souls! Oh, shadows which seek each other on nights of sadness and weeping! (Translated by Ruth J. Warner)

NOTES TO CHAPTER V

Martín Fierro

(Pages 88–105)

[1] E. Tiscornia, *Martín Fierro* (Buenos Aires, 1925): "In Camarones and Laguna de los Padres he learned how to control a horse; he observed and even took part in the crude tasks of cattle raising, which were performed by the gauchos, under the direction of his father. Thus did he spend his boyhood, receiving a hearty preparation for life."

[2] Loose trousers fastened at the bottom.

[3] Improvised song of the *payador,* gaucho singer of the plains.

[4] I use this term in paraphrase of that applied to the old popular epic genre of the Spanish Middle Ages, *mester de juglaría,* and to the cultured, generally clerical form, employing the Alexandrine, *mester de clerecía.*

[5] Rural general stores.

[6] The quotations marked with note numbers 6 to 30 and 33 to 35 are from José Hernández, *Martín Fierro*. The translations in the notes are from *The Gaucho Martin Fierro,* adapted from the Spanish and rendered into English verse by Walter Owen (New York, Farrar and Rinehart, 1936), xxiv + 326 pp., the specific pages as indicated. Thus the first:

There was a time when I knew this land
As the gaucho's own domain;
With children and wife, he had joy in life,
And law was kept by the ready knife
Far better than now; alas, no more
That time shall come again.

I mind me well when the star of dawn
Gleamed high in the holy sky,
And the cock's shrill crow and the cattle's low
Rose up like a hail in the morning glow,
How the hands to the kitchen's cheery blaze,
In the paling dusk went by.

And scarcely daybreak's red had paled
To the blue of the full-blown dawn,
And the birds to sing as they took to wing,
And the hens began their foraging,
When each with a cheery hail went off,
And the morning's work was on. (Translated by Owen, pp. 6–7)

[7] When work was o'er, in the village store,
'Twas my delight to sing.
I would warm my throat with a glass or two,
And sing as now I sing to you,
When I'm primed, the couplets bubble out
Like water from a spring. (Translated by Owen, p. 15)

[8] Only a few bare poles were left,
And the thatch and nothing more;
Christ knows it was a mournful sight,
It withered my heart up like a blight,
And there in the wreck of my ruined home,
To be revenged I swore. (Translated by Owen, p. 45)

[9] I cleaned my knife on a clump of grass,
I untethered my nag from the rail;
I took my time to mount, and then,
At a canter I hit the trail. (Translated by Owen, p. 55)

[10] Come then my luck; let's be off together,
Since together we began.
Together we must lose or win,
And stick it out through thick and thin.
If they bar my path, I will open it up
With my knife, as befits a man. (Translated by Owen, p. 61)

[11] I gathered together their remains,
And I knelt and said a prayer;
. . .
And then I asked God to forgive my soul
For killing so many there. (Translated by Owen, p. 71)

[12] "We're chips, said I, of the selfsame block,—
We'd might as well match our plans;
I'm a gaucho that's got an evil name
And more or less you're much the same;
And as for me—to end this mess,
I'm off to the Indians." (Translated by Owen, p. 91)

[13] When he got to this point the singer stopped,
And grabbed for the liquor jar;
Straight up to heaven he tipped his chin,
And when he had sluiced his pipes with gin,—
On the ground with a crash, at a single bash,
He shivered his guitar.
"Lie there," he said to the instrument;
"Don't tempt your master more;
I'll not have another twang your strings,
And fondle you, while his songs he sings,
Nor ever another shall take up
That song that here is o'er!" (Translated by Owen, p. 96)

[14] And then one day, when the sun's first ray
Made the plain like a sheet of gold,
Cruz pointed back where the eye scarce caught
The last ranch stand like a tiny dot,
And as he looked, two burning tears
Down the cheeks of Fierro rolled. (Translated by Owen, p. 97)

[15] Man's first look-out is to see he keeps
His hide from getting holed;
. . .
The devil is sly, for he's built that way,
But he's slyer because he's old. (Translated by Owen, p. 197)

[16] Just look at the rat—it's sleek and fat
Though it dens in dirt and grime;
You copy it—don't change your lair,
Stay put where your nose first sniffed the air;
The cow that's changed from her grazing ground
Gets late in the calving-time. (Translated by Owen, p. 197)

[17] By a woman that weeps or a hound that limps
Don't ever be taken in. (Translated by Owen, p. 198)

[18] The pig may be greedy that eats its young
But what does it care?—it's fatter! (Translated by Owen, p. 198)

[19] The cow that gives the richest milk
Is the one that longest chews. (Translated by Owen, p. 198)

[20] For each little pig at his private tit
Is the proper way to suck. (Translated by Owen, p. 199)

[21] And woman's an animal, my boy.
I don't get any road,
She'll fall for the man that's quick and game,
But keep your eye on her all the same
For her heart's as roomy and big and soft
As the belly of any toad. (Translated by Owen, p. 199)

[22] You can work like a slave, but unless you save
Some day you'll beg your clothes,
If you haven't got thrift in your bone and blood
Some day with your muzzle you'll plough the mud.
"Pot-belly born, puts belts to scorn,"
The good old saying goes.
Blow here, blow there, it's little I care,—
Come rain on my weathered pelt;—
If I hit bad luck I tip my chair
And take a good swig at my crock of gin;
If I'm wet outside I even up
With a sousing inside my belt. (Translated by Owen, p. 200)

[23] Just tell me now, what in all the world
Is the song that the earth is singing? (Translated by Owen, p. 274)

[24] Her song is the voice of motherhood
In the bearing pangs of her mighty brood,
The last death-sighs and the first birth-cries
Of her countless generations. (Translated by Owen, p. 274)

[25] And quick on the spot, just tell me what
Is the song that's the Ocean's song. (Translated by Owen, p. 275)

[26] When the mighty winds o'er the ocean blow,
The waters all round the earth
Rise up and sing with a dreadful roar,
Till the whole world trembles from shore to shore,
Like a beast it howls in earth's rocky bowels
As if raging to come to birth. (Translated by Owen, p. 275)

[27] They're the whisperings of the secret things
That the shadows of night enclose,
The phantom voices that haunt the ear,

When a cry goes up in the midnight clear,
Like the muffled tone of an endless moan
From a source that no man knows. (Translated by Owen, p. 276)

[28] The shining fish that swim the sea
Have their loves, just the same as man;
From the ocean's deeps to the skies above,
There's nothing's got life that hasn't love;
God made them together and yoked them up,
The day that the world began. (Translated by Owen, p. 278)

[29] They would gather there the blaze around,
Till the sun rose round and red;
The kettle sang, and piping hot,
They sucked at the circling 'mate' pot,
While their 'chinas,' rolled in their 'poncho's' folds,
Lay snugly yet abed. (Translated by Owen, p. 7)

[30] Till with crops well-gorged with meat and wine,
When the embered fire grew dim,
Each doffed his jacket and boots and belt,
And snugged him down on a fleecy pelt.
With his 'china' beside him, many a lord
Might well have envied him. (Translated by Owen, p. 10)

[31] Eleuterio Tiscornia, who has devoted a book to the language of *Martín Fierro,* sums up thus his ideas on the subject:

"*Martín Fierro* is written in a mixed tongue, composed of Spanish archaisms and of American indigenous expressions, a dialect that we commonly call 'gauchesque language.' This mode of speaking, inherited from the early colonizers, was conserved in our rural districts, and was transmitted, with the modifications of the environment, from father to son until the disappearance of the gauchos. No one speaks that language any more. A small portion of its vulgar pronunciations and of its vocabulary may still be recognized in the popular speech of Argentina, but the standardizing desire of the public schools and the leveling power of urban education tend increasingly to improve the national language and to make it conform with the exigencies of culture.

"The gauchesque language, which now neither exists nor carries weight socially, persists in its own expression in literary texts. It is, then, a historic fact which, only in this respect, should be rightly considered and studied."

[32] Ricardo Rojas, *La Literatura argentina,* Vol. II (Buenos Aires, 1924), pp. 840–841.

[33] I will sing my song till my breath gives out,
I will sing when they bury me;
And singing I'll come where the angels roam
The rolling plains of their starry home,—
Into this world I came to sing,
As I sang on my mother's knee. (Translated by Owen, p. 2)

[34] 'Tis little I have of bookman's craft,
Yet once let me warm to the swing
And the lilt and beat of the plainsman's song,—
I will sing you strong, I will sing you long,
And the words will out like the tumbling rout
Of waters from a spring. (Translated by Owen, p. 3)

[35] With my mellow guitar across my knee,
The flies even give me room,
And the talk is stilled, and the laugh and jest,
As I draw the notes from its sounding breast;
The high string sighs, and the middles weep,
And the low strings mourn and boom. (Translated by Owen, p. 3)

NOTES TO CHAPTER VII

A Reëvaluation of Rubén Darío

(Pages 120–137)

[1] Darío's *Triumphal March* reads, in English, as follows:
They're coming! They're coming!
They march in procession! Already we hear the ringing bugles.
We catch the reflected gleam from their sabers;
with iron and gold arrayed the paladins' corps is approaching.
Now they are passing under the arches embellished in marble with Mars and Minerva,
those arches triumphal where Fame lifts high her far-sounding trumpet,
and in solemn grandeur the standards are raised
by the brawny hands of heroic athletes.
We hear the sound the accouterments of the horsemen are making,
the champing of bits by the powerful, warlike horses,
the clack of their hoofs as they strike on the ground,
and the beat of the drummers
keeping the step with the rhythm of their martial music.
Thus under the arches triumphal
are passing our war-hardened veterans.

Now the clear-sounding clarions are raising their voices,
their clamor sonorous,
their heartwarming chorus,
which enfolds in a golden thunder
the majestical pride of the banners.
It speaks of the combat, of vengeance provoked,
of the horses' harsh manes,
of the rough-fashioned plumes, the pike and the lance,
of the blood that streams in heroic carmine
over the earth,
of the grim mastiffs
which death incites and war controls.

The bugles' golden notes
are announcing now the arrival
triumphant of the Flag;
leaving the lofty peak that guards their nests,
and spreading to the breeze their wings enormous,
the eagles descend, for victory has come!

The parade now is passing.
The grandsire points out the heroes to the child.
See, how the beard of the old man
surrounds with ermine his grandson's golden curls.
The lovely women fashion their wreaths of flowers,
and under the doorways we see their rosy faces;
and the most beautiful
smiles at the fiercest among the conquerors.
Honor to him who bears captive the flag of the enemy!
Honor the wounded, and honor the faithful
soldiers who met their deaths at the hand of the stranger!
Clarions! laurels!

The noble swords of other glorious times
from their place on the wall salute the new-won crowns and laurels—
those ancient swords of grenadiers stronger than bears,
brothers, they, of those lancers who were centaurs—
The warlike trumpets reëcho;
they fill the air with their voices . . .
Those ancient swords,
those famous blades of steel
embodying the glories of past days . . .
And the sun that shines today on the victories newly gained,
the hero who leads his troop of fierce young warriors,
him who loves the flag of his motherland,
him who, girded with steel, with weapons in his hands,
has dared the burning sun of summer,
the snows and freezing winds of winter,
the night, the hoarfrost,
and hate and death, to become for his country immortal:
all these the horns of war with brazen throats
salute as they sound the march
triumphal! . . . (Translated by G. Dundas Craig)

[2] The symbol of the swan, French-inspired and used to the point of abuse to represent grace and purity, was highly popular among the modernists, who followed the lead of Darío in its adaptation. For "wringing the swan's neck" González Martínez was indebted to Verlaine's line in *Art poétique:* "Prends l'éloquence et tords-lui son cou (Take Eloquence and wring his neck)."

[3] A fourteen-syllable line, stemming originally from the erudite *mester de clerecía,* but utilized and varied by subsequent schools.

[4] The title of the poem means "My Beloved speaks." It reads, in English: My poor pale soul was a chrysalis. Then a rosy-colored butterfly. A restless breeze told my secret . . . "Hast thou known thy secret one day? Oh, my beloved! Thy secret is a melody fashioned of a moon ray." "A melody?"

[5] Love your rhythm and rhyme your deeds according to your law, as you do your verses: you are a universe comprising other universes, and your soul is a fountain of songs.

The heavenly unity which you presuppose will cause different worlds to come forth from you, and when your dispersed parts resound it demonstrates Pythagorean theories in your constellations.

Listen to the divine rhetoric of the birds of the air and conjecture about the geometric irradiation of the night; extinguish taciturn indifference and link pearl with crystalline pearl into which truth pours its treasure.

(Translated by Ruth J. Warner)

[6] I seek an elusive form for my style, bud of thought which desires to be a rose; it is announced by a kiss which is placed on my lips when Venus de Milo bestows her impossible embrace.

Green palms adorn the white peristyle; the stars have foretold to me the vision of the goddess; and in my soul there reposes a light as the bird of the moon rests on a tranquil lake.

And I find only that the word escapes, the melodic beginning which flows from the flute and the dream boat which glides in space; and under the window of my Sleeping Beauty, the continuous sobbing of the fountain's jet and the neck of the great white swan which interrogates me. (Translated by Ruth J. Warner)

[7] In my garden people saw a beautiful statue; they thought it marble and it was living flesh; a young soul lived within; sentimental, sympathetic, sensitive.

(Translated by Ruth J. Warner)

[8] The title of the poem means "The Sweetness of the Angelus." It reads, in English:

The sweetness of the angelus divine
That simple rustic bells diffuse each morn
In an air of innocence, of roses born,
Of prayers, of virgin dreams, and rapture fine

Of nightingale, opposed to fate malign
That fears not God . . . The evening's golden skein
Coiled up behind the night's dark crystal bourne
To spin the seamless web of our lot forlorn,

With flesh inwoven, and scented all with wine . . .
And the bitterness of finding joy in naught,
Of knowing not whither to steer our way

While the poor bark in night's deep darkness caught
Makes fight against the billows, orphan'd of day . . .
(Oh, soothing of the bells by morning brought!)

Translated by G. Dundas Craig, in *The Modernist Trend in Spanish-American Poetry* (Berkeley, University of California Press, 1934), p. 65.

[9] Spider, salute the Sun! No rancor show.
Give God your thanks, O toad, that you exist.
The hirsute crab has such thorns as has the rose.
In the mollusk reminiscence of woman is.

Since shapes are mysteries, learn to wear your own;
The responsibility is of the Norms alone,
Which they in turn leave to the All-Powerful's care.
Fiddle, cricket, in the moonlight; dance on, bear.

(Translated by Muna Lee)

[10] Cleopompo and Heliodemo, whose philosophies are the same, take pleasure in talking together beneath the green canopy of the banana grove. There Cleopompo bites into the Epicurean apple and Heliodemo airs his confidence in eternal harmony. Woe to that inhuman one who remembers the Fates! If he loses one sonorous drop of the water clock, it will not be offered again by the hand from which it comes.

A cow appears, twilight-like. It is the hour when the cricket sings praises to Flora, and in the blue a lofty diamond comes into flower. And in the large eye of the peaceful animal, Cleopompo and Heliodemo watch how the music of the world revolves in visible rhythm. (Translated by Ruth J. Warner)

"That tree which moves its leaf is hankering for something. That tree of the handsome look acts as though it wants to put forth flowers. It longs for something. (Translated by Ruth J. Warner)

[12] Unhappy he who his inner sphinx one day
Observes and questions deeply. Lost is he.
Alas for who believes that Grief or Joy will stay.
Ignorance and Forgetfulness: two gods have we.

What the tree desires to say and says to the wind,
That for which animals by instinct expression find,
Into thought and into speech we must crystallize—
Yet only in manner of saying a difference lies.

(Translated by Muna Lee)

[13] The title of the poem means "Doom." It reads, in English:

Happy the tree that scarcely feels,
And happier hard stone that feels not at all,
Since no pain is greater than pain of being alive,
Nor burden heavier than conscious life.

To be, and to know nothing, with the goal unsure,
And the fear of having been, and a future terror . . .
And the frightful certainty of being dead tomorrow,
And to suffer for life and for the shadow and for

What we know not and hardly suspect,
And the flesh that tempts us with its bright clusters,

And the tomb that waits with its funeral wreaths,
And not to know whither we go,
Nor whence we come— (Translated by Muna Lee)

[14] Nevertheless, life is beautiful, for it possesses pearl, rose, star, and woman.

And we feel life to be pure, clear, genuine, when it is surrounded by springtime sweetness.

Enjoy the flesh, that treasure which bewitches us today and later will turn to dust and ashes.

Enjoy the sun, the pagan light of its blaze; enjoy the sun, for tomorrow you will be blind.

Enjoy the sweet harmony which Apollo invokes; enjoy singing, for one day you will have no mouth.

Enjoy the earth, which contains a positive good; enjoy the earth because you are not yet beneath it.

Life pours into us force and warmth. Let us go to the Kingdom of Death by the highway of Love. (Translated by Ruth J. Warner)

[15] Into the west sinks the setting sun; clothed in gold and royal dignity it will return tomorrow. In life there are twilight hours which make us weep, for there are suns which depart and never again return.

The magic illusion disappears in a passionate ending, and it is accompanied by a song from the heart.

There was a king of Colchis or perhaps of Thule; a king of lyrical dreams who smiled one time. Concerning this hermetical smile it was never well known whether it was painful or wan or whether it sprang from pleasure.

The magic illusion disappears in a passionate ending, and it is accompanied by a song from the heart.

The melancholy evening sobs o'er the sea. The Evening Star in the sky shines in godlike peace. And in the quivering air there are deep desires to sigh because it passes with Zephyr like the autumnal soul.

The magic illusion disappears in a passionate ending, and it is accompanied by a song from the heart. (Translated by Ruth J. Warner)

[16] Which path is indicated, which is the holy road, when Jesus preaches or when Nietzsche praises?

The way of affection or the way of work? The way of power or the way of love?

Find rapture in the opium which calms one's sadness. Be the martyr of one's soul or be the hero one's self.

Martyrize one's life against one's judgment, and make it resolved to go to the sacrifice.

Have one's will power made of steel and gold; possess honesty as an inward treasure.

Or else be the tyrant who suddenly rises, with project in mind or sword in hand.

(Translated by Ruth J. Warner)

[17] Ramiro de Maeztu, "El Clasicismo y el Romanticismo de Rubén Darío," in *Nosotros* (Buenos Aires, January, 1922).

[18] One twilight-time I thought to compose a song in which all my personal essence would be expressed by my word; St. Paul's preaching or the lamentations of Job, evangelical verses or precepts of Solomon, O Lord!

Toward what indefinite Compostela was I bound in pilgrimage? With Valle Inclan or with St. Roch, whither were we bound, Master? Could the little dog which followed us possibly be a lion? We were following a vast multitude from all parts of the world, arriving for the great pilgrimage. It was a black, black night, for the sun had perished: we communicated with gestures, for speech had died. In everything there reigned a fearful and profound desolation, O Lord!

(Translated by Ruth J. Warner)

[19] The cathedral towers appeared. The divine hours of pure morning, the silks of the dawn greeted our arrival with bells and singing swallows, O Lord!

(Translated by Ruth J. Warner)

[20] I continue to cry peace, peace, peace. (Translated by Ruth J. Warner)

[21] . . . hateful to the sweet creatures since you are the giver of arrows and bullets, may you be cursed . . . (Translated by Ruth J. Warner)

[22] . . . putting dagger to throat or unsheathing sword; and in God's name, houses of God in Rheims and Louvain are being tumbled down by the 42 howitzer.

(Translated by Ruth J. Warner)

[23] It is certain that war is infernal; certain that there dwells a wolf in the mortal soul of unredeemed man; but Jesus Christ is not dead, and against killing, hating, robbing, He is the Light, the Way, and the Life.

(Translated by Ruth J. Warner)

NOTES TO CHAPTER VIII

José Enrique Rodó

(Pages 138–153)

[1] See note 7 to chapter vii.

[2] José Enrique Rodó, *Ariel*, translated by F. J. Stimson (Boston, Houghton Mifflin, 1922), p. 4.

[3] *Ibid.*, pp. 33–34.

[4] Gonzalo Zaldumbide, *Montalvo y Rodó* (New York, Instituto de las Españas, 1938), p. 275.

[5] Rodó (Stimson), *op. cit.*, pp. 14 ff.

NOTES TO CHAPTER IX

Social Poetry

(Pages 154–184)

[1] My country has palm trees where the *sabiá* bird sings . . .
(Translated by A. T.-R.)

[2] The princess is sad; what ails the princess? (Translated by A. T.-R.)

[3] This was a blue fly, golden and red wings, daughter of China or Hindustan, born among the petals of a red rose, a certain summer night.
(Translated by A. T.-R.)

[4] Our skies have more stars, our meadows have more flowers, our forests have more life, our life has more love. (Translated by A. T.-R.)

[5] It is sweet to think of Death when our body, exhausted from pleasure or pain, suffers to the utmost. It is sweet to think of Death.
(Translated by A. T.-R.)

[6] O lips that I shall never kiss, another's lips, laughing at me, in the fraction of space that separates us all depth is contained! (Translated by A. T.-R.)

[7] I, with this coldness growing in my heart, so full of you, long for the horror of the tomb! You, seeing the mouth twisting in agony that was kissed by your burning lips, the mouth that was yours. (Translated by A. T.-R.)

[8] If your nude and green presence, if your boundless apple, if your mazurka in the darkness, where is your origin? (Translated by A. T.-R.)

[9] Cecília Meireles, *Poetas novos de Portugal* (Edicões Dois Mundos; Rio Janeiro, 1944), p. 18.

[10] *Ibid.*, p. 18.

[11] *Ibid.*, p. 19.

[12] *Ibid.*, p. 19.

[13] Yesterday they called me "nigger" so that I should get mad; but he who called me thus was as black as I am. You pretend to be so white—but I know your grandmother. (Translated by A. T.-R.)

[14] With so much English you knew, Bito Manue, with so much English, now you don't know how to say "yes."

The American girl goes after you, but you have to run from her, your English was only "strike one, strike one," and "one, two, three."

Bito Manue, you don't know English. Never fall in love, Bito Manue, if you don't know English. (Translated by A. T.-R.)

[15] On what a Yankee drinks in one visit to the bar, anyone else could eat for a whole year. (Translated by A. T.-R.)

[16] Soldier, I can't figure why
you should think I hate you,—
why, we are the same, we two,
me,
you.

You are poor, and so am I;
I'm from down under, so are you;
where in the world did you get the idea,
soldier, that I hate you?

I'm sorry that you sometimes
can forget who I am; why,
hell, man! but I *am* you,
just the same as you are me.

But that's no reason why I should
have a grudge against *you:*
if we are the same, we two,
me,
you,
soldier, I can't figure why
you should think I hate you.

We'll see each other, you and me,
out in the same street together,
shoulder to shoulder, you and me!
With no hatreds, me or you,
but knowing well, you and me,
where we're going, me and you . . .

Soldier, I can't figure why
you should think I hate you!

(Translated by H. R. Hays in Dudley Fitts, *Anthology of Contemporary Latin-American Poetry* (New Directions, Norfolk, Conn., 1942), p. 245.

[17] Pertaining to *Apra,* which is derived from the initials of the name of the party, *Asociación Popular Revolucionaria Americana* (Popular American Revolutionary Association).

[18] Muledriver, you are incredibly glazed with sweat. The Menocucho Plantation collects a thousand daily sorrows for your life. Noontime. We are in the middle of the day. The sun hurts a lot. Muledriver, you trudge away in your bright-hued blanket, relishing the Peruvian romance you find in your wad of coca leaves. (Translated by Ruth J. Warner)

[19] When the battle was finished,
and the fighter dead, a man came toward him
and to him said, "Do not die, I love you so!"
But the corpse, alas, went on dying!

Then two drew near to say once more,
"Do not leave us! Courage! Come back to life!"
But the corpse, alas, went on dying.

Then twenty, a hundred, a thousand, five hundred thousand came,
clamoring, "So much love and against death to no avail!"
But the corpse, alas, went on dying.

Millions of individuals surrounded him,
beseeching as one: "Stay, brother!"
But the corpse, alas, went on dying.

Then all the men in the earth
surrounded him; the corpse looked at them sadly, deeply moved;
sat up slowly,
embraced the first man; and began to walk . . .

(Translated by Kenneth Edwards)

[20] León Felipe. See *El Payaso de las bofetadas y El Pescador de caña* (México, 1938); *Ganarás la Luz* (México, 1943).

[21] Gentle caressing love, sweet and fair, I shall go away, and you too will go away, my love.

[22] I depart. I am sad; but I am always sad. I come from your arms. I know not where I go. A child bids me farewell from your heart and I tell him good-bye.

[23] I understand, friends, I understand it all. Another's words united with mine, I understand that, friends! As if I were wanting to fly and the wings of birds arrived to help me, all the wings; thus came these alien words to unleash the confused intoxication of my soul. (Translated by Ruth J. Warner)

[24] "And thus some evening–cruel-handed love–kneeling, I shall thank thee." . . . Friend, banish with the evening this desire of mine that every rosebush belong to me. Friend, if you are hungry, eat of my food.

(Translated by Ruth J. Warner)

[25] Cities–soot and vengeance–gray filthiness of suburbs, the office which makes shoulders droop, the boss with troubled eyes. (Translated by Ruth J. Warner)

[26] In the heavens there is a vast country with fabled flowery fields of the rainbow and evening vegetation: thither will I go, not without some anguish, treading earth removed from recent graves; in confused fashion I dream among those vegetable plants. (Translated by Ruth J. Warner)

[27] I am encompassed by one thing, one single movement; the mineral's weight, the skin's sheen adhere to the meaning of the word–night: the color of wheat, of ivory, of weeping, leather, wooden, woolen things, old, discolored, worn smooth, they unite around me like walls– (Translated by Ruth J. Warner)

[28] I am in the presence of your wave of dying odors,
enveloped in autumn and resistance.
I am setting out on a funeral journey
amid your yellow scars.
I, with my laments without origin,
without food, sleepless, lonesome,
am entering darkened corridors,
arriving at your mysterious substance.

(Translated by Kenneth Edwards)

[29] From the pure center that sounds never
penetrate, from the untouched wax,
come forth bright linear lightning flashes,
doves bent on endless spiraling,
toward sluggish streets with the odor
given off by fish and shadow.

They are the veins of celery! They are the foam, the laughter,
the hats of celery!
They are the marks of celery, its savor
of fireflies, its maps
of inundated color,
and its green angel's head droops,
and its delicate curls are grieving,
and the feet of celery enter the markets
of the wounded morning, amid sobs,
and the doors close upon its passing,
and the docile horses kneel down.

Their feet are cut from them, their green eyes
are scattered about, submerged in them forever
are their secrets and their drops of water.
The sea's tunnels from which emerge
the stairways that celery prescribes,
unhappy submerged shadows,
resolutions suspended in midair,
kisses in the heart of stones.

At midnight, with drenched hands
someone in the mist pounds upon my door,
and I hear the voice of celery, an unfathomable voice,
a harsh voice of wind imprisoned,
complains, wounded by water and roots,
buries in my bed its bitter misfortunes,
and its lawless scissors are thrust into my breast,
searching for the opening of my oppressed heart.

What do you wish, O fragile corseted guest
in my funeral chambers?
What shattered girdle encompasses you?
Fibers of opacity and weeping light,
blind bindings, vexed energies,
river of life and essential filaments,
green stalks of caressed sunlight,
here am I, in the night, listening to secrets,
vigils, solitudes,
and you enter in the midst of the sunken mist,
until you grow in me, until you communicate to me
your obscure light and the rose of the earth.

(Translated by Kenneth Edwards)

[30] A black hiccough of generals and a wave of rabid cassocks.

[31] The title of the poem means "I Explain Some Things." It reads, in English:

You will ask: And where are the lilacs?
And the poppy-covered metaphysics?
And the rain that so often beat against
Its words, filling them
With holes and with birds?

I am going to tell you everything that happens to me.

I was living in a suburb
Of Madrid, with its church bells,
With its clocktowers, with its trees.

From this district one could see
The barren face that is Castile
Like a vast, brown leather ocean.

My house used to be called
The house of flowers, because geraniums used to sprout
In every nook and corner: it was
A beautiful house
With dogs and little children.

Raúl, you remember?
You remember, Rafael?
Federico, you remember
There under the earth,
You remember my house with the balconies where
The June light used to deluge flowers into your mouth?

(Translated by Kenneth Edwards)

[32] Our father who art in the earth, in the water, in the air—
throughout our extended silent latitude,
all things bear thy name, father, in our land:
the reeds raise thy surname to sweetness:
tin bolivar has a fulgency bolivar,
the bird bolivar soars over the volcano bolivar,
the potato, saltpeter, special shadows,
the currents, the veins of phosphoric stone—
all that is ours comes from thy extinguished life:
thy heritage was rivers, plains, bell towers;
thy heritage is our bread of every day, father.

In death, thy small brave captain's body
has extended its metallic form into immensity:
suddenly thy fingers come from out the snow
and the austral fisherman draws thy smile out to light—
suddenly thy voice is trembling in the nets.

Of what color shall be the rose that we gather near thy soul?
Red will be the rose that remembers thy passing.
And how the hands that shall touch thine ashes?
Red will be the hands that are born in thine ashes.

And how is the seed of thy dead heart?
Red is the seed of thy living heart.

For that reason the circle of hands is next to thee today;
next to my hand there is another, and another next to that,
and yet another, unto the depth of the dark continent.
And another hand that thou didst not know in thy time
comes also, Bolivar, to clasp itself in thine.
From Teruel, from Madrid, from the Jarama, from the Ebro,
from the prison, from the air, from those the dead of Spain
comes this red hand that is the very child of thine.

Captain, fighter, where one single mouth
cries Liberty, where one ear listens,
where one red soldier breaks one brown forehead,
where one laurel of free men puts forth shoots, where one new
banner is adorned with the blood of our heroic dawn—
there Bolivar, captain, in the distance thy face is seen.
Amidst gunpowder and smoke thy sword once more is born.
Once more thy banner has been wreathed with blood.
Evil men attack thy seed again;
nailed on another cross is the son of man.

But toward hope thy spirit leads us on:
with thine own glance it follows the laurel
and the light of thy red army through America's night.
Thine eyes keep watch from far beyond the seas,
beyond the peoples wounded and oppressed,
beyond blackened cities all in flames.
Thy voice is born anew, again thy hand is raised:
thine army defends the sacred banners: and a sound terrible with sorrows heralds
the dawn reddened by the blood of man.
Liberator, in thine arms is born a world of peace.
For peace and bread and wheat from thy blood sprung:
and our young blood from thine transfused
shall bring forth peace, bread, wheat for the world we build.

. . .

In Madrid on one long morning
I met Bolivar, at the head of the Fifth Regiment.
"Father," I said to him, "art thou or art thou not, or who art thou?"
And looking up at the Mountain Headquarters, he said to me:
"I awaken every hundred years when the people rise."

(Translated by Kenneth Edwards)

[33] I see a rose near the water, a tiny goblet of reddish eyelids, sustained on high by an aerial sound . . .

[34] The title of the poem means "Hymn and Return." It reads, in English:

Native land, my native land, I give back my blood to you.
But I beseech you, as a child of its mother
full of tears,
cherish this mute guitar
and this wounded forehead.

I went out to find your children through the earth,
I went out to care for the fallen with your spotless name,
I went out to build a house with your solid wood,
I went out to carry your star to the wounded heroes.

Now I wish to sleep within your substance.
Give me your clear night of pervading sounds,
your armor-clad night, your star-studded stature.

My native land: I wish to move from shadow.
My native land: I wish to change from rose.
I wish to put my arm about your slender waist
and sit upon your rocks calcined by the sea,
and check the wheat and look at it inside.
I am going to gather your slender flora from the nitrate,
I am going to spin the glacial yarn of the country,
and looking at your glorious solitary foam
I will weave a seashore garland to your beauty.

Native land, my native land
surrounded completely by contending water
and hostile snow,
in you the eagle is united to sulphur,
and in your antarctic hand of ermine and sapphire
burns one drop of pure human light,
lighting up the enemy sky.

Watch over your light, O native land! keep
your hard tassel of hope in the midst
of the blind portentous air.
Upon your far-off land has fallen all this difficult light,
this destiny of men,
enjoining you to defend one mysterious flower
alone, in the immensity of sleeping America.

(Translated by Kenneth Edwards)

NOTES TO CHAPTER X

The Poetry of the Future

(Pages 185–195)

[1] The poem reads, in English, as follows:

I am dying strangely . . . For it is not life
Nor Death nor Love which now is killing me;
A silent thought wounds me like a knife . . .
Have you not felt the novel agony

Of thought immense and rooted deep in life,
devouring flesh and spirit barrenly?
Or borne within a dormant star, rife
With fire that burned but gave no fulgency? . . .

O apogee of Martyrdoms . . . The need
To feel eternally the tragic seed,
A cruel tooth within its carnal bed! . . .

To make it bear a bloom, inviolate,
Miraculous! . . . Ah, then no greater fate
Although you held between your hands God's head!
(Translated by Cyrene Smith)

[2] The title of the poem means "The Miraculous Bark." It reads, in English:

Prepare for me a bark like a wondrous thought . . .
"The Shadow" or "The Star" the name to bear.
A hand's or wind's caprice will count for naught,
I want it conscious, indomitable, and fair!

The rhythm will move it of a spirit fraught
With superhuman life; in it I'll fare
As strong as in the arms of God! In aught
Of winds, trim its scintillant prow to the air!

The load will be my sorrow, and, rudderless,
I'll go with a shattered nelumbo's progress,
Beyond the liquid horizon of the sea . . .
Bark, sister soul: toward what lands never seen,
Of deep revelations, of things unforeseen
Shall we go? . . . I die from living dreamily . . .
(Translated by Cyrene Smith)

[3] The title of the poem means "Thirst." It reads, in English:

"I feel an ardent thirst," I told the sprite,
And she offered nectar. "No, that palls on me!"
A rare fruit with her magic fingers shortly
She pressed into a goblet starry bright.

The lovely goblet held a ruby light.
I sipped. " 'Tis sweet. Some days alluringly
Such honey sates, but now repugnantly!"
I saw a sparkle in the fairy's sight.

And through a valley, perfumed and agleam,
She led me to a clear, diamantine stream.
"Drink!" she said. A forge was my burning breast.

I drank, I drank the crystalline libation . . .
Oh, coolness! Oh, purity! Oh, divine sensation!
"Thank you, sprite, may limpid water be blest!"
(Translated by Cyrene Smith)

NOTES TO CHAPTER XI

The Parallel between Brazilian and Spanish American Literature

(Pages 196–213)

[1] José de Anchieta. See Ronald de Carvalho, *Pequena Historia da literatura brasileira* (Rio de Janeiro, 1935), p. 16.

[2] Ronald de Carvalho, *op. cit.*, p. 86.

[3] Author of *Música do Parnasso, dividido en cuatro grupos de rimas, portuguesas, castelhanas, italianas e latinas* (Music of Parnassus, Divided into Four Groups: of Portuguese, Castilian, Italian, and Latin Verse). This work is like that of other pedantic writers of Hispanic America.

[4] M. Oliveira Lima. See: *Aspectos da literatura colonial* (Leipzig, 1896). See also: *Aspectos da historia e da cultura do Brasil* (Lisboa, 1923).

[5] I am he who, during the past years, has praised in my biting poetry the apathy, vice, and deceit in Brazil. (Translated by Ruth J. Warner)

[6] Where, at the entrance to a grotto, there is a hoarsely whispering spring, covered by an arched trellis of jasmine and roses. (Translated by Ruth J. Warner)

[7] What lily or white rose, cut down by the unmannerly plow that is breaking open the field, fell to the grass so beautiful as she? Or what heavy-headed poppy bends its crown the way Gualeva laid down her beautiful face above that weary and weak yet sculpture-like throat? (Translated by Ruth J. Warner)

[8] Volumes of poetry, especially of the fifteenth and sixteenth centuries.

[9] Collections of ballads.

INDEX

INDEX